LA MANO DERECHA

THE RIGHT HAND MAN

CILLIAN DUNNE

TO CARLOS WITTGREEN

"Ni milliones, ni limosnas, queremos justicia."
"Neither millions, nor alms, we want justice."
– General Remon Cantera
16th President of Panama

Contents

Preface

P anama is the playground for international intelligence. The knowledge that passes through this country has a ripple effect that touches the politics of every nation in the world. Panamanians earned their freedom from Colombia in 1903 with the help of the United States. The prospect of the canal was too great for the Americans to ignore, so they invested heavily in the budding Central American government and forcefully edged out their South American opponents. Control over the canal was essential for the United States. It needed the fifty-mile stretch that connected the Americas. So, with little pushback, it turned the canal and ten miles on either side of it into American territory, known as the Canal Zone, and its inhabitants, Zonians.

After Panama gained independence, US presidents played with the strings that controlled leaders of the "crossroads of the worlds" for many years. Whether an affair was domestic or foreign, the American interest came first. No Panamanian dared to oppose the puppeteers until a coup erupted in 1968, which ultimately saw the introduction of Panama's first de facto leader, Omar Torrijos. The people wanted a Panamanian in power solely focused on Panamanian issues. That, however, wouldn't always be the case, as the United States still owned the canal. Though steadfast in his desire to develop a unique cultural identity for his home, Omar Torrijos found himself at the beck and call of Washington.

Standing by Omar's side was Manuel Noriega, chief of intelligence, CIA asset, and military strongman who would ultimately succeed him. Noriega is a name many know. He is one of the most vilified people in modern American history. It's well-known that Noriega went to the grave with most of his secrets.

Years before the United States launched a full-scale invasion of Panama, Noriega was its most crucial intelligence asset. Every CIA and DEA director from 1970 to 1986 knew they had to keep Noriega happy. He was their man in Central America. When the United States needed its trash taken out, Manuel was the man they called. America needed Noriega, and when shit hit the fan, it turned on him.

Standing right by Noriega's side was a Panamanian named Carlos Wittgreen. Carlitos was Manuel's right-hand man. Señor Wittgreen stood by Noriega as he became one of the most infamous political targets the US government had ever issued, and he never left his post. The two weathered the storm of countless assassination attempts and insurrections and an invasion on their home soil, America's largest military exercise since the Vietnam War.

Carlos's story has never been told before. He trained with the Panama National Guard, Mossad in Israel, and the DEA to become an asset for Panama, America, and Fidel Castro's Cuba. Carlos was a strategic point of intelligence for many. Still, his loyalty to his nation and people never faltered at the tension and aggression of those who wanted to see him imprisoned or dead. The ferocity is very much still alive. Yet, for all his machismo and the trauma endured by a life of military and covert servitude, he remains one of the most intensely caring and loyal individuals I have ever met.

I spent several months in Panama. I even lived with Señor Wittgreen and his partner, Natasha, for a stretch. I had the opportunity to interview him and record his life story. I was twenty-seven years old when I began my work on this book. I wanted to not only do Carlos's story justice but also to find as much truth as I possibly could about the betrayal by the United States.

Day in and day out, I interviewed Carlos. I consider myself lucky to have had this experience at such a young age. To help build the world around Carlos's story, I also interviewed a series of former Panamanian military aides, American soldiers involved in the invasion, journalists, authors, former intelligence assets, members of Noriega's family, Panamanian civilians, and family and friends of Manuel Noriega and Señor Wittgreen.

Carlos told me his life story in his own words. This book is written from my perspective in certain chapters and Carlos's perspective in others. I knew that, in order to effectively maintain accuracy while writing this book, I would need to back up Carlos's story using verified, undisputed evidence. So, with the help of author, historian, and former mayor of Panama City, Jose Hilario Trujillo, I was able to implement real, verified documentation into the book. This documentation consists of letters sent between the

DEA, DOJ, and Noriega, research conducted by international human rights organizations, historical reports, and archived articles written by major publications such as the *New York Times*.

Introduction
A Gringo's First Week in Panama

My friend Jack Moran called me out of the blue one day in October 2023 with the opportunity to write this book. It was around the time of the October 7 attacks in Israel. About six months prior, I had quit my job so I could pursue writing full-time. I had already released four books by that point, two with low levels of success. A week before Jack reached out, I had held a book signing at my friend Conor Holway's party at SkyBar on the Sunset Strip in Los Angeles. I didn't even sell enough copies of *Dreams in Incarceration* to cover my bar tab that night, but Jack had seen a picture from the event, and so he got in touch with me after several months of not having spoken with each other.

"Listen, my business partner, Jose Goldner, has access to this incredible story down in Panama. Are you interested in speaking with him about it?"

Jack had no idea at the time, but I had about five hundred dollars in my bank account, and rent was due in a couple weeks. "Absolutely," I responded.

Within five minutes, Jose called, and he wasted no breath getting right into the meat and potatoes of what would eventually become this book. He spoke of major world events like the Iran-Contra Affair, the Bay of Pigs, and the Panama Papers. Names like Fidel Castro, Muammar Gaddafi, and Ronald Reagan were thrown around. The conversation lasted about twenty minutes, and in the final moments of the call, Jose said he could get me access to people who could tell me the true story behind Manuel Noriega's rise, rule, and fall, the US invasion, and Panama's involvement in world politics and intelligence.

I was immediately hooked, even if I didn't fully understand everything I was told.

"When can you come to Panama?" Jose asked.

I told him I needed twenty-four hours to make the decision. I had never been to Central America. Truthfully, the majority of what I thought I knew about that part of the world was negative. The media often painted it as a dangerous place for gringos like me to go to. "If you go to Central America with two arms, you'll return to the US with only one." This was the sentiment, but thankfully, I knew Jack considered Panama a second home, and I had heard only wonderful things about the country, so there was never any discomfort with the idea of traveling there. Still, I was a twenty-seven-year-old man from Dublin, Ireland, and I was nervous about undertaking a project like this in a country where the native language was something I barely knew how to speak. That night, I sat silently on the couch in my Santa Monica apartment alongside my friends Mark Gildea, Liam Daly, and Alec Flynn. I was lost in my own mind, thinking of everything that could go wrong, when I finally spoke up and told my friends about the call. Mark, Alec, and I had all known Jack since we were fifteen, so they were just as shocked as I was to learn that Moran had introduced me to an opportunity like this. "Manuel Noriega, the dictator?" They couldn't believe it. I asked them what they thought, and the response was a resounding "holy shit, you need to do this." I knew they were right. I needed to be the one to write this story, and I understood that in order to do so, I would have a lot of learning to do. I called Jose the next day and told him I would be in Panama City by the weekend.

There was so much to cover in such a short amount of time. I decided to work backward at first, starting with the US invasion of Panama in 1989. There was a lot of free access to videos, published articles, and books on the subject that were available to me. It was not difficult to familiarize myself with the event, but I quickly realized that every story had the same narrative. *Manuel Noriega is an evil dictator who is an enemy of America, and so we must send our troops to Panama so we can rid their people of his authoritarian leadership.* "Sounds familiar," I thought to myself. I was always taught that America was the good guy and its job was to ensure all the bad guys in the world were dealt with. I was never naive enough to fully believe that, but I still held an ingrained notion that the United States was the big brother of the world, stepping into conflicts so it could bully nations and terrorist organizations who were a threat to national and international security. I didn't yet realize the extent to which my entire worldview was going to change by undertaking this project.

As I began to work back through the years, from the invasion in 1989 to Noriega's consolidation of power in 1983 and to the Torrijos coups of 1968 and 1969, I found many stories and articles that highlighted Noriega's wrongdoings. With the accusation of his throwing the Priest Hector Gallego out of a helicopter in 1971, brutally mutilating and murdering Hugo Spadafora in 1985, and the conspiracy of Noriega's involvement in the 1981 plane crash of the previous de facto leader, Omar Torrijos, I was growing increasingly worried about what I had agreed to do. The world's spotlight shone on Panama between 1983 and 1989 for all the wrong reasons, and I was about to spend an unknown amount of time in the middle of the hemisphere with the men who stood in circles around Noriega throughout all these years. Yet, my excitement and curiosity outweighed any negative feelings within me. Still, I knew that trying to change the narrative set in stone for decades would be a mountainous obstacle to overcome.

A Colombian-American filmmaker and friend of mine was somebody I knew I could contact for advice on how to get a different insight into what I would be researching in Panama. I called him up, and we exchanged pleasantries for a few minutes before he asked, "So, what's up?"

I told him about my upcoming trip. As I suspected, he was familiar with the history of Panama, but his knowledge was more related to Omar Torrijos and his relationship with the United States government.

"I recently interviewed a man by the name of John Perkins. Have you heard of him?" he asked.

Truthfully, I hadn't, but I was by my computer and quickly Googled him. "Of course I have," I responded, eyes scanning through Wikipedia, flash-learning about Perkins's malicious deeds performed in third-world countries on behalf of the United States government.

"Perkins told me that, after he released his book *Confessions of an Economic Hit Man*, he was at a restaurant in Manhattan one night where he got poisoned."

If I wasn't nervous before, I was now.

Departure day soon came, and I boarded my flight to Atlanta before connecting to Panama City. The second leg was empty. I had a whole row to myself. I couldn't sleep; there was too much anticipation. The anti-Noriega headlines flashed with every bump of turbulence. When I arrived at Tocumen Airport, I was exhausted but kept awake by a pounding heart. There were three layers of customs waiting for me. The moment I stepped off the plane, an airport worker singled me out and asked to see my passport. Nobody else around me was asked, though I'm sure a couple other gringos on the jet were stopped as I was. Then, the true customs agents welcomed me with a smile and stamped my passport. However, in order to leave the airport, there was a third, small security section where my carry-on would be scanned one last time. A Panamanian in his thirties sat behind a desk next to an x-ray. His eyes were glued to the screen as I put my bag through. His pupils flicked back and forth, and then they expanded before he slammed his hand onto a button that halted the conveyor belt. "Come," he said, grabbing my backpack. I was nervous but not necessarily worried. The man didn't speak any English. I could barely understand what he was asking. He slipped his hand into my bag and pulled out five copies of my book *Dreams in Incarceration*.

I had brought them as gifts for Jose's family, as well as added proof that I could, in fact, write a book and write it well, at that. "Escribo el libro," I said, using as few words as possible. Having taken Spanish for six years in secondary school, I retained just enough to converse with the guard before he called another employee over to check out the book. "Regalos, regalos," I said, offering them a copy each if they would just let me get on my way to Jose's apartment. I had no idea where it was in relation to Tocumen, and I didn't want to keep him waiting. The guards asked me to sign their copies, and then I was on my way. Jose called and told me what to say to the taxi driver so he wouldn't shake me down for more than the ride was worth. I was given exact instructions, and within twenty-five minutes, I found myself at the base of Jose's apartment building, my wallet twenty dollars lighter instead of what could have been fifty dollars.

"I drove six hours to meet you," Jose told me right away. He had been at his beach house near Pedasi, a place I would come to know. We spoke for about thirty minutes before Jose gave me a card and told me which hotel to go to. "Come back at 7 a.m. We have a lot of work to do," he said before retreating to his bedroom.

I once read that our prey instincts kick in when we're in a new and unfamiliar place. I wasn't afraid, but my body wouldn't allow me to sleep that night, even in my nice hotel room. My mind spun. I had no idea what to expect the following day.

The first order of business was meeting Carlos Wittgreen. I was immediately told that he was the story. "Carlitos sat in rooms where some of the most important political decisions of the twentieth century were made. He was there for everything." I sat and spoke with Jose's son, Diego, as the rest of Jose's family got ready for school and work. Diego and I mostly talked about our mutual friend, Jack, and all the fun they had on surf and party trips around Panama. I learned about the popular tourist places like Playa Venao and Bocas del Toro, but I was more interested in where the locals would go. Diego showed me some locations on Google Maps.

Then Jose came charging out of the kitchen and said it was time to go. "We're meeting Carlos for an early lunch," he exclaimed before we jumped into an Uber and shot out onto the street.

Driving in Panama City was a culture shock for me. Diego explained it as "defensive driving." Cars whizzed through lanes, and they stopped at the last second. It was nothing like the places I had previously lived: Dublin, Boston, Los Angeles. We arrived at an Italian restaurant around eleven o'clock. I stepped out of the car to the beating hot sun and I fanned my body using my T-shirt, but it did no good. I was sweating like a dog on my first day in Central America, like a true gringo. We arrived early on purpose.

"In my community, this man is like a celebrity," Jose said, ensuring I would acknowledge the importance of this introduction.

I understood he was subtly prepping me for the meeting. All Jose knew about me was what Jack had told him, so Jose was presenting his trust by introducing me to such an important man, whom he clearly considered a dear friend. The moment Carlos entered the restaurant, I could see he was enigmatic, extremely personable, and, for lack of a better way to put it, a very fun person. He was delighted to see Jose. They exchanged hugs. I am not sure how long it had been since they had been in each other's company, but they immediately delved into personal conversation, which I could hardly understand. Their chatter was alien to me, but Carlos still involved me in the conversation. It was clearly a conscious effort to make sure I was included in one way or another. I even became the brunt of a few jokes. In Ireland, someone having a laugh at your expense in a non-malicious way is a sign of acceptance. I took the jokes as just that, even if they weren't, laughing along and allowing my ego to disappear.

"Carlitos, Cillian is a young writer from Ireland who lives in America. He is very interested in writing your story," Jose suddenly interjected.

The joking stopped. Carlos became more serious. I noticed his eyes were sharper. He was thinking. There was a moment's silence before Carlos nodded and accepted the proposal. "You will do a good job," Carlos said to me in English.

I suspected that Señor Wittgreen spoke more English than he let on, but I was in his country, and I spoke as much Spanish as I possibly could. "*Si, señor, me encantaria escribirlo,*" I told him.

We agreed that my interview process would take place at Jose's beach house. I would bring Diego with me to help translate, and Carlos would bring his girlfriend, Natasha, so they could also enjoy the time as a vacation away from the chaos of the city. The lunch was not nearly as intense as I had assumed it would be, but the work hadn't even started. Jose was happy that Carlos took enough liking to me to allow me to write his story. Carlitos offered to drive us back to Jose's apartment. We were out of the way for him, as he lived just around the corner from the Italian restaurant, but Carlos insisted. I could see he was a man who did many favors for his friends. I knew that loyalty and personability would be two defining traits of his character when I began writing the book. I sat in the back seat of his car, thinking about how his character's dialogue would read on the page when he looked into the rearview mirror and locked eyes with me.

"I am very fond of the Irish people," he said.

The surname Wittgreen intrigued me from the moment I heard it. It didn't sound like a Spanish name, and it wasn't, as Carlos then explained to me that his ancestors on his father's side came from Ireland a long time ago and found themselves on Panama's northern coast. I don't think Wittgreen is an Irish name, but Carlos was making a clear effort to connect with me. I immediately took a liking to him.

A few days went by, and I was doing as much research from my hotel room as I possibly could. Diego and I hung out several times, too. We got to know each other before undergoing the six-hour drive to Pedasi, which he was all too familiar with. I sat in the passenger seat as he drove me around the city, showing me various landmarks and taking me to some bars where we conversed over Balboas, a beer I became fond of. Jose's children were nice enough to let me borrow one of their books. It was *In the Time of the Tyrants: Panama, 1968-1990* by Richard M. Koster, an American journalist and veteran who had spent decades living in Panama. He wrote a comprehensive history book that would provide me with the necessary background of the nation before my interviews with Carlos.

The weekend was approaching, and we were due to pick up Carlos and Natasha at their apartment at seven on Saturday morning. I sat in my hotel room, watching videos of Noriega's speeches on YouTube. My phone vibrated atop the bedsheets.

"We're going to meet Richard Koster tomorrow at noon. Make sure you do your homework," Jose's voice echoed through the speaker.

I turned to look at the 430-page beast staring at me. I couldn't meet Koster not having read his work. From the first page, I knew it would be a dense read. Richard had clearly written a detailed account of Panama's modern history and had even been there to see it with his own eyes. I didn't want to waste a second, so I dove in, reading as fast as possible while ensuring I was taking notes throughout the book. Day turned to night, and my fingers were strained by keeping the book open and steady in my hands as I paced around my hotel room in my boxers like a madman. I felt like Martin Sheehan at the beginning of *Apocalypse Now*. I knew I couldn't retain everything, but I was sure there were nuggets of vital importance in there that I needed to understand before meeting the man. After hours of reading, I finished the book, and a jolt of energy suddenly shot through me. I picked up my phone and called Jose, telling him I knew exactly what to call our book. "La Mano Derecha, The Right-Hand Man," I exclaimed. From that moment on, I never even thought about changing the title.

The following day, we met at a Cuban restaurant on Via Argentina that was mostly empty. Diego sat with us. He was interested in pursuing a career as a writer and wanted a glimpse of the work behind the page. The three of us sat at a table in the corner next to a wall of glass, from which we could see the bustling street and sidewalk.

Jose continuously scanned through the window, turning to speak to me and Diego every other moment, preparing us for the meeting. "Richard is tough. I've been in rooms with him where he's singled somebody out and questioned them until they broke," he stated.

My heart raced. Every cell inside me was working to keep composure.

"Here he is," Jose exclaimed, sitting upright, watching as Koster stepped through the glass doors and shifted toward our table.

He was an old man when I met him. I believe he had just beaten cancer around that time. Still, he moved around the table to shake all of our hands. Jose introduced Diego and me before pulling out Richard's seat. Koster immediately began cracking jokes, ones I didn't understand, even though they were told in English. They were local anecdotes that only a Panamanian would know. Koster had ingrained himself so much in the local culture that, in many ways, he was a Panamanian. "Don't worry, I've been living here for decades, and even I don't fully understand Panamanians," he turned and said to me. He didn't know what the reason for the get-together was at first, and it didn't seem like he cared. We all joked and laughed while Richard told us stories from the past.

Jose nudged me, gesturing toward my phone. He wanted me to take note of what Richard was saying, whether it was relevant to our project or not. Koster's stories were so beautifully detailed that I wished I could pause mid-sentence to catch up on my notes.

Then, Richard flipped a switch, and the stories became darker and more relatable to my research. It was as if he realized why I was there. "The fucked-up things that happen in the world . . . we don't know the half of it," he exclaimed. Koster told us horrifying stories about authoritarian rule in the Middle East and how dictators kept their power by silencing the people in the streets through violent oppression. He began by mentioning that, in Iran, during the rule of the shahs, people were kept in order by trained dogs who understood what it meant to rape and kill. He led us off with that horrible fact. It was clear he had strong feelings about the shah of Iran and the way he and his father had kept their status as rulers decades earlier. Richard was passionate, reciting specific incidents and gesturing with his hands as if he were living within his own story.

Then Richard pivoted, telling me about a weapons smuggling operation from Bovina, Texas, to airstrips in Honduras and Costa Rica to supply the Contras in the early 1980s. The weapons had originally been seized by the Israelis from Palestinians and then handed over to the Contras, a detail he found especially relevant, given current events at the time. He said Russian weapons were also prevalent in Nicaragua, with the Sandinistas caught using AK-47s and other Soviet arms. Richard stated that, while working for *Newsweek* in Panama, he had to stop writing about the country when he returned to the United States because Panama passed a law making foreign journalists legally liable for anything they published about the country, effectively silencing outside reporting. He also had deep criticisms of Henry Kissinger's books, claiming they were half true and half fabricated, a conclusion he reached because he and Kissinger had both entered World War II counterintelligence at the same time.

Koster then quickly moved on from Kissinger, landing on the topic of US intelligence within Panama. He explained how knowledge moved from the mouths of gringos on Central American soil back to Washington. Richard mentioned a specific offer he received from a man named Dick Dillinger, who had built a hotel by Tocumen Airport and wanted Koster to take a cut of the profits in exchange for acting as an intelligence source, but

Richard declined and didn't elaborate further. He was clearly insinuating that Panama was the epicenter of world intelligence, and although he was just an American journalist, he was very much involved. I didn't notice that the tables around me had become filled with parties of Panamanians, laughing and speaking loudly. "Kissinger influenced Jimmy Carter to allow the shah of Iran, who was in Mexico at the time, to come to the US for medical treatment," he stated, citing it as one of the key moments that sparked the Iran hostage crisis, before quickly finishing his thought.

"Richard, we're writing a book about all this: Iran-Contra, the US invasion, Noriega," Jose spoke.

I was waiting to be challenged, perhaps even scolded. My palms were sweating. I struggled not to rub them against the fabric of my pants.

"Well, you know, writing a book is a difficult thing," he said as the waiter approached and placed the check on the table.

"I know, sir. This is actually my fifth book," I responded, waiting for the strike.

"I had written the same number at your age," he said with a smile.

Whether the intention of his response was acceptance or not, those words gave me a lot of confidence in what I was doing, and my fear of being questioned like an inmate in Guantanamo lessened. Koster was one of the most resourceful sources of information when it came to Central American politics in the 1970s and 1980s. Not only did he live through it, but he also reported on it. His job was to find the truth as it was happening. I was on cloud nine.

As we all hopped into a taxi to accompany Richard back to his home, we spoke about our respective cities. Koster grew up in Brooklyn in the 1940s. "I remember seeing Jackie Robinson play for the Dodgers," he said with fondness in his eyes. He knew a little about Ireland, enough to recite stories he had of the old neighborhood, where he and his friends would clash with the Irish over territory. I still had my phone out, and he could see I was rapidly taking note of everything he said.

*"When you work in intelligence, you're
lying all the time. I am a very good liar."*
"Reality does not exist; what exists are realities."
*"Hugo Spadafora's death was the USA's
divorce from Noriega and Panama."*
*"What you're going to find doing this research is that
this whole topic—Panama, Iran-Contra—is something
that people know a little about but not much, even the
people who were directly involved."*
*"Get rid of all prejudice. You will be able
to see a lot more without prejudice."*
"If it looks like a pistol, you'll be afraid of it."
*"I think because I didn't pay attention to the cancer,
it just said fuck this and left my body."*

I was intrigued by everything that man said. Meeting R. M. Koster would be a defining moment in my life. Before we arrived at Richard's house, we told him about the upcoming trip with Carlos. He knew of Señor Wittgreen and even chuckled when he heard his name. There was no noticeable animosity there. It was clear Koster had memories of Carlos and his brother Gaspar, but the one that came to his mind and out his mouth first was about the invasion. "If I remember correctly, Carlos was robbing banks during the invasion." I would later find this was not true. Still, Koster knew that Señor Wittgreen's story was niche, unique enough to create a new angle into a narrative different from the one the world had heard thousands of times before. "You'll face some challenges doing this. Some years back, Panama's ambassador to England, Guillermo Vega, who married into the Sainsbury family, the big supermarket chain in Britain, sued me for defamation, and because of that, my book, *In the Time of the Tyrants*, isn't allowed to be sold in England."

Koster and I took a picture together. We exchanged phone numbers, and by the time the sun had set, he was home with his wife, and the rest of us returned to Jose's apartment.

Richard Koster (left) and Cillian Dunne, 2023.

Before that Saturday morning, Jose introduced me to several other local figures I would be able to question. One of interest was a man who had spent several years working for the CIA, and he had retired in Panama.

"There's a young writer visiting here who is researching Panama and Iran-Contra. Can I put you guys in touch?" Jose turned his phone speaker high, telling me to be quiet as the man on the other line went silent.

"Who the hell is this guy?" the man asked.

"A writer. Are you open to speaking with him or not?" Jose responded.

I didn't make a sound. A slight static echoed from the device.

"I'm going to need a scan of his passport, his social security number, a picture, the address of where he's staying in Panama ."

I knew that there was no chance I could speak with the man. Besides, we didn't deem it necessary, but I often wondered what he knew that made him so paranoid.

"And don't tell him my real name," he said as he finished his rant.

That former CIA agent would have never told me anything, so we decided to begin searching for alternative sources of information on American covert intelligence operations in Central America. The night before departure day, I was able to have drinks with Edgar Noriega, Manuel's nephew. We did not spend too much time speaking about his uncle or politics in general, but rather, he introduced me to a variety of Panamanians, some of whom were more than willing to tell me everything they thought I should know about Panama. I was most interested in the sentiment they held for those who ran the country. "The government is a joke. They're thieves," they said. As the night went on, more and more women began to show, and Panama's sex work culture stepped into the spotlight.

I didn't get as much sleep that night as I would have liked, but when the next morning came around, I felt I had done as much as I possibly could to prepare myself for the next several weeks of interviews. It was time for Diego and me to pick up Carlos and Natasha.

Chapter 1
A Gringo Digs Up the Past

A drive had never felt so long. It had been hours since we had left the city, and I could see Diego's wrists were cramping up. "At least the air inside the car is cool," I thought. Outside of the auto was hell. The sweltering heat caused bullets of sweat to rush down my forehead and soak my collar. Carlos and Natasha sat peacefully in the back seat. She gazed out the window at the rainforest vegetation we passed by; the Panamanian landscape's palm trees and thick green brush hypnotized her into a silent trance. Carlos, on the other hand, was talkative. He told us story after story using a mixture of Spanish and English, making Diego and me laugh for hours on end.

We were one of a few cars on the road. The city was a circus when we left. It felt like something was brewing. Maybe it was just my own anxiety, but the air felt tense. There were upcoming elections in Panama in December, so I asked Carlos and Diego about their significance. They both seemed to hold the same sentiment that the government wasn't necessarily to be trusted. "Too many riots have sparked before my eyes. Flag Day and Martyr's Day; Protests are a part of our nature as a people. It's a different feeling out here," Carlos said as we drove along a highway from the city to Divisa, the border of the Veraguas Province and the Herrera Province. We turned left and went straight for another 150 kilometers on Highway 2. Highway 1 is the infamous Pan-American Highway. Chitre was the first major town we passed through.

"The Government is a joke, con artists, criminals who steal from the people and give back to themselves. I knew better men on Coiba Island. I don't trust the politicians one bit," Carlos said.

Showers of rain would spurt every other hour. We had expected showers, so all our bags in the truck bed were covered in plastic. But I was worried my recording device back there would get waterlogged and I would have to take all my notes freehand.

"How far away are we?" Natasha asked.

"We'll be there soon, *mi amor*," Carlos responded.

Cars gradually vanished from our sight the closer we got to our destination. We were off the beaten path. In my peripheral, the trees grew taller, and their brush thickened.

"We're getting close," Diego stated. I remember looking into the rearview mirror and seeing a 4x4 Jeep with surfboards attached to the roof. They pulled left and whizzed right by us, spitting out fumes that briefly blinded my line of sight. They were gringos like me, but they were in Panama to surf the waves and stretch their dollar, not to speak with the people whose lives had paved the foundation for the land we stood on. I made it a personal goal to think like a Panamanian, so when I saw a group of gringos, I tried to think as I would imagine someone like Carlos would think.

"Fucking gringos." A dirt road with a white sign came into sight. The interior of the car shook. I rattled in my seat. Natasha put her hand on Carlos's shoulder and rubbed it gently. We drove through a shaded darkness; the leaves blocked the light of the burning sun. We passed over small streams of water that rushed through the woods, sticks and twigs snapping under the weight of the tires. I could smell the ocean air. The path opened before us, and a beautiful yellow house sat atop a field of immaculate green grass, among the greenest I have ever seen. The Nicaraguan house workers spotted us approaching and waved us in.

"Hola, Diego!" they yelled.

I shook their hands and kissed their cheeks.

"Nicaraguans are amazing humans," Carlos said. "Their nation has endured a lot, I know firsthand."

I watched as they took everyone's bags and brought them inside. "Would you like something to eat?" they asked us.

"Seco is fine for now," Carlos responded, putting his arm around Natasha.

A chilled glass of Seco and agua de pipa was placed into my hands. The ice cubes crackled. For an alcoholic beverage, I didn't expect it to be as refreshing as it was.

"You can drink a whole bottle of seco and not be hungover," Carlos joked.

On that first day, we decided not to dive into anything serious; instead, we enjoyed each other's company and became more comfortable with each other. We walked across the grass to where the property met the beach. The sight was beautiful, with waves thunderously crashing at the shoreline and rushing to meet our bare feet. Natasha tapped Carlos's shoulder and pointed to our left, where turtles dragged themselves along the sand to pits on the ground where they had laid their eggs. I took a deep breath and allowed my body to relax. This wasn't the city where my thoughts were pent up like cocks in a cage. This was the real Panama, and I was there for the real story.

I felt a warm wind blow; it rustled the palm tree leaves surrounding us. A particular but unique smell lingered in the air.

"There's a storm coming," Carlos stated.

Natasha squinted her eyes and looked to the horizon. I understood that, after eight decades in Panama, Carlos knew everything there was to know about the nation. He was certain the storm would form by nightfall, so he told Diego and me to get back into the car and we'd see him in the morning. Jose had another house close by that we could stay in to give Carlos and Natasha some space. The Nicaraguans would cook and clean for them. All Diego and I had to worry about were the interviews that would follow. This isolation from the subject also allowed me to prepare for the conversations every day. Although I was familiar with all the major and some of the minor events I was certain correlated with Carlos's story, I needed to be more confident in my knowledge. The only way to do that was to continue to read documents available to me, study archived interviews of Panamanian and American officials, and watch documentaries such as *The Panama Deception*, which an American girl working for the Peace Corps in Las Tablas had told me about a few days prior.

"They make all the newbies watch it during their first week in Panama," she said. "It's important because it was the poorest of Panamanians that suffered the most during the US invasion."

The next day, I awoke to find the walls of the home shaking and the sound of slashing rain pounding outside. A rumble of thunder shook my bed, and shards of lightning sliced through the gray skies and shone flashing rays through my white blinds. It felt like Armageddon, but to the locals, it was just winter. Diego and I got breakfast at a local establishment in Pedasi before heading out to meet Carlos. The restaurant also had a daily deal called *comida del dia* (first meal of the day)," which I ate every single day while I was in Pedasi. Fueled up and ready to go, Diego and I drove to meet Carlos and Natasha. I clung to my recording device, checking it every other moment to make sure it hadn't gotten wet from the drive.

I sat opposite Carlos on a table covered by a wooden gazebo, the wind whistling and the white-tipped waves thrashing before us. I knew I had to ease into it. I couldn't just start firing questions like, "Did the CIA blow up Torrijos's plane?" or "Did the US invade Panama only because George Bush had personal issues with Noriega?" I needed to create a conversation, not an inquisition. So I turned my recording device on and slid it toward Carlos. He stared at the flashing red light on the recorder for a moment, and then I finally asked him the question that would kick everything off: "So how did you meet him?"

Chapter 2
My Friend Manuel

The flash from a firing pistol reflected in my glistening eyes. My limbs froze in place. I could hear my muscles straining as I leaned. The other runners sprinted forward; I stayed still. The pistol, the noise it made, the smell of gunpowder—I was taken.

"Run, Carlos!" my coach screamed.

His words were muffled. My eardrums rang from the thunderous power of the weapon. I stared at it. The trigger was a dull gray, but the barrel still had some shine. The handle boasted a wooden design with organic carvings that looked to have been scratched by the overgrown nails of the gunslinger. When the flash dimmed, the race was over, and I hadn't moved an inch. I think of my entire childhood when I think of this, right up until I met Noriega.

My mother told me I was born blue. My skin, eyes, hair . . . I came out of the womb like a character from a horror movie. It was November 7, 1942. I was a miracle in her eyes. She had had three stillbirths before I was born. Much later in life, she told me she thought she was cursed and my birth brought light back into her life. From that day forth, her arms were wide to all who sought her affection.

My father was a true man, a strict man. He wanted many children because a great man needs to have a legacy. I was the black sheep of our family. *Mi hermano*, Gaspar, was the golden child. Everybody—teachers, our parents, priests, store owners—loved him. It was clear to us all that Gaspar would go on to do important things. I was a real bastard. When out of their sight, I knew my parents had palpitations thinking about what I might be doing. I couldn't help it. I loved to cause trouble. By the age of eight, I was a fighter. Nobody could cross me, and many people tried. My fists were constantly aching. My neighborhood enemies fueled my passion to establish my dominance however I could. I was destined for combat. It couldn't have been more apparent. Yet, in Panama at this time, a boy who fought in school was reprimanded in more ways than one. The priests would hit me with sticks, and when I got home, my father would make me kneel atop corn kernels and hold my arms out wide while he placed calculus books in my palms. It was a Panamanian crucifixion, fucking torture. I was lucky to have such a sweet mother. When my father wasn't looking, she would lift the books out of my hands and bear the weight of my responsibility for as long as she could. My father had no idea.

My father worked on the canal when I was a boy. He was a strong, loyal, good man. He was also a tough caballero, a family-first kind of guy, the head of the pack. "Life is not easy, Carlitos," he would tell me. Even as a boy, I knew he was right. None of us children disobeyed him in his home. I would watch as he stained his uniform with blood and sweat every single day to feed us. There was honor in the work he did; I just didn't want it for myself. I needed more power.

The years passed, and I grew stronger than the other boys in Chiriqui. Physically, I was a beast. Mentally, I was cunning. I had fought to channel my physical rage, but it wasn't until I was eleven years old that I found something that would become a lifelong passion, a marriage in some ways.

"I want you to have this, Carlitos," my father said to me as he handed me a knife with a silver blade and a corked handle.

"It's heavy," I responded.

"It's a hunting knife," his voice boomed.

It stayed with me everywhere I went, strapped to my side. I never drew it to harm another person, but then again, I didn't own it for very long. I walked down the main *calle* in town one day as a young boy. It was winter. Some older boys had these cages down by their feet. They were kicking them. The piercing pitch of roosters' screams echoed in my eardrums.

"What are you doing?" I asked the boys.

"Cockfighting, *cabron*," they responded with a snub.

I saw one rooster per cage. They had sharp claws, like knives. I noticed scars and indentations in their flesh. "How much are you selling them for?" I asked.

The boys all laughed at me.

I was considerably younger. I didn't care. I could have beat the shit out of any of them.

"*Chucha madre*, go home, kid," one fucker told me.

The balls on that asshole. I had to show him I meant business, so I slung out my glistening knife from my waistband and extended it toward their faces. The boys all took a step back. A jolt of energy struck my heart, and electricity pumped through my veins. I felt alive. "I'll trade you this knife for your best rooster," I said. It was a no-brainer. I wanted the best and only the best, the one that would make me a champion of that town and the whole province of Chiriqui.

"This is the king, you see. Look at his claws, his beak . . . he's been champion for six months," they said as they lifted a cage and presented a rooster to me.

After all these years, it pains me that I forget that fucking bird's name. I've had so many since. I've trained national champions, but that bird, that fucking bird, I just can't remember. I told the kid he had a deal, and we swapped. I carried that rooster right to the nearest *gallera*. It was just off the main street. The inside was an oven. Almost every old, dirty bastard in there smoked cigars or cigarettes, and some men were so drunk they would forget which rooster was theirs. The stench was near unbearable, the air hung heavy, and the lights were dim around the stands. Only inside the arena was lit.

I walked right into the middle of that place and opened my lungs. "Who wants to fight?" I screamed.

Wiser men than I jumped in my direction. Rafael, a caballero in his thirties, got there first. The Devil's advocate. It boils my blood just thinking of him. . . . I put my rooster right into the arena and stood back, arms crossed, awaiting my award. My rooster was the best, after all. It had been champion for six months. Well, the bell rang, and I heard my rooster squawk like a chick while it ran in circles, flapping its wings like a fucking duck. Rafael's rooster submitted mine in no more than ten seconds. *Chucha.* My fucking rooster was useless! I stuck him back in that arena two more times, and then he died. In two hours, I lost all my money, my knife, and my "champion." He was a shit rooster. End of story. I learned two valuable lessons that day. Never trust a man by his word; trust him only by his actions. And I learned not to buy roosters from fucking punks. *Puta madre.*

I wasn't somebody who ever cared what people thought of him. I had confidence. My father cared deeply about politics and the world around him. When the Cubans had their revolution in 1959, my father practically pinned me next to the radio so I could hear about this monumental event. Radio Soberana, it was biased toward America. Even I knew that as a young boy. In some ways, I wish I had paid more attention at the time because of how important Castro would become to me later in life. But, as a young man, I cared about only fighting, roosters, and women. Chucha, I've had more wives than nose jobs. That first surgery came a few years after that whole gallera experience. I was more of a man by then, more of a fighter, a force to be reckoned with. People were afraid of me. I was the champion of the pueblo. People threw money over my head, chanting, "Carlitos!" Sometimes, it would feel like rain, the cash fluttering down from above.

That day, a jab to the nose knocked me back a few steps. Blood rushed from my left nostril and dripped to the mud below. "*Puta madre*," I said as I spat red. Fury ran through me. I could feel the sparks in my fingertips. My opponent awaited my move. I knew then to be patient. I could see his legs were growing tired. The mud fatigued him; I had the advantage. I went for the death blow but slid on the surface, and I caught nothing but air, fist striking nothing. It didn't matter. My opponent was clearly exhausted. Every inhale sounded like a whistle. I picked myself up. He stood back. We locked eyes. His were wide open and bloodshot.

"*A BALAZO!*" the children in the crowd screamed.

My opponent fell right back and crashed into the mud. "Fucking *cocobolo*, go work a fucking job," I said before turning my back to the asshole to collect my winnings. I never had respect for the older boys who didn't work. That motherfucker didn't even have hair on his head, and he would spend his days trying to scam a *pelao* like me. He learned a lesson that day.

I was seventeen. I was becoming a man, but I was directionless. This is when Noriega came into my life. The end of the school year was approaching, and I didn't know how I would spend my summer. In my teenage years, I worked every blue-collar job available. Stores, farms, bookstores, in the church . . . I was a breadwinner. I paid rent to my parents as soon as I could earn.

Gaspar was like this, too. He studied more than I did and exercised his brain more than his muscles. "Carlos, the bookstore owners need to know if you are returning," Gaspar once told me.

I was almost offended by such a notion! My hands were thick, and my skin was coarse. I was a physical worker, and I knew I could make money in the way I wanted to. Self-sufficiency was my goal. By age seventeen, I had figured out I could make money two ways. The first was fighting, but even I knew I should fight only once daily; otherwise I might scramble my brain. My second realization came when I picked up a pool cue inside one of the town's saloons. I had skill, but more importantly, local men had a fresh paycheck and a stomach full of liquor. Their egos plagued their minds. I would play them like a fiddle. This was when I started to make real money.

My fingers gripped around the wooden handle of an old saloon door in the heart of town one day. I entered to a musk of cigarette smoke that hung over a couple of dozen men in dirty clothes. The floorboards creaked as I approached the bartender. Behind the man, there were three shelves of liquor. The top shelf was for whiskey, the vodka and gin in the middle, and finally, on the bottom row, a beautiful bottle of seco sat staring right back at me. It was unopened. Fresh. My mouth salivated at the thought of it.

"Two seco," I demanded, handing the bartender money. I rested my seco glasses on a splintering wooden ledge opposite the saloon pool table where the velvet lining was red and the balls were scuffed from years of use.

"Hey, *zambito*," a familiar voice yelled to me from across the table.

That motherfucker, Rafael. . . . He held a pool cue and stood alongside three of his caballeros. I hated that asshole.

"You want to lose money again, cabron?" he asked.

"Line them up, puta," I responded.

Twenty American dollars. That was a lot of money back then for a kid like me. Rafael had to use balboa, the currency that now exists only in my memory. It's cambiar. It's change, useless. I played him with all of his friends watching, and I won. The floorboards creaked as I went for the money.

"What do you think you're doing, Carlos?" Rafael boomed as the cabron pushed me away.

I punched him right in the lip, and he tackled me to the ground. The music stopped, men swarmed, money fluttered from above, and we rolled around in it until a giant, veiny hand planted on my shoulder and ripped me off the floor and to my feet.

"Carlitos!" It was my father.

He dragged me out of the saloon, all before I could even finish my second shot of seco. Rafael wiped the blood from his lip and counted his cash with a fucking smirk on his face as my dad kicked the door open and threw me onto the dusty ground outside.

"What the fuck do you think you're doing, Carlitos?"

"That motherfucker just hustled me!"

"I don't care. Why do you spend your time here? These cabrons? They're losers. They're all losers. If you want to be different, you have to act differently. Do you understand?"

"Yes, Papa," I responded with my head low.

"This country needs people who can change it, not people who contribute to its submission."

I was locked away for the first time in my life. Grounded. When my father left the house, my mother would come into my room with fresh pineapple juice. "Don't tell your papa," she would say before kissing my forehead. With my father, I had the truth. My mother was an idealist, a beautiful soul. I had a spectrum of love and harshness that many do not get. Still, I was bored. I felt how a prisoner does on Coiba Island. I would dream of women while I sat in my bedroom. There was a girl I was seeing, Gracia. I needed to see her, and I found my way by sneaking through the window late at night and returning before my father awoke. We would fuck wherever we could. It didn't matter. Nobody but the town drunks were awake, and they would never remember seeing us. By the time I was eighteen, she had already given birth to my first child, Yolanda.

All these moments in my childhood led me to meeting the most important figure in my life. The summer was coming to an end, and my father had arranged for some extended family members to come to our house for a party. He gave me money to pick up lamb meat from a farm just outside town. The heat swelled as I shifted my body along the dirt road with a bag slung over my aching shoulder. Bullets of sweat ran down my forehead. I could hear a car revving behind me. It was approaching fast. I turned, and a beat-up pickup truck skidded right alongside me.

Rafael sat in the driver's seat. "Need a ride, Carlos?" he asked.

Gravity beat me down, and my spine was hunched. My eyes vibrated from the headache that pounded against the innards of my skull. "Go fuck yourself," I responded. Chucha. I would never get in that car. He laughed like a fucking hyena. I wanted to fucking kill him, but my house shimmered in the distance like a mirage.

"Carlos, Carlos!" my mother's voice screamed. "Your cousins are here, Carlos; come inside with the meat quickly."

A blast of cool air from a spinning fan struck me as I entered my home.

"Buenas, Carlitos," my aunties and uncles yelled as they rushed me with hugs and kisses.

Music played from my father's old radio. My mother cooked in the kitchen. The smell of the various stews and meats bubbling and brewing in the pots lingered in the air.

"Que pasa?" they all asked me.

I was the center of attention.

Gaspar had already been berated with inquisitions. "I need a break," he told me as he exited the house.

My parents treated our home like a hotel. Our guests were always front of mind. It was very important to them that people saw how we lived and how we treated those in our circle. I never complained about the affection. I was social. I enjoyed the conversation. As I spoke with a *tio* of mine, I could see a man in uniform sitting on my sofa alongside my cousin Felicidad. Her nickname in the family was Muneca. She was introducing this suited man to my father on this day. His outfit was almost entirely beige. Every aspect of it caught my eye. The neatly tucked shirt, the black leather belt that held his pants. I noticed glistening medals pinned to his breast, and stitched patterns ran along the sleeves. He looked unlike any man I had ever seen before.

"Come over here, Carlitos. There's somebody I want to introduce you to," my father yelled.

The man's grip was tight, and he didn't break his intense but not unfriendly stare. His smile was infectious.

"Carlitos, this is Manuel Noriega," my father said.

"It's nice to meet you, Manuel," I told him.

His smile never faded. His grip remained firm. "I hear you like to fight," Manuel said.

Felicidad shook her head. It was clear my father had told her about my behavior. It was no secret that I was a wild child.

"Do you box?" Noriega asked.

"Yes," I responded.

"Good. Only an idiot fights for no benefit."

"I agree," I responded.

"Don't act righteous, Carlitos," my father butted in.

"Even the craziest animals can be tamed," Noriega began. "During my time in the Chorrillos Military Academy, I stood alongside some of the most vicious men I have ever met. Within four years, not only had they been tamed, but they had also been programmed to use their power for duty."

"That's what my boy needs," my father said.

"You know, it was only in 1946 that our country focused on strengthening the minds of our soldiers. That is when the School of the Americas was established, which led to the creation of Law 44 in 1953."

"Law 44?" I asked.

"An intelligence branch within the National Guard. Right now it is weak, but one day, it will be strong. Trust me. I have stood next to the men who have been trained in these covert arts."

"I've been trying to tell Carlos to do something more with his life," my father said.

"Have you ever thought about joining the military?" Noriega asked.

"I would make a good fighter. The best," I responded.

"I recently worked for the US Army Map Service here in Panama. Truthfully, I did so because they paid four times the salary of a man in the National Guard. However, it was never my plan to do this for my entire life. Not every Panamanian needs to always act in the interest of the gringos. . . . I am soon joining the National Guard, and one day, I could use a man like you in my corner," he exclaimed.

Noriega convinced me to alter my life in a moment. I was sold on the prospect of the military. Manuel knew how to speak to me, and I could feel his respect for my family. I took a liking to him instantly. He and I spent hours that evening conversing and laughing. Muneca acted like a princess. She wanted him all for herself. Manuel was a man of men. He told her to be quiet and that he was there to make friends with the family with whom he would one day come to share blood. His presence entranced me. When night fell, fireworks lit up the sky, and the booming echo sprayed over our village. Noriega and I were drunk. We sang. We danced. We told jokes.

My childhood seemed to come and go quickly. It was my last day at home. My bags were packed, and I would travel wherever Noriega needed me. President Roberto Chiari was giving a speech the same morning. For the first time, I tuned into Radio Soberana with genuine interest. I could hear the Americans in his rhetoric. It was raining on this day. The smell of the rainforest hung in the air inside my home. My father was working.

My mother sat by the window and watched the droplets fall. "I'm going to miss you, Carlitos," she said repeatedly. I deeply felt that a young man must leave home if he wishes to make something of himself. She knew that. She understood me better than anyone.

I couldn't listen to the thrashing drops any longer. I needed to take care of something before I left home for good. "I'll be back soon, Mama," I told her as I rose to my feet. The door slammed before she could ask me where I was going. Droplets of mud sprayed onto my pants as I charged down the street, right toward the saloon where I had been hustled. I whipped the door open. Rainwater dripped from my clothes.

"Look who it is," Rafael echoed across the bar. The cabron held a pool cue in his right hand. Three of his amigos stood behind him, holding cans of Balboa. "Did you come to lose more money?" he asked.

The floorboards creaked as I stomped over them. I could see the bartender reaching for the Bowie knife that rested underneath the bar. I picked up a pool cue that rested atop a red velvet table. My hands clenched around the indented base. The organic wooden carvings scratched against my palm. I swung. The vibration of the strike reverberated along the cue and rippled against my hand. Rafael fell straight onto his back and thumped against the ground. He groaned and held the side of his cut and bleeding face. I swung into the open air, and his amigos jumped.

The bartender whipped the knife out from under the bar. "Stay right there, Carlos," he yelled to me. I stood over Rafael. He trembled between my legs. My body blocked the dull light above, and my shadow engulfed the rat bastard. "Pussy," I scoffed as I reached into his pocket and took back my money.

I would return to my home many times, but I would never look back. I left to join Noriega with wide eyes and a thumping heart. The image of the firing pistol flashed in my memory every month of my life. In many ways, it was that moment that defined me. I loved nothing more than the feeling of power that jolted through me when I held a weapon. My purpose was revealing itself.

Chapter 3
Change Is Brewing

Bullets of sweat rushed along my skin. I stuck to the concrete floor. My spine was bent, and my muscles throbbed at the rate of my heart. The cell containing me was small and stank of shit and piss. I had gotten arrested for carrying a military-issued pistol without military identification. My timing was not ideal. There had been a riot at the American Embassy sometime prior. Students, men, and women alike protested in the name of our people. This scared the Americans. It was the first time the gringos could genuinely feel our anguish. Yet, because of this, everything became more tense. I was a young man living in a contentious country in the sixties. It didn't matter that I was working under Manuel in a military unit. I was in Chiriqui, near the town of David, and the presence of danger was about, just as it was in the Ciudad. There were enemies everywhere. Political opposition was mounting, and it was clear the National Guard would have to be the anchor. I placed much of the blame on Arnulfo Arias. Ever since the 1940s, his convoluted national ideals caused disruption domestically and abroad. While I was in that cell, rumor of his return escalated the already contentious nation. The American-bought media sought for his Panamenista Party to rule, but the public largely disagreed, and within that disagreement birthed bandidos and aggression that rattled society. It was not a safe time. We desperately needed stability.

Some years earlier, Noriega had met Omar Torrijos in Colon during Carnival. I know Torrijos instantly took a liking to Manuel, who was soon tasked with overseeing the region of Chiriqui. Manuel wanted someone he trusted to provide him with intelligence in this part of my country. Few men were as close to him as I was. My role was simple: tell Noriega everything I learned about the people, the gringos, and even the police, as you never knew who was conspiring to hurt the nation. With that knowledge, Noriega could make informed, high-level decisions. There were significant problems that men like him would tackle. His time in Chorrillos provided him with worthwhile connections to the CIA and DEA. That was where he met Richard Helms, who would later introduce him to men like George Bush and William Casey. Manuel and Richard were introduced at the Military Academy. I was on the outskirts of some of those high-level conversations, but Manuel would only divulge the important information with Torrijos and other superiors like Federico Boyd and Boris Martinez. My job was to make sure the smaller problems didn't get bigger. Most of the non-consequential issues I would provide knowledge on were just local crimes or minor political interferences. Yet times were changing, and I needed that fucking gun more than ever.

"Can I get some fucking water? It's a hundred degrees in here. I'm ready to boil," I yelled to the overweight guard sitting in a wooden chair outside the cell door.

He scoffed at me and repositioned his stomach, so it would press into his belt instead of bulging over it. That's when I noticed the Panamenista Party badge on his desk. The fucker was an Arnulfista, a devout one. He had no reason to hate the National Guard. I knew men just like him. They did what was easy.

My blood bubbled. "Puta madre," I screamed as I smashed my fist into the wall. I have always loved my people and my country, but some motherfuckers didn't deserve respect. It was men like these who became submissive, rolling over for the Americans like a dog. "Hey, you've got some shit on your desk," I said, pointing at the badge.

A pen was launched at my eyes. It barely scratched the tip of my nose. "Shut the fuck up, *ladrona*," he yelled at me.

Arnulfistas were a confused people led by a madman who had already been ousted twice. They were idiots, snakes in the grass, fucking *culebras*. If only that fat bastard could see into the future, he'd burn that badge and open his fucking eyes.

"You know what Arias plans to do?" I spoke up.

"What?" The guard responded.

"He's going to cheat his way into power, and he will succeed because he sucks America's dick. We will be living in a dictatorship sponsored by the gringos. And you and me? We won't be able to change anything because America has its hand up Arias like a smiling puppet."

"You forget that in World War Two Arias told the Americans no when they asked him to build more military bases on Panamanian land. He is anti-imperialist."

"And yet there are still multiple American bases on our land today. Fucking idiot."

The National Guard was still relatively new. Our influence was growing, and it was because of our leaders. At the time, Torrijos called most of the shots, but there were historically key figures like Paredes Del Rio, Florencio Flores, Boris Martinez, and Diaz Duque who were just as close to the government, if not closer. Omar was older than Manuel. Yet, I could see that Manuel was the most promising. He had the strongest, most genuine connections to our friends and our enemies. I knew he made it a point to plant the seeds of friendship early. Manuel was necessary for the National Guard. I was under Noriega's wing, an apprentice of sorts. People knew me because of this.

I always had strong feelings about Arias and his crazed mind. Yet, I had strong opinions about every leader. I could never imitate respect. Before I was in that jail cell in Chiriqui, the president was Marco Aurelio Robles. He led the National Liberal Party after Chiari, and he did what he could for a man attached by strings. It was all the same, really. There was only so much change a Panamanian could instill without the action being intervened by our overseers. Chiari signed the first major Canal Treaty, which gave my country more rights in the zone, but then, these riots in the canal zone happened, and everything seemed to wash away as

Robles stepped into power. The last thing the Americans ever wanted was our people in their zone.

Now, I just wanted to get out of that fucking cell. "Open the door, you fat asshole," I yelled to the guard.

"I have no problem tying you up and tossing you in with the crocodiles in the river outside of town. People who serve this country go missing every day," he responded.

He wasn't wrong about that, though I knew that if the asshole put a finger on me, my superiors would hunt him down.

The phone rang. It rumbled atop the wooden table the cop sat at. I could smell the stench of rum and cigarettes from the bastard's mouth. "What now?" he mumbled, lifting the phone to his ear. "Yes?" he began.

I could hear water dripping from the pipes that hid behind the walls and circulated the building. What a shithole. I groaned as I pushed myself to my feet and gripped the rusted bars. Shavings of brown dust stuck to my hands. I pressed my face between the rusty gaps.

The guard gulped and looked at me. His eyes grew wide. Sweat bubbled on his forehead and rushed down those fat fucking cheeks of his. The drops fell to the chipped floorboards and soaked between the splinters and into the dirt the foundation rested upon. "Yes, it was me," he mumbled. "Francisco, yes, that's me," he said with a shake in his voice. I could hear the bones in the guard's neck creak. "I didn't know he was one of *your* men." The floorboards squeaked as he set the phone atop the wooden table and shimmied toward my cell.

I smiled at the cabron while he slotted the key into the lock and opened my cell door. A gust of fresh air whistled and wrapped around my bare feet.

"He wants to speak with you," the guard said, pointing at the phone.

I navigated through splinters and nails, careful not to lose a foot. The black phone calmly rested atop the cluttered table, the guard breathing heavily in my direction. "Hello," I said as I picked up the phone.

"Hola, Carlitos."

"Manuel." I knew it was him.

"There's a car waiting for you outside. These fuckers need to learn to respect us," he followed.

"Thank you," I responded.

"Give the phone back to the pig, *por favor*."

The chord extended into a straight line as I reached the phone toward the cop.

"Manuel still wants to speak with me?" he asked nervously.

I nodded.

He gulped. I could practically see his heart beating through his chest. He looked uncomfortable just being alive.

I turned and walked right out of the police station. The air outside the station was dry. Warm winds rustled my hair. A green military vehicle pulled up before me and skidded in the dirt. Dust lifted and hung in suspension until the driver opened the passenger door window.

"Carlitos?"

I heard a yell. I could see two Panamanian men in the back. A pair of military boots were immediately handed to me. The interior of the car was black, and the leather seats were hot to the touch. The light could barely enter through the tinted windows I sat by. The two men behind me carried pistols and smoked cheap cigarettes. The driver didn't look at me once.

"Where are we going?" I asked.

"David. Headquarters," the driver responded.

Our vehicle stopped outside of an old Spanish building, a beige structure with Galician arches and large wooden doors akin to those guarding the entrance to a Gothic church. The ground was level when my feet struck the earth, paved and polished. The noises of the city were muffled in my ears; I heard only the sound of palm trees swaying in the breeze like a symphony. We charged toward the doors. The shadow of the structure engulfed us in its shade from the beating sun and cooled our boiling bodies. We entered, and my gaze was brought up toward the ceiling, dozens of feet in the air, before I heard a familiar voice.

"Carlitos! Welcome, my friend," Manuel boomed. A set of doors opened from the other end of the hallway, and Manuel's silhouette shimmered alongside a half-dozen armed guards. He stepped into the light and threw his arms in the air. "How are you feeling?"

"I'm fine, sir," I responded. My back was straight. I looked him in the eyes.

He chuckled and gently slapped my face. "You smell like a whorehouse, mi amigo. You can take a shower here."

Manuel trusted me, and so he treated me differently from the others around him. We knew many good and loyal men, just like the many faceless and nameless men I would encounter in my life, but none of them would ever have his trust as I did. Noriega and I both knew deep down that if Boris Martinez came walking through those doors and demanded the guards wring Manuel by his neck and slice him open, those soldiers surrounding us would have taken out their knives before even drawing a breath. I was different. I followed only Manuel.

"Carlos, let me talk with you alone for one moment," Noriega said, gesturing for me to follow him into the corner. "You are doing a good job," he told me.

"I wish I could do more."

"Let me tell you a few things, my friend. It may seem like chaos, but we have not seen true anarchy yet. Look at our friends in Cuba. After their revolution in 1959, Fidel knew that enemies would quickly surround him. The betrayal that was the Bay of Pigs proved to him that if he wanted to stay above the chaos, he would have to support the Soviets. Castro understands he must fight an ideological battle in order for his country to be free."

"I understand."

"Do you know of the National Security Doctrine?"

"Yes, it means the Americans can squash Marxist uprisings in Central America because Communism is a human threat."

"The soldiers they send to slaughter thousands of innocent men, women, and children stand on our land."

"What can we do about it?"

"Fidel once told me that if America wants to crush you, it will find a way to do it and to make it your fault. He said one must work with Americans enough to postpone the inevitable.. Do you think we are any different?"

"We are a third-world country with a golden crown."

"I've been given orders from the very top, Carlos—Martinez, Boyd, Torrijos, . . . In the next few years, you will see much change. It begins now. The National Guard must put its foot down and do what our government cannot."

"I am ready."

"Jorge Samudio's tax reforms purposely hurt the rich. Samudio knows he is poking the white bear by attacking the elite. There is less incentive for wealthy businessmen to invest here, hurting the nation, the canal, and ultimately, the United States. We can expect to see a push for the Panamenista party. The Americans will back them."

Even then, it was evident Manuel was going to rise in the ranks and become a great leader. He started building the foundation around him, and I was one of his architects. His inner circle was tight and impenetrable, and I was there. My life had promise. I would have done anything for him. Everything Manuel told me began to come true. The American and Panamanian elite responded to social change with media corruption and fraud. They barely tried to hide it. There were only two television stations, and both of them spoke only of American-backed candidates in the Liberal Party. Radio Soberana had become especially one-sided. Between 1964 and 1968, it became apparent not only to us in the

National Guard but also to the public that Panamanian issues would never come first unless a true statement was made by the people. With this societal change came even more tension, some of which sparked violence. This was my first significant chance to prove myself to people like Torrijos. Manuel knew me; he trusted me, but I desired growth through independent action. We needed to prove we could take care of ourselves.

Chapter 4
The Coup

The sound of gunfire in the streets pounded my eardrums. I watched Panama change forever after the coup of 1968. Boris Martinez overthrew the crazed President Arnulfo Arias after only eleven days in office, and still, it was too many. Just as I had always known, Arnulfistas turned the election into a fraud, and the people could smell it from a mile away. On October 1, 1968, Arias assumed his throne and began dismantling the government piece by piece, starting with his greatest threat, the National Guard. I saw how he toppled the leadership with my own two eyes. He knew that men like Martinez, Boyd, and Torrijos were not likely to submit, so he chose Diaz Duque. This did not sit well with me. Duque was an outsider, more loyal to the dictators of Chile and Argentina than to the democratic Panama. The decision violated agreements between the government and the National Guard. I had never seen someone as infuriated as General Bolívar Vallarino. The military elites knew they had to intervene, and so the National Guard stepped in. Ultimately, it was Boris Martinez, head of the Chiriqui Military Zone, who made the final decision to overthrow Arias about a week later. I was there for the exact moment of realization, too. We were all in the Baru Brewery on October 6. Arnulfo gave a speech to the National Guard, which he was planning to dismantle, and he purposely disregarded Martinez of his much deserved military honors for serving the nation. Arias turned his cheek on Martinez. That was enough for whispers to begin in small circles, holding covert meetings at Olmedo Miranda's La Pollera Colorada estate. I was there for the conspiracy, and I was involved in the coup, but I thought Boris was just as mad as Arias.

We all understood it needed to be Torrijos to ultimately come out on top. Boris Martinez was unlikeable. He was abrasive, and he certainly had trouble communicating. It was his problem. He couldn't express himself or his ideals in a motivating way. Something had to be done before Boris could start implementing his policies. Noriega was hearing whispers from the United States; it was waiting for us to figure out our problems before deciding whom to support. Torrijos had been in El Salvador at the time as a military attaché, and he soon returned to Panama, where he was promoted to full colonel and named commandant of the National Guard. We could see the threat that loomed over Martinez's head from a mile away.

I remember those days all too well. Lieutenant Colonels Amado Sanjur, Ramiro Silvera, and Luis Nentzen Franco, men who had once stood by Torrijos against Boris Martinez, were now secretly plotting another coup, this time against Torrijos. I was there as the operation unfolded, and I know this was no spur-of-the-moment uprising; it was a carefully orchestrated plan backed by the CIA and US military intelligence. The United States had lent its support to these conspirators, claiming that Torrijos was either a communist sympathizer or at least a leftist, and he needed to go.

On December 15, 1969, Torrijos left for Mexico, his mind weighed down by the unrest in Panama, yet completely unaware of the treachery brewing in his absence. I remember the shock that ran through our ranks when, as he was far away, the conspirators stormed into our headquarters and boldly declared that Torrijos had been deposed on account of his supposed communist leanings.

But their coup never gained the traction they had hoped for. I, along with many other lower-ranking officers, refused to abandon our leader. The answer to all the madness was a thousand miles north of us. Manuel contacted Torrijos and told him it was time to return. "It needs to be you," he said. I was right by Noriega's side when he made contact. Omar had a personality, and the gringos could communicate with him.

FBI, CIA, DEA, ATF . . . Torrijos was someone who provided them with knowledge from Central America. I was young, and much of what Torrijos worked toward didn't concern me directly. At this time, I was more of a pawn than a king. I served Omar, who, in turn, served the United States. For the United States, the threat of communism was too great not to have people in its corner in Central America. Omar was a point of contact. He was a lightning rod for Manuel in many ways. It was Noriega who orchestrated the web of intelligence that centered on Panama and expanded all across the world. Yet, it was Omar Torrijos who stood at the podium and led the people. It was a symbiotic partnership, and both men understood what the other brought to the table.

We waited in Chiriqui for Torrijos to return. It was not easy to bring him back into the country. The military was told to look for him. Martinez would have imprisoned Torrijos at the first chance, maybe even killed him. We arranged for a private plane to pick Torrijos up in Mexico and fly him to Chiriqui. Few of us knew. Only men whom Noriega trusted were involved. We were all at the airstrip. It was the middle of the night. The headlights of our cars lit up a section of the runway. I stood next to Manuel, a team of trained soldiers behind us. Our gaze looked to the night sky. The stars hid from us. Clouds covered the moon.

"History is happening, Carlos," Manuel said to me.

I could feel the change. Shivers slithered along my skin. The air was cool that night. Hours of darkness passed when, suddenly, two glimmers of light appeared in the sky. Their luminescence grew brighter with each second that passed.

Manuel turned and nodded to the men. "As soon as that plane lands, we're moving," he said.

I understood completely. We had to make sure nobody saw us from the moment Torrijos landed until he stood at the podium of this nation. The rubber tires of the Cessna screeched upon touchdown. A staircase extended from the plane, and Torrijos sauntered down it in civilian clothing. He wore American jeans and a brown suede jacket, and his polished black shoes glistened even in the darkness. "It's good to see you, Manuel," he said as he hugged Noriega.

"We're taking you to the city now. We cannot let anyone set eyes on you until we know it is safe," Manuel responded.

"I know the drill," said Omar. "What are the newspapers saying?"

"*El Mundo* was on board with the first coup. The world knew Arias violated constitutional laws. This coup is in the interest of the Americans. They do not want you, Torrijos."

"What do we do with Boris?" Torrijos asked.

"We won't reinvent the wheel."

"We'll find him somewhere nice to live," said Torrijos. Then, to me, he said, "Señor Carlos Wittgreen! Mi amigo. How are you, kid?"

"I'm well, señor. It's good to see you," I responded.

"I'm hearing good things about you. Keep it up."

Boris could not make a rational decision, and because of that, Torrijos had no choice but to take his seat. I helped him do it. Before Omar's consolidation of our government, the people were scared. Rumors of rights being stripped away and the constitution being shredded circulated in society. I never paid attention, knowing what I knew, but families hid, scared, and I never wanted a fellow Panamanian to fear their leaders. Martinez had crazy bastards like Colonel José María Pinilla and Colonel Bolívar Urrutia lead a junta to assume power, claiming to restore constitutional order while consolidating military control but doing the exact opposite. I stood before our new government with wide eyes. I felt the change.

Over the next several years, Torrijos directed the people. Presidents came and went before my eyes, but it was Omar who made the decisions. Noriega was under his wing alongside Ruben Dario Paredes del Rio and Diaz Herrera. I swam in the wake, doing whatever I could for Manuel. Noriega found himself at a lot of important gatherings that I had to attend with him. Manuel had become chief of intelligence, the head of G-2, the most important intelligence agency in the Americas for two decades. He leaned on me during this time. I was exposed to information that separated my name from the rest. I gave orders. My men would sniff out knowledge like dogs, and then the information would pass to me, and Manuel would pass it to Torrijos if necessary. We had a system. We let Torrijos focus on larger issues, like bringing the canal back into our hands or removing American troops. We knew it was time to strengthen ourselves, and to do that, we needed to wine and dine our overseers.

"They need to feel comfortable enough to forget that we are not submissive animals."

One Flag Day, November 4, several years into Torrijos's leadership, I did not party as I should have. The holiday felt different back then. Everybody was drunk off their asses, but on this day, I was not. I had information for Noriega—a rumor of an American conspiracy to kill Omar Torrijos, perhaps Manuel, too. Rumors were difficult to deal with. I couldn't just point a finger at the United States. They would have bitten it off. Most of the time, these conspiracies were just rumors. However, even if the conspiracy was baseless, you could find some truth in a rumor. I didn't understand why the United States would even want to do such a thing to one of its most valuable assets. Torrijos did what they asked from day one. Whenever a member of the American government took a trip south, Torrijos himself would meet the person at the gates, and if, for whatever reason, he couldn't, Manuel would assume the greeting role in his place, usually alongside our president.

I rushed to an event where the country's most important people were. Hordes of drunk people blocked the streets in Casco Viejo. It took me forever to maneuver through them. "Get the fuck out of my way," I screamed from my car. The string of holidays starting from the third and ending at the tenth attracted everyone to the city's party center. It was chaos.

The soldiers guarding the building let me in right away. They knew who I was. Most people did by then. I was always with Noriega, and he was a figurehead. I was a sponge, learning all I could from such a wise man. Every major decision, in one way or another, started with him. Torrijos was the diplomat, and Manuel was the brain. I had to find him immediately. The hallway was lined with incredible artwork. Two oakwood doors opened before me, and a thunderous unleash of chatter and laughter exploded in my eardrums. There were hundreds of people in attendance. To my right, a group of American military officials drank whiskey with their gorgeous blond wives. They always seemed to be blondes. Women like that were the main import in the canal zone.

"Carlitos!"

I turned to my left, and Torrijos came crashing into me with a bear hug. He was drunk. A charming smile was painted on his face. I could see the wrinkles at the sides of his eyes were bulging.

"Where's your drink, Carlos?" he asked. Before I could even answer, Torrijos grabbed the sleeve of a waiter and snapped his fingers. "What do you want, Carlos?"

I wanted to find Manuel but didn't see him anywhere. "There are a lot of gringos here," I said.

Torrijos chuckled, patting my shoulder with force. It didn't need to be said. Everybody in that room was there to seduce each other. The Americans didn't want to talk to National Guardsmen like me. They didn't want to see the men who fought; they barely even wanted to hear about them. They were interested only in knowing that somebody was delivering on their interests. Torrijos was having a good time because that's what was required of him. His left-leaning ideals put a tag on him, and so he needed to charm the Americans in order to keep the relationship balanced.

I could see eyes in my direction, Panamanian eyes. Members of our government knew me. To them, I was the dog who chased when Noriega pointed. Those people often felt they were better than that, though they were doing the exact same thing for the Americans. "Have you seen Manuel?" I asked Omar.

"Manuel, Manuel . . . I just saw him, yes, yes. I think he's . . . maybe he's outside," he responded.

The waiter returned with my drink.

"Gracias," I said. The cool cubes of ice numbed my lips. The taste of the liquor was immaculate. It must have been a rare bottle. Still, I had a mission. "I'm going to go find Manuel," I told Torrijos. I stepped away.

He was instantly swarmed by a group of Americans. They wore navy suits and brown shoes. No military man had such taste. I sensed they were government, perhaps intelligence. CIA, DEA, ATF, FBI. Whoever they were, they had much to say to Torrijos, who listened with a glare in his eye. They were like piranhas to flesh. I walked through a pair of silk curtains that fluttered in a gentle breeze and left our nation's leader in my wake. My trail led out to a balcony. Manuel leaned against the barrier and smoked a cigar with a gringo. They were laughing.

Noriega spotted me instantly. "Carlitos! Come here, my friend," he yelled.

The American had a receding hairline. I could tell that he gelled it down so his head would look flat. The way his lips puckered reminded me of Nixon. He had a smirk on his face.

Noriega could make anybody laugh. He knew where your funny bone was. He'd grab it and not let go. "Carlitos, this is Richard Helms," Noriega introduced.

"It's nice to meet you," Helms said as he reached his hand out to me. There was a sleek, silk touch to his handshake. He looked me right in the eyes with a cracked smile.

"Richard and I met at Chorrillos," Noriega stated.

"We go back farther than I'd care to admit," Helms joked.

"This is the man you want to know if you're ever in trouble," Noriega said with a smile.

"Yeah, yeah, yeah. . . . I'm going to get another. We'll talk later, Manuel. It was nice to meet you, Carlos," Helms said before walking inside.

"That man is the director of the CIA."

My gaze on Manuel lingered as he took a drag from his cigar. His eyes followed Helms until he completely stepped out of sight. I'd come to know just how important Richard was to us. Manuel's genuine friendship with the man was not something to be overlooked, for us or for the Americans.

Manuel and I marinated in the silence for a moment, the muffled sounds of chatter and laughter dancing through the air. "Those men inside, they swarm Torrijos, making demands that are masked as favors," he said.

I was climbing the ranks. Not too long before that, I was getting in bar fights and buying shit roosters from spineless street urchins. I had developed. I was becoming a trusted man with a purpose. I could do anything those other men could do, and I would do it better. "What do you think of the conspiracy to assassinate you and Omar?" I asked.

"Moises Torrijos and his bodyguard, Guillermo, might be mixed up in some bad shit, drugs . . . I've heard rumors that the Americans are conspiring to assassinate Omar because of this. Me? It is likely. But where this rumor originated from? I do not know. I will be fine, mi amigo."

Manuel wanted to know every piece of information, true or not. False information could still paint a picture of what was happening on the ground floor of the nation. I bet he knew who wanted to make the call, but I also knew Manuel was not one to have a loud response.

Noriega led me inside, his arm over my shoulders. "There are many important people here tonight."

It was an honor to be in that room. Whispers sang from ear to ear, the kind of chatter that could shatter nations.

Manuel pointed to a well-dressed man standing at the bar. "You see that man? He's with Mossad, the finest intelligence agency there is."

That's the last I remember of the night. Once the bottle of seco was opened, my memory was wiped. Nobody partied harder than us. We showed our guests the night of their lives. I awoke in my bed the next morning with bags under my eyes and a naked woman by my side. "Chucha," I mumbled to myself as I arose and walked to the window. Rays of light shone through the glass and illuminated particles of dust that hung in suspension before me. I lifted the pane, and then I silently scanned the room. There were empty bottles of beer on the ground. The woman's dress was torn and flung against the wall. The heels she wore were carelessly tossed atop a bundle of my clothes. I lifted them out and set them by the bed.

"What time is it?" the woman asked as her eyes gradually opened.

"I don't know, *guapa*," I responded. My brain thumped against my skull like a beating heart.

"Guapa, guapa, you call me guapa all night and not once by my name," she complained.

I was too hung over for an argument. She was right. She knew she was. Arguing was pointless. A knock at the door. My feet felt heavy as I walked. I peeked through the peephole. A young boy with newspapers stood there patiently. He tapped his fingers against the wood. The pitter-patter was constant. I ripped the door open. The kid's arm hung in place.

"Anything interesting?" I asked as I snatched a newspaper from his hands.

He didn't respond at first. He just watched me as I flicked through headlines. Sometimes, intelligence slipped through the cracks and went to the media. I checked the papers first thing every morning.

"Carlos Wittgreen?" the boy asked.

"Yeah," I responded without lifting my head.

"I hear you're a very good boxer."

"You heard that, did you?"

"Yes."

"From whom?"

"My father . . . you know him from the cockfights in El Chorrillo."

"What's your name, kid?"

"Roberto."

"Roberto Duran?"

41

"Si, yes, that's me."

Roberto was in his late teens when I met him. He was just an amateur then, a nobody who lost his first three amateur fights. The kid sold newspapers to make some money. I wasn't on his route, but he still delivered to me. I had a reputation for fighting. Sure, I threw on the gloves every now and again, but my talents lay in physical psychology. I knew what move my opponent would make. There was an innate primal drive to the boy. It was palpable. He reminded me a lot of myself when I was young.

"I can't help you, kid," I said.

"Come on, man."

"If I could, I would. . . . Maybe in a few years when—"

"Come to my fight this week in El Chorrillo."

The phone in my apartment rang.

Roberto stared at me.

"Okay, kid. I'll go. Now, finish your job," I said.

He zipped up his satchel of newspapers and walked down the hall.

I closed the door. Ringing echoed. My head was already pounding. "Hello?" I spoke into the device. The ceramic casing was warm against my cheek.

"Carlos, it's Manuel. Come see me on Via Argentina. The Galician restaurant."

I set the phone down. The woman in my room sneezed. The floorboards creaked as I approached the doorway.

"Put your clothes on. I'll call you a taxi."

Traffic was heavy that morning. Exhaust stunk up the air. It was mayhem. My taxi driver barely spoke. He smoked a cigarette and listened to the radio. Venezuelan music played. The air was sweltering. Drops of sweat rolled down my cheek. I gripped the rotator attached to the door. The window wouldn't open. Chucha, it was a fucking shit box. "Can you open the window?" I asked.

"It doesn't open anymore," the driver responded.

"So fix it, you fucking bum," I said.

The rubber tires screeched. I jolted forward, hitting my head on the back of the driver's seat. He turned to me with rage in his eyes. "Nobody disrespects me in my own cab," he yelled. He was holding up traffic. Cars honked loudly behind us. I could see in the rearview mirror that the line of vehicles was piling up. My hand clenched into a fist. I felt the strain in my fingers. The skin over my knuckles stretched. The driver's eyes shot wide open. I pumped him. Blood exploded from his nose and sprayed onto the windows. A throbbing pounded in my arm. "What the fuck?" the driver yelled as he held his hands to his face.

"Drive! People have places to be," I yelled.

We arrived at the Galician restaurant in record time. I handed the driver three dollars. His wheels spun, dust kicked up behind them, and I never saw him again.

The restaurant was empty. It was still morning, after all. A doorman saw me on the sidewalk and yelled out to me. "Are you coming in, señor?"

I nodded to him.

His arm extended out as he welcomed me inside. The overhead lights had a warm red hue to them. Ember rays graced the open dining room.

Manuel sat with his back to the wall at the far end of the room. He had been reading a newspaper, a steaming cup of Peruvian coffee before him. "Carlitos, join me!" Manuel yelled.

The waiter pulled my chair out.

I sat down. "Two seco, por favor."

Manuel leaned back with a smile. He put his hands behind his head. "You had a fun night, no?"

Chucha, I couldn't contain myself. We both broke into hysterical laughter. He knew I had no fucking idea what he was talking about. The last thing I remembered was ordering two seco, one for me and one for the Mossad agent.

Our waiter swiftly returned with our drinks. Manuel and I fell silent as we sipped from the crackling glass. Satisfied exhales came from our mouths. The muffled sounds of the street hung in the air.

"I spoke with your father this morning," Manuel exclaimed.

"He told you about Gaspar's interest in politics?" I responded.

"That boy is going to be a very important man one day," Noriega said with a smile. Manuel coughed the phlegm out from his throat. He leaned forward. "You were right. Apparently, there has been some discussions about Omar from within Nixon's team. Maybe Mitchell; he is not a friend of ours. Even Helms is frustrated with us," he whispered.

"Why?"

"It is mainly because of Torrijos's beliefs, but there is discontent over Moises's drug trafficking allegations, which they feel is part of a larger problem," he told me.

The headache that corroded my brain suddenly vanished. A wave of clarity washed over. I almost fell out of my chair. "Motherfuckers," I mumbled.

Noriega exhaled, then finished his drink. He lifted the glass and tapped against it. The waiter nodded and scurried off.

"They are wrapped up in the early days of a scandal. We agitate them, yes, but they have no proof," Manuel said. "We are the crossroads of the worlds. Everybody is, one way or another, plotting to take a piece of us. That's why our intelligence is so important. If we can understand the state of international affairs from inside the walls of allies, we can know which direction our enemies are coming from."

There were still people who were mad about Arnulfo Arias's excommunication. Our country remained contentious, but it was getting better. Our most active units, the Tigres and the Pumas, were hunting down guerrillas, and the streets were safe from violent crime. The guerrillas were led by Walter Sardinas; he was from Uruguay. People continued to voice concerns about us, but our country was becoming stable. It felt like we were governing ourselves and taking the challenges as they came on every level. We wanted to be our own people.

I celebrated the rest of the festivities of that week until November 10. On the last day, Roberto had his eleventh amateur fight. I promised the boy I'd attend. All I had was my loyalty and my drive. Roberto Duran shared the same interests as I did. I sensed greatness in him, but he was a loose cannon, a hound who could not be tamed by just one man. He would need a team of people who were loyal to him. I knew his father well. He was a sociable man who loved to gamble and make money.

A single bright light shone down on the ring as I entered. I was surrounded by dozens of men, each giving off a different stink. A bookie slipped right by me and roamed through the crowd, taking bets. Duran was the favorite. His opponent had eight years on him. Chucha, I forget the fucker's name. He was too old to be taken seriously. Roberto was young; he had a future. A bell rang. Duran walked into the ring. His gloves had gray tape around the base. There were gashes in the material; I could see his skin. Duran jabbed like a scorpion. Sweat exploded from his opponent's face. I was hooked. Blood trickled down from their noses and dripped to the ring floor. Whispers of chatter echoed. "It could go either way" were the words spoken. I knew I would miss it all, everything about those days. Panama was my home. My roots were deep within its soil, and to extract them was sacrilege. I watched as Duran's opponent came crashing down, and the crowd around me shot up to their feet. Duran raised his arms high in the air. Money fluttered before me like rain. I stared at the victor, clapping my hands, creating thunder between my palms.

Chapter 5
Cocalequa

Iwas tasked with hunting down the guerrillas that caused havoc in Panama in the early 1970s. Some of those men were Arnulfistas who refused to see the National Guard in power, some were supporters of Martinez, and the rest were simply deranged. It was a contentious time, but luckily, our military had become more advanced with a recent shipment of American weapons. They still did not trust us completely, but we were a clear ally, and they rewarded us with their artillery.

Cocalequa . . . he was the greatest son of a bitch I could have ever imagined, a chaotic bandido. I could never pin my finger on his intentions. Yet I understood with certainty that Cocalequa was somebody who acted beyond the walls of society, and for that, he needed to be stopped. The guerrillas we were chasing gave Panama a bad name, especially with gringos; a small drop in the sea of international opinion sent media tidal waves across the globe. "This Central American nation is filled with fiery chaos," the headlines would read one day; "Thank God for the American fire extinguisher," they would read the next. That was why it was important for the National Guard to squash crimes against the government. If we wanted real change to happen, we had to sweep the nation clean. I would give my life to hunt those bandidos down.

Those ladronas hid from us like a rat hides from a cat. They caused chaos and stole riches from the perpetually poor. Times were changing and not for the better. My fears over political fraud had come to realization. Before the coup, American-backed presidents like Marco Robles undermined the public's intelligence and blatantly controlled electoral processes. Votes were thrown away, the media silenced the opposition, and heaps of resources were sent from Washington to ensure the Liberal Party stayed in power. The criminals I tracked were taking advantage of this chaotic climate that has followed this period of American control. My nation's greatest trait was and always will be the ability to protest; change is in our blood. Bribery, oppression, and murder ran amuck in politics at that time, and the eyes of Washington watched us as we began to clean it up.

I was a hunter who did what he was told and forwarded those orders. The winter had passed into summer, and the air stood dead one hot evening in Chiriqui. My men followed close. Rifles were gripped in our steady hands. We would never find Cocalequa simply roaming the landscape. He would need to screw up. Besides, other guerrillas needed to be cleansed. Many passed through Chiriqui, and we'd trail them wherever they went. I drove. I was the lead hound. Chucha, Cocalequa. What a son of a bitch. Other guerrillas were easy to capture, but not that motherfucker.

One day, the radio suddenly started to echo static. I fidgeted with the buttons and dials until an unfamiliar voice came onto the speaker.

"Carlos Wittgreen? Are you there, Carlos?" The voice spoke through the static.

"Who is this?" I responded.

"I'm police, in David. . . . Are you Carlos Wittgreen?"

"What is it?" I asked.

"Cocalequa. You are still looking for him, yes? We found him."

"Where?"

"He's here, in David. He robbed a bar, and now he's running through town. He just passed by the church."

It took me only ten minutes to get into the city. I had never driven so fast. That motherfucker Cocalequa was a bastard. He murdered people, and then he would rob them. The man had no respect for human life. A month prior, he killed men of the National Guard with a homemade bomb in an attempt to rob a train. Ever since that happened, he was my number one target. I wanted to trap him like the rat he was, to make him suffer like the families of the departed had.

The streets before me were full of men, women, and children. It was the weekend. They were there for the fruit markets in David. The sea of bodies scattered before me as I drove through. Men and women ran to the sidewalks and watched me pass through like Moses. Drums beat, and guitar strings strummed, reverberating in my ears. The city of David moved as if it had legs.

As the street came to an end, the road split in two. Both of my options were blocked by military units. Chucha, fucking American soldiers.

"*Déjanos pasar*," I demanded.

"In English, buddy," the gringo responded.

"Let us through, motherfucker. There is a guerrilla on the run."

The asshole puckered his lips and tilted his head to get a better look at our car. It was a standard military vehicle. Any man with two working eyes knew what it was; he was just being a motherfucker. The country was riddled with them by '68. The gringos had just gotten active in Vietnam, so the ones that were stationed in Panama lived with a sense of guilt and a need to prove themselves to Uncle Sam vicariously.

"Let me see some ID first," he said, extending his arm through my window. One of the National Guardsmen nudged my shoulder. The others stayed quiet in the back. We wanted to get out and fight these motherfuckers, but that would have put us in jeopardy. Not even Manuel could have gotten us out of that pinch. Fucking with a gringo was suicide.

"You're Noriega's guy," he said with a smile as he held onto my ID.

"Do I need to call him?" I responded.

"Give him my best."

"Give me back my ID."

The Americans watched as we passed through their brigade and drove off. I could see their gaze in the reflection of my rearview mirror. There was no trust. I was doing my job. I didn't understand what they were doing in David. It was normal to see them more and more as time progressed. Noriega's actions have always been a lesson to me. He would remain calm around Americans, always. Even if I could see something bothering him, he would wait for the gringos to leave his presence before he plotted a solution. They never realized he was ten steps ahead of them.

Many of us were quick to accuse the gringos of infesting a land they were not native to. I did not fully disagree. There were many men I respected. They were soldiers, after all. However, there were things no Panamanian could overlook. Our women were playthings to them, and our men were lesser unless they had received a gringo education. This had been the way since the dawn of my nation. The United States interjected itself in our war for freedom with its own motivations. Without them, we would have never won. Yet we didn't need them afterwards. They required the canal, and we were still a newborn child cradled in the arms of a giant.

During the Second World War, we were involved against our will. The Japanese were going to bomb the canal and parts of Panama City as a strategic move to injure the Americans. We weren't seen as an independent nation; we were just a port, a strategic target waiting to be hit. In 1945, there was even a Japanese plan to use a giant submarine to transport floatplane bombers across the Pacific. From the edges of Central America, they would be equipped with bombs and flown over the city.

Nobody would have thought about us, the people of Panama; they would have cared only for the lives of the gringo soldiers like the ones in my rearview mirror.

"Stop the car!" Luis yelled.

The rubber screeched. The wheels skidded. Our bodies jolted with whiplash.

"There he is," Luis said.

My eyes couldn't comprehend it. I opened the door and lifted my gaze until it met the fourth floor of the yellow apartment block. Chucha, Cocalequa, what a bastard. The man swung from a balcony like a monkey. We stood down below like fools. "What do we do?" Javier asked. Cocalequa flung himself to another balcony and then scaled to the top of the residential jungle.

"I hope you fall, asshole," I yelled.

The butt of my gun was warm to touch. I closed one eye over and watched as Cocalequa made it to the top of the five-story building. My breathing was slow and steady. I had him in my sight, but just by his body was an open window with the head of a young girl sticking out of it. "Move, kid," I screamed. The sight of us froze the child, four weapons pointed right at her. Before I could open my mouth again, Cocalequa had vanished from our sight. We rushed into the apartment block and sprinted up the staircase. I could smell nothing but bleach the entire way to the top. My reflection moved in the glistening tiles. We reached the roof. One of the guardsmen, Christopher, kicked the door down, and we spilled into the light. Cocalequa was gone. There was an escape in every direction. "Fuck!" I screamed.

That role was hard. I wanted to get the job done. I promised I would. We were always on the move. At night, we'd get drunk in some random place. If a bar was nearby, we'd clear it of its liquor and put our hands on the finest women within sight. If there was nowhere to gather and nobody to fuck, we would drink what we could find and where we could find it. We were in our late twenties, after all. The beach towns were my favorite. After a day of hunting, falling onto the sand and hearing the waves crash while gazing up at the stars was hypnotizing. The moon's glow would cast shimmering light spells across the glistening sky. It would chill my body. We would exist in mostly silence, thinking about women and romanticizing life. That's all any of us ever thought about. It was our vice. Not alcohol, certainly not narcotics, but beautiful temptresses. We couldn't help it. We were just as our ancestors had molded us, passionate in every facet of life. It was all because of the Spanish. That's what my father and his friends would say. As a boy, I learned that back when the Spanish invaded this part of the world, they saw an opportunity to broaden the influence of their culture and diaspora, and so Spanish men were encouraged to fuck everything that walked.

The sun rose one morning, and I awoke in a hammock that swung between two coconut trees. Christopher slept in the sand using his jacket as a blanket and a bottle of rum as a pillow. I believe two others, Luis and Javier, swam in the Pacific. The car engine rumbled. Radio Soberana gently filled the silence. Panamanian music riddled the air, and when the song finished, the voice of a reporter spoke.

"Yet another rally in Panama City turns violent as anti-government protestors take to Avenida Balboa. The crowd was mostly made up of people from Chorrera and highly dense neighborhoods. Talk of increased police presence is being discussed. The protestors are acting out against the National Guard . . ."

Our internal radio system began echoing static. I couldn't listen to that garbage any longer. I stumbled to the vehicle and opened the door. "Hello?" I spoke into the internal radio.

"Carlos?" the man on the line quickly responded.

My head felt like it weighed fifty tons. There was crust in the corners of my eyes.

"Carlos, it's Manuel."

Just like that, I was awake. "Manuel, good morning, my friend," I exclaimed.

"How are you and the men?" he asked.

"Good, we're just getting up now," I responded. I slipped my shoe off and threw it at Christopher. It hit him right in the head.

He arose frazzled and covered in sand. "What the fuck was that, Carlos?" he screamed.

I removed the car keys from my pocket and jingled them in his direction.

A sigh left his mouth; then he turned to Luis and Javier. "Get out of the water; we have to go," he yelled to them.

"There is a group of guerrillas in the city that are causing problems. They are trying to make a statement to the government by robbing banks and American trade ships. The gringos are barking at us. I have told them to leave it to me. Torrijos has already given the green light," Manuel exclaimed.

Panama City was different for a man like me. Chiriqui was rural; the city was chaos. Our military vehicle didn't have the presence it did in David. Civilians barely batted an eye when we drove by, especially in Chorrera, where the most impoverished of us lived. The people there have endured so much in their time. The families had been deeply rooted in that community. No matter how poor they were, they stayed and never looked for opportunities elsewhere. I always respected them. Being so close to the Howard Air Base, they were used to seeing men in uniform, both American and Panamanian. I wasn't surprised to hear that Chorrera guerrillas were lashing out at the system.

The smell of exhaust was pungent in the air I breathed. We parked our car outside of a small motel and booked a room. I did a lot of waiting in my twenties. Orders were passed down, and then I'd move. Patience was key. That motel room was small and unpleasant, but I wasn't there for a vacation. I prayed for action, for a chance to exercise duty.

"Guerrillas have just robbed Riba Smith on Calle Thirty-Seven!"

"Where are they heading?" I spoke into the radio.

"It looks like toward La Cresta, on the university campus," the correspondent replied.

I spun our car as fast as it could go. It was a miracle we even caught up to the guerrillas as fast as we did. The leader of the bandidos saw our military vehicle and knew he had to find a way out. Our car was faster than his. It could take more of a hit, too. They were outmatched. "Everybody, make sure your guns are loaded," I said to my men.

Clicks and clanks of metal echoed as we all checked our weapons.

"What about these, Carlos?" Christopher asked me. He held two grenades, one in each hand. Imprinted on the metal was English. Americans provided us with weapons to defend their interests.

"Keep them in the car," I said. My eyes stayed on course. The nose of my vehicle was inches from ramming into the bumper of the bandidos'. I could see the driver gaze back at me through his rearview mirror. He was afraid. In a flash movement, the wheels locked, and he turned left with all his force. I spun with him, and a wall of smoke rose into the air. The steam dissipated. All five bandidos ran for a school building made of red brick. It was a student living center for young girls. The bandidos had kicked in the door and hid from us. We exited our vehicle slowly, guns in hand.

"If you come any closer, we're killing every single girl in here," one of the bandidos yelled.

"What do we do, Carlos?" Luis asked me.

I scanned the property for entry points. The house had two floors. Eight windows faced the street, four on top, two on the bottom. Pairs of eyes watched us from half of them. They could see every move we made. Discretion was impossible. Chucha. I couldn't afford to let another guerrilla get away. Cocalequa had made me look like a fool. Noriega had placed his faith in me. I couldn't return to Chiqirui with my tail between my legs. I would have rather died.

"You have nowhere to go," I yelled to them.

"So get out of our way!"

If young women were killed on my account, I would never be able to lift my head again. Those girls were the future of our country. I thought about every possible angle and couldn't think of a single way to ensure their safety. Chucha, I was at a low. Pride held my words hostage. My men looked to me for answers. I knew what I had to do, so I took a step forward and lay down my gun. I put my hands in the air, far and wide. Just as my mouth opened to speak, I heard the low and raspy voice of an old man in a janitor's uniform yelling from across the street.

"They're lying to you; there's nobody in there!"

The air stood still. We all turned.

"What did you say?" I asked.

"There are no girls in that house. It's vacation; they're all at home," he responded.

"You're sure about this?"

"This is one of the few days a year when I don't have to clean up after those little shits," he exclaimed before taking a drag from his cigarette.

"Get me the grenades," I demanded. When Christopher handed them to me, I turned my back so the little eyes gazing out from the house would be obstructed. The cold steel in my hand made me feel powerful. Electricity rushed through my veins. My eyes lit up. The pin slid out easily, and my throw had the perfect weight. The first grenade smashed through a window upstairs, and the second one skidded right into the hallway where the door had been kicked down. The explosions were quick, briefly bright, and powerful enough for shards of glass and splinters of wood to spray onto the front lawn. Screams of agony riddled the air, and bloody bandidos stumbled toward me with tinnitus ringing in the beating eardrums. Only two survived the blast. The others lay in a pool of their blood, clutching bags of money. Those men had no political affiliation. They took advantage of unrest, and as good as it felt to stop them in their tracks, it only made my desire to catch Cocalequa greater.

Hunting became easier after that. Guerrillas knew my unit. We were killers. They feared us. Noriega was pleased. He began to buy us more alcohol, introduce us to more women, give us more responsibilities. Life became better and better, and people in high positions began to hear about how capable the young Carlos Wittgreen was. Yet, in the back of my mind, I was unfulfilled. That bastard was still out there. Cocalequa. No matter how many bandidos we wrung by the neck, I knew I wouldn't be happy until we found him. We were known as Tigres and Pumas, highly specialized groups of men like me that were responsible for tracking the rats in our nation and ridding of them. I have fond memories of those times. We showed civil support as opposed to institutional one. We made it clear that the military would lead from then on. I was still a speck of dust on our nation's chessboard, but I felt pride serving how I served. I knew that if I could just get my hands on Cocalequa, I would be as complete as any man could be.

My men and I were near Colon, on the Caribbean side of the country, where I first realized how much money could be made through the busy ports. The Colon Free Trade Zone was the second largest of its kind. It brought us thousands of foreign corporations operating on our soil. It was summer when we were at the Caribbean end of the canal. The sun was beating hot, and the ground we walked on was dry. When guerrilla activity rose in the area, the poor were the first to be affected. Cocalequa, I knew the bastard was responsible. I could smell him from miles away. We arrived to the sight of torched and charred boats docked at the harbor. The Americans had already shown up to investigate whether the ships or cargo belonged to them. I moved to find witnesses. Cocalequa had been active for years; people could always provide sketch art. He was the Jesse James of Panama, the ultimate bandit. I wanted to be the one to kill him.

Activity in Colon wound down. We moved constantly. We frequented a fine little taverna by the Pacific shores of Playa Marchena. The structure had sat there for decades. I would drink and long for my family. I enjoyed the chaos of my twenties but sought something more stable. I wanted to be a provider to those I loved. My parents, my brother, and my extended family all received gifts from me whenever I could give. There was too much instability at this time. I couldn't lose focus. I had to find Cocalequa.

All hope seemed lost when, one day, we heard gunshots. Something in my gut told me it was him. No call came, but we went anyway. We drove to the outskirts of town to where an old Asian man sat outside of a *chino* with his head in his hands. "You're too late," he mumbled. Christopher consoled him while I stepped through the shattered door of the structure to find glass scattered across the floor. I tilted my neck back, and light shone through bullet holes in the ceiling. It was the work of Cocalequa; I could feel it.

"When we find the man who did this to your chino, we are not going to arrest him. We are going to kill him," I told him with passion in my lungs.

"He moved toward the mangroves."

I have always believed the mangroves in the Gulf of Panama were ecological masterpieces manufactured by God. We arrived to quite a picturesque sight with sinewy roots snaking through shallow waters, intertwining like a labyrinth before my eyes. We tip-toed along the dense, emerald canopy covering the waters, filtering the sunlight into a mosaic of flickering shadows. The deeper we moved into the forestry, the closer I felt myself getting to him.

"Look, Carlos, the footprints," Luis pointed out.

Cocalequa had small feet. We tracked every step he took through the shaded terrain. Christopher wielded a machete and sliced his way through the brush. I followed closely behind with my pistol held out from my body. My heart thumped against my chest. The ocean was near; I could smell it. I knew it meant the trail was coming to an end. A burst of light pierced and blinded me. I shielded the rays with my forearm, still gripping the pistol tightly.

"*Jefe*, over there," Javier whispered.

Sitting on a rock, washing his filthy feet in the water was Cocalequa, right in front of my eyes. He was tiny, no more than five foot five. His clothes were ragged. Blood dripped from fresh wounds on his biceps. It was clear he had been torn up by the mangrove. We took in the moment. All that time chasing this one fucker, and there he was, trapped like a cock. He had nowhere to run. I could have painted a picture.

"Stay right there, Cocalequa. We found you," I yelled.

Cocalequa's eyes jolted wide open, and he gasped. He jumped to his feet and stood in the shallow waters. I sized him up. The waves brushed against his knees. His fingers wiggled. I waited for movement. He leaned forward.

"You're trapped," I said.

Cocalequa scanned his surroundings—the sea to one side, the mangrove to the other. "Fuck you, assholes," he yelled before turning his back and sprinting through the waters.

We must have fired thirty shots into him. The water rushed red, and his body floated in the gentle current until he bounced against the curling branches of the mangrove. It was over. The wildlife would finish the job. His body would be gone by midnight. All that time chasing one man, and I had succeeded, we all had. Noriega showered us with compliments and exclaimed that we were making a difference.

A few months later, after many mornings of heavy heads, I found myself with Noriega and his peers at a cockfight in the city. Those men were our leaders, and they liked me. I was no longer a boy. I had earned a milestone of respect that took me to a whole new level of responsibility.

"Carlos, come here. Let me get you a drink," Noriega yelled with a smile.

We were drunk as can be. Some of us were winning money left and right. Noriega held hundreds in one pocket. He treated me like a younger brother, buying me a seco and doubling my bets.

Later that night, Noriega put his hand on me and said, "I'll be right back," and went to the bathroom.

I leaned against the railing separating the man from the rooster. The moment I was alone, I felt a tap on my shoulder. It was weak as if it came from a child or an elderly woman, but when I turned, my eyes lit up, and I broke into laughter. Standing before me, beat to shit, hanging on by a thread, and leaning over a set of crutches, was Cocalequa. The little bastard had survived. Scars covered him from head to toe, his eyes drooped down on either side. He was a living skeleton.

"You motherfucker," he mumbled.

I didn't know what to say. We shot that man over thirty times. I saw his flaccid body float for minutes. Yet there he was, standing before me, ready to fight. I laughed so hard my stomach hurt. The alcohol in my blood had gone to my head. I could hardly stand anymore. Noriega returned, and when I told him the story, he put his arm around the cripple, and we got him so drunk he couldn't use his crutches anymore. A taxi came and picked him up, and when he arose the next day, I called his doctors and paid his hospital bills. I assured Cocalequa that he would continue to live as long as he kept good behavior. I grew to admire the little guy. Any man who could take that many bullets and not only survive but also come and confront the man who shot him deserved to live. Cocalequa . . . the greatest son of a bitch I could have imagined.

Chapter 6
A Gringo Caught in Civil Unrest

I watched as particles of sand rolled toward the house. The waves thumped against the shore, thunderous thrashing echoing in my ears. The red light on the voice recorder flashed as Carlos finished telling me about his introduction to the world of military intelligence. He spoke so colorfully that I became entranced by his storytelling and could almost picture myself there. I had a strong feeling that Carlitos was embellishing much of his narrative, but I knew it was too early to contest him on facts. I would have to do my own research to back his story up. We had barely made a dent in the book. Still, spirits were high, even if I found myself dancing around eggshells with the fear of being struck by Señor Wittgreen's mammoth fists.

Water droplets sprayed onto my face. The smell of grilled and broiled meats and vegetables floated through the air and landed in my nostrils. Natasha and the Nicaraguans were cooking inside while I sat with Diego and Señor Wittgreen under the gazebo outside. It had been just over a week of interviews, and I had recorded some amazing stories. I knew I would have to transcribe the audio from Spanish to English to entirely understand the anecdotes I was being told. I had been able to translate and document Carlos's stories about his youth. Still, because of the inclement weather and the rural location, the Wi-Fi was too sparse to translate and transcribe using various software efficiently. I would have to do a lot of work upon my return to Panama City and, subsequently, Los Angeles, where I would start writing this book. Still, even though I had documented only a small portion of Carlos's story, I recognized I had recorded anecdotes nobody else knew of. Stories like that would make this book different.

"Noriega and I traveled this whole country together. When we had the opportunity to let loose, we would seize it. Beaches like these would be crawling with gorgeous women from all over the world. Colombia, Costa Rica, France, Argentina . . . everywhere. With my friend, it was always a party. Yet, in those moments, some of the most important decisions about this country had ever been made. It is all flooding back to me. Politicians flocked to us from countries all over the world. They loved to come to Panama. Chinese, Japanese, Australians, Israelis, and Europeans would call us up and ask to block off a section of days for a vacation, sometimes even weeks. Royal families, heirs to great fortunes, and significant politicians and their aides would step onto the runway at Tocumen Airport and be taken to a beehive of debauchery in one of our helicopters or armed cars. Yes, I provided intelligence, but one of my roles was to show people a good time. I would party with these people from morning to night in my younger days. My body was fueled by pure adrenaline."

Natasha stepped outside with Carlos's phone in her hands. "You missed a call from Trujillo," she yelled out. Jose Hilario Trujillo and Carlos were very good friends. I would know the man well in future trips to Panama, and his archived documents would help build the foundation of this book. However, back in October 2023, he was just a name. I hadn't yet seen documents like this, where influential Americans quite literally stated they could use information against Panama in the interest of the United States.

TOP SECRET

UNITED STATES DEPARTMENT OF JUSTICE
DRUG ENFORCEMENT ADMINISTRATION
Washington, D.C. 20537

3649

January 25, 1978

The Honorable
Griffin B. Bell
Attorney General
Department of Justice
Washington, D.C.

Sir:

As agreed at our last meeting on January 23, I am putting into writing the details of the alleged involvement of Moises Torrijos, brother of General Omar Torrijos, in drug trafficking into the United States, to be used in your report to the President.

On July 8, 1971, customs agents at Kennedy Airport arrested two Panamanians who were trying to smuggle 154 pounds of heroin into this country. Subsequent investigations resulted in the arrest of the suspected ringleader in heroin smuggling, Guillermo Gonzalez, a former bodyguard of Moises Torrijos. No evidence whatever was uncovered to link the latter to this illicit activity.

In October, 1971, the chief of the CIA field station in Panama, Stanley R. Burnett, reported to Washington on Moises Torrijos's connections with the drug smugglers. The relevant information, already known to you, was conveyed to John Ingersoll with a note from the former CIA Director, Richard Helms:"The President is informed. The information may be used in the national interests of the United States".

Mr. Ingersoll personally instructed our agents in the Panama DO to verify the information. No confirmatory evidence was found.

However, on the direct instruction of the former Attorney General, John Mitchell, the information was filed as unimpeachable and led to Moises Torrijos's indictment by a grand jury in the Eastern District of New York in May, 1972, and the issue of a bench warrant for his arrest.

The Drug Enforcement Administration believes that the dubious and unproven character of the available information makes its presentation to General Omar Torrijos at his request undesirable as being potentially damaging to the prestige of the American Executive.

Sincerely,

Peter B. Bensinger
Administrator

ARCHIVADO JUL 5 1980

TOP SECRET

Figure 6.1. Letter from Peter B. Bensinger, Administrator of the US Drug Enforcement Administration, to Attorney General Griffin Bell, January 25, 1978, detailing allegations of Moises Torrijos's involvement in drug trafficking and the subsequent investigations.

"Trujillo was once the mayor of Panama City. He has published several books, too. I will try to get my hands on one for you," Carlos said.

"Thank you, señor."

"He is very knowledgeable. Noriega himself gave him access to many, many documents."

"What kind of documents?"

"He's got direct correspondence between DEA directors, Department of Justice, and Noriega, never published publicly; Bensinger, Bartels, all of them. There are several hundred, and they tell the true story of America's betrayal. They're some of the letters Manuel wanted to use in his defense at his trial in Miami, but he was not allowed to. He held onto them for a purpose. Collateral. Safety. The Americans thought they had all been eradicated, shredded. Chucha madre," Carlos responded.

Trujillo was clearly a historian, and those documents intrigued me. Still, I focused solely on Carlos's story over the following days. I came prepared every day, writing a list of ten to fifteen questions designed to direct the conversation. Carlos and Natasha would eventually get cabin fever. Then we would have to return to the city, regardless of where I was in the interview, so I needed to get as much as I possibly could while we were in Pedasi. Yet Señor Wittgreen said what he wanted to say. He would answer my questions; then he would go on tangents, touching on an important topic before slipping a joke or a funny anecdote into his response. A response was direct if I made the same inquiry twice. Señor Wittgreen was a man who did not like to be asked the same thing more than once. It became clear to me that, although I was getting what I needed, I could not corroborate any of it, so I didn't know what was true, what was half-accurate, and what was a fabrication designed to paint a prettier picture than what occurred. I do not think Carlos actively lied to me. I think he told his truth and perhaps spared me from knowing information that would get me in trouble. He considered this book his legacy, and there were certainly parts of his life he didn't want to shine a light on, but I trusted his story as much as I was entertained by it.

"In 1903, my people rebelled against our oppressive government and broke free from the bounds of Colombia. Of course, we all know the United States quickly moved in and established a home away from home. Men like my father helped build the canal for them, and many died. Those who lived protested their deaths, but they would soon be forced to go back to work. Trujillo and I always speak of happenings like these and how they led to 1964 when a group of high school students raised a Panamanian flag in place of a United States flag at Balboa High School in the Canal Zone and were murdered by US troops. I walked with the protestors in the aftermath. Now, we call it Martyrs' Day, November 3, every year. Since then, we have protested in the streets almost every year, and every time one sparks up, I find myself wondering if it will make any difference at all."

What happened at the end of the second week felt like irony at its finest. Diego had just celebrated his twenty-first birthday in Playa Venao with his friends. I wanted to join, but I felt behind in what I was in Panama to do. So I bought him a bottle of seco and told him not to worry about work. Every second of every day, I was focused on this book. I knew I couldn't go back to Los Angeles with wide gaps of knowledge.

One morning, a ring of static jolted in my eardrum. A radio in the house was struggling to find a frequency when the voice of an announcer suddenly sparked.

"Civilians have taken to the streets of Panama City in protest of the government. The approval ratings of the current president and his party are the lowest since the time of the invasion of 1989. Hordes of protestors congregated on Calle Fifty by Parque Harry Strunz roughly thirty minutes ago, and now they're heading toward Avenida Balboa. Traffic in the area has come to a standstill. Police units are out and have advised people to stay at home."

"What's happening?" I asked Diego.

"Something about politicians accepting bribes from foreign governments. The protests are spreading everywhere. People are pissed," he responded.

The news showed clips and images of large protests quickly forming all over the country. In a flash, almost all infrastructure was blocked. Protestors stood in the middle of highways, refusing to let cars through. Taxis and buses stopped their services. All supply chains were immediately halted. Gas stations had no gas. Grocery stores had no inventory. There were stories popping up of dairy farmers attempting to transport their produce, being stopped by protestors, and pouring the milk out onto the gravel as a form of protesting the protest. Everything happened so quickly, and I felt I was getting a glimpse into what made Panama, Panama. Still, on that night, right after the government's wrongdoings were outed to the public, Diego and I called Jose and asked what we should do.

"You need to get the hell out of there as soon as possible," Jose told us.

The protests were intensifying by the hour. Even in the smallest, most remote communities of Panama, people were flocking in droves to block infrastructure and make a statement to the government. It seemed as if the entire population of the country was on board. One of the Nicaraguans dropped Carlos and Natasha off at the house Diego and I were staying in. It was close to ten at night. Carlos recommended we wait another hour before getting on the road. We were fleeing in the middle of the night. The thought process was that the protestors would have to take a break at some point, so if we could get back to the city before sunrise, we could avoid everything. Still, our collective news sources showed us that, no matter our direction, we would hit blockades. There was no point in waiting around. We jumped into the car. Diego sat behind the wheel. Carlos and Natasha were in the back. I was in the passenger seat, promising to help Diego out as much as I could by keeping an eye on Waze GPS, which had a sort of geographical comment section where drivers could chat with each other. It was beneficial because I could see where cars were stopped and for how long they had been stationary. As the vehicle pulled out onto the road, I could see that vehicles had been halted by Chitre, which wasn't too far away. Drivers angrily flooded the comment forum, claiming the protestors should be run over. It was a tense time for me, and Carlos picked up on that immediately.

"In the 1960s, protests like these were very common. Everybody protested: Arnulfistas, pro-America, anti-America, pro-Torrijos, anti-Torrijos. This is normal. There is nothing to worry about," Carlos told me.

"Everything changed in the 1970s, didn't it? That's when the Americans started asking for more favors," I responded.

"I have had countless people approach me in my lifetime and beg for information about Noriega. Not all of those people walked away unscathed. People can be soulless and irreverent to the idea that loyalty cannot falter even in death. They have it all wrong. They have made video game villains out of him, for fuck sake. Nothing is going to change Manuel's image; it is projected across history. . . . One day, Bush is asking for a favor; the next, he's sending thirty thousand troops to bomb civilians."

"So you think the narrative is set in stone?" I asked.

"By the time the seventies came, I was a man who stood alongside the driving force behind anti-narcotrafficking initiatives in North, Central, and South America. That was Noriega. My time with Mossad in Israel made me special. The DEA had just been founded. The coup had come and gone, and so did many of the struggles that came with it. The seventies were a different decade for my people. The international climate was shifting. We were ahead of the curve."

"Why did the Americans need Panama?"

"Nobody knew the game yet, but we knew all the players. We held US troops on our land; we used the American dollar. Because of Manuel, we had the strongest intelligence in the Americas. It made the most sense."

"I read that, in 1973, Noriega took the stage at an anti-narcotic conference in Vienna. He gave a speech about the threat of drugs that, at the time, was somewhat revolutionary," I mentioned.

"He called drugs "the fifth horseman of the apocalypse." He saw the road ten years ahead of everyone. Richard Severo from the *New York Times* wrote an article titled "Panama Praised for Drug Curbs, for Christ's sake.""

We reached Chitre around midnight. A line of parked cars stretched for about a mile. We were far back, and we couldn't see the protestors. Diego's friends, who had been in Playa Venao for his birthday, were also caught in the blockade. They told him about a secret shortcut through the woods. If it were just Diego and me, I'm sure we would have followed, but it was too risky with Carlos and Natasha, given that it was pitch black out and nobody was sure where the backroad would spit us out. We were forced to wait. There was a chicken shop a hundred yards from our car. Its sign shone a bright neon red. "Come, come, let's eat," Carlos exclaimed. He knew there was no point in us waiting around for movement. It would happen when it would happen. He bought us dinner. I was so exhausted that I could barely taste the spice, but that didn't matter. I still wanted to squeeze every last drop of conversation I could.

"I am interested in hearing more about your training with Mossad. How did that come to be?"

"I knew I would become an asset to them here in Panama, just as Manuelito was, but they would also become an asset to me like they were to him. You'll have friends all over the world you can call at a moment's notice to access information otherwise considered inaccessible," Manuel told me. I froze up. It was a big decision to make. One day, I lay in bed all day. I gazed up at my ceiling fan spin. I did that for hours, pondering my life. Nobody called me. Not my ex-wife, my girlfriend at the time, my mother, my father, Gaspar, Noriega . . . nobody. I watched as the sun's rays shone through my window and climbed along my walls before disappearing as time passed. Horns sang in the street; I closed my window. It was the first night I spent in solitude in years. When the sun rose, I still lay awake. My crusted eyes stung, but the rays were warm and inviting. I sat on the edge of my bed, staring at my feet. Chucha, I remember it well, all of it. The phone felt heavy when I lifted it. The dial tone rang for what seemed like an eternity, and then I said four words that would change the trajectory of my life: 'I'm going to Israel.' I left shortly after, and I would return a stronger man."

The blockade was dismantled around one in the morning, and we were back on the road. There was a collective sigh of relief. Our car was moving close to one hundred miles per hour at one point along Highway 2. We were making good time. Carlos and Natasha snoozed in the back seat. Diego did a great job staying awake, strategically sipping on a coffee. I didn't sleep, either. I wanted to keep Diego company, talking about anything that would take our minds off the remaining stretch: girls, surfing, partying. The chatter flowed until we hit another blockade on the highway in the middle of nowhere. We had about two and a half hours of driving left. It was around two in the morning. The others were just as surprised to see protestors out so late. It was the dead of night, and they didn't want to budge an inch. I checked the GPS comment forum, and people had been held up for hours. Fights had sparked at the picket line. The men and women who created the blockade were ready and willing to spend the night at their post.

Diego got out of the car at one point to meet his friends, who had made it out of the woods, and they skateboarded to the top of the line. "People are going crazy up here," he called and told me. Thankfully, Carlos and Natasha were at ease the whole time. They were extremely pleasant, never once complaining. After a couple of hours, the protestors agreed to stand aside and let the cars through. We made it back to the city just as the sun rose. I slept like a log for almost the entirety of that day in my hotel room.

At some point in the evening, I was awoken by gunshots. I rushed to my hotel window. I was on the twentieth floor. People flooded the streets below. Some wore balaclavas and masks, holding weapons. Teenagers shot fireworks into the sky. I distinctly remember a school bus spray-painted green, white, and neon yellow circling the streets, blasting Panamanian music at full volume. I decided to walk out into the crowd, and after five minutes or so, I realized that it might not have been the safest thing to do. After all, it wasn't my country, and it was people who looked like me who had bribed the Panamanian government, which had sparked the whole fiasco in the first place. All it could take was for me to look at a local the wrong way or to say something stupid, and it would not be good for me. So I retreated to my hotel room and spent hours just watching the streets below flood with protestors chanting for change.

The US embassy released a statement calling for American tourists to return to the States. I took that as my sign to flee. So I booked the next flight out, and in the middle of the night, I hopped into a cab and made my way to Tocumen Airport, thankfully traveling while the city blockades were void of protestors until the sun rose. I sat at my gate for hours on end that morning, waiting for my flight. My heart was racing. I didn't relax until I passed through customs at LAX. I knew I would have to return to get more, but I was ready to start digging into the material I had acquired and to see what I would need to attain on my next trip. Those protests ended up lasting for months. The president had been bribed by a Canadian mining company to allow severe excavations on Panamanian land, effectively destroying massive areas of the country's climate and geography. It did make me wonder if things had really changed from the days of Carlos's youth.

Chapter 7
The Panamanian Sayanim

I was once told that the best intelligence comes from everyday human interactions. No longer in Panama, I was in Israel, where everyone listened. The Sayanim, they called them. They were civilians who performed as intelligence for Mossad, volunteers who acted out of pure patriotism. It was instantly clear to me that Mossad ran the country. I respected their duty to protect a religion.

I arrived in Tel Aviv. The Mediterranean climate was easy to adjust to. The sea brought warm winds that didn't stick to my skin. The air smelled clean. The people were friendly. I sat in the back of an armed, solid-black car. The driver did not speak Spanish. It didn't matter; I was too busy soaking in my surroundings. Noriega told me not to ask questions. I was to immerse myself fully. To do that, I needed to rid myself of all inhibitions and expectations for what might be. I was a blank canvas, ready to learn.

We drove north for about thirty minutes. Through the window, I saw us pass by a sign which read Herzliya. It was a town I had read about in a book on the flight. I learned the prime minister owned a vacation home in Herzliya. We maneuvered through narrow streets, and then our surroundings opened up. In the distance sat a white building. It looked old. The paint was peeling off the bricks, and some of the shingles on the roof had detached from the structure and slid off the edge, falling to the green grass below. I knew that's where I was going.

An armed officer stopped our car. My driver rolled down the window and said, "I'm dropping off a new recruit, Carlos Wittgreen."

My window slid down, and the armed guard gazed at me with a tilt. "Carlos Wittgreen?" he asked me.

"That's me," I responded. With a flash of my passport, we were through.

"The Midrasha," the driver muttered as he unlocked my door.

The Midrasha. Mossad Academy. I entered the building and was met by agents who quietly led me through corridors. The tiles covering the floors sang with every tap of my feet. The sounds echoed along the walls until they stopped at a double set of large brown doors. "Go in," one of the agents said. My heart beat faster. I gripped the knob and spun it. The door squealed as it opened, revealing a thin man behind a metallic, chrome desk. It warped my reflection in its mirror-like exterior, almost resembling a Picasso painting.

"My name is Michael Harari. I will be your supervisor. . . . You're Noriega's man?" Harari asked.

"Yes."

"I've heard good things."

Training started how I expected it to. A trainer shoved a gun into our hands. We all lined up side-to-side inside an empty garage that sat at the edge of the compound. Harari paced back and forth before us. He was the leader. "This country is constantly under attack; that means you are constantly under attack," he yelled, body cast in shadows. "You are each holding an IMI Galil, one of the finest Israeli weapons of the last decade."

I rubbed my fingers along the weapon. My pupils dilated. It was immaculate. The craftsmanship highlighted the passion that clearly went into the design. I wanted nothing more than to test it.

"Disassemble your weapon. I'll be back in five minutes," the trainer said before exiting.

I could see the cocking handle was attached to the bolt carrier on the right side of the receiver. I disassembled it easily. The door opened slowly. A strand of light moved along the ground until it met our bodies and blinded our vision. I raised my forearm to shield my eyes. The door closed, and darkness set over us once more.

"Disassembling your weapon is not supposed to be difficult," our trainer said. He moved from man to man, visually inspecting the parts of each gun. The rubber material of his soles screeched when he stopped. He lifted his eyes to match my gaze. "Why might you have to disassemble your weapon?" he asked me.

Every pair of eyes continued to look forward.

I breathed through my nose. "Transportation," I responded.

"More often than not, your weapon is not going to be welcome where you need it. And, when you arrive at your destination, what must you do?"

"Reassemble it," I exclaimed.

"This is not always easy. Our agents find themselves in dangerous conditions. There are obstructions."

Harari pulled six blindfolds out from his pockets. He tossed them at our feet. My blindfold landed atop loose pieces of my gun. I was the first to bend down and pick it up. The others followed my lead. Harari continued to pace back and forth. Each step he took was now soft and made no sound. "Put them on," he said. The silk touch felt smooth against my eyelids. I tied the knot tight behind my head. I could feel the pressure of the material against my skull.

"Now, assemble your weapon. You have one minute," I heard through the darkness.

The sound of the metal door slamming shut echoed. Nobody moved for a moment. I was trying to visualize where everything was. That minute felt like seconds. Yet, when Harari and our trainer returned, I was the only one to have successfully assembled his weapon. We were all considered somebody's most trustworthy adversary. If I looked good, so did Noriega, Torrijos, and the nation of Panama. I wanted to have some fun while I was in Israel, but my duties came first. I needed to earn that respect.

I learned how to read people. I could understand what someone's motivations were by how they moved. My superiors opened my eyes to everyday things that are hidden in plain sight.

The techniques embedded themselves into me. I would never let anybody walk behind me ever again. The others I trained with seemed to be good men. It wasn't easy to make it to Mossad. Sometimes, we would play card games and gamble with money if we had it and booze if we didn't. Every other week, I'd have cigars to play with. Manuel mailed them to me. He'd include a letter, too.

One night, they rounded everyone up in the dark. There were often tests at strange hours. Fatigue was no such thing during this time of my life. I always had to be ready. I stood amongst the other trainees as Harari opened a folder in his hands. He handed us each a piece of paper with the image of a beautiful Israeli woman with a martini glass in her hand printed at the top.

"You're being put to the test. This woman is an enemy of the state. Her husband is a member of Fatah. He left for Jordan last night and will not return for two days. Extract whatever intelligence you can and report back to me," Harari yelled.

"Yes, sir," we responded in unison.

The night had already fallen upon us all. We stumbled into each other as we passed under the archway in the wall. The air was cool; I shivered, and the others did, too. We all looked at each other with a glaze in our eyes. It was time to split up.

Passing through dark streets on the edge of the city caused discomfort in my gut. An explosion of chills stemmed from my stomach and squirmed across my skin until it reached the tips of my toes and fingers. My breathing was steady. My eyes opened wide with a sting. Everything around me was foreign. The street signs were in Hebrew. My thoughts sporadically vanished and returned without reason. The buildings were made from material I had never touched before. The mixture crumbled in my hand. Even the moon hung in the sky differently. I stopped to think. The picture of the gorgeous woman was taken at a bar. She held a martini glass in her hand. She was dressed well for the occasion. I squinted my eyes to find more detail. I did not know that city, but I had to go somewhere. I couldn't keep walking around with my dick in my hands all night.

Ahead of me, there was a racket. Men and women laughed and yelled in the street. I could not see them at first; they were behind a corner. I sprinted toward them, and right as their group came into sight, a man stepped out from behind the corner, and I crashed into him. His friends whipped their heads toward me. Both the man and I were on our backs, scratched from the pebbled street.

My head was all over the place. I stood to my feet, but before I knew it, I was in a fight with several gringos. The big one stumbled over himself and fell face-first into the ground. His chin was scratched up, and blood seeped through his skin. "You motherfucker," he yelled.

The other three men quickly jumped me. They weighed me down to the ground. Two of them pinned my arms, and one pounded me in the face over and over. I could taste the blood salivating in my mouth and staining my teeth. I kicked the fucker on top of me in the groin. My palms sprained as I pushed myself to my feet. I limped, a sting shooting up my leg with every ounce of pressure placed on it. A woman shrieked. I darted down the first alley I saw. It was pitch-black.

"Where did he go?" the gringos yelled.

I panted with every breath, running deeper into the darkness. Just as the blackness of night was about to swallow me, I tripped and skidded across the ground. My neck creaked. Before me were the shimmering red and yellow lights of a bar. Chucha. I wiped the gravel off my clothes and gripped my hand around the iron handle. A waft of cigarette smoke rushed up my nostrils as I entered. Behind the bar, a bartender paced along a mirror. I sat on a chipped wooden stool painted in black. My head leaned into my palms, and I took a deep breath.

"What can I get for you, sir?" the bartender asked.

When I lifted my head, the bartender's eyes jolted wide open. He grabbed a white rag from behind the bar and tossed it at me. I caught it with my right hand and dabbed it against my lip. "Thanks," I said.

Some chatter lit up in the back. Two Middle Eastern men were sitting at a rickety booth. They drank a dark beer that I had never seen before. An oil lamp hung on the wall between them and cast shadows over their bearded faces.

"Do you have seco?" I asked the bartender.

"Seco?"

"Just give me a whiskey," I muttered.

The Middle Eastern men broke out into laughter once more. I turned to face them. As I opened my mouth to yell, the bartender placed a glass of whiskey down before me.

"I wouldn't do that, sir," the bartender warned.

The stool creaked as I turned to face him. My hand wrapped around the glass. "Who are they?" I asked. The whiskey burned my throat. I squinted. The bartender already had the bottle ready for me by the time I opened my eyes.

"That's a problem you certainly don't need," he said, gesturing to my black eye.

I was a foreigner in a new place and didn't want any more trouble. So I finished half the bottle and left quietly. I shifted along a main road. Camp shimmered in the distance like a mirage. I was all alone. My mind wandered home to Panama. The palm trees, the people, even the humidity, I missed it all. I knew what I was doing in Israel was important. Panama needed people to leave and then return. Cultural understanding was the most important piece of our growth. If we wanted to prove ourselves, we had to grow. Our population needed to be exposed to life outside of our country. I was becoming stronger and smarter by the day.

The silence of the building was almost deafening when I entered. All the trainees were told to see Harari, one by one, to report their findings. I sat outside of his office, face throbbing. I wanted to go home.

"Carlos, come on," Harari said, poking his head into the room.

The chair was warm when I sat on it. I rested my hands on the sides.

Harari leaned back. "You don't look good," he said.

I nodded my head. "I got into a fight with gringos."

"You Panamanians are hot-blooded. Did you find anything?"

84

"I went to a bar . . . after the fight last night. There were two Middle Eastern men there. The bartender said they were dangerous. That's all I know."

Harari opened a notepad on his desk. Ink covered the tip of his pen. I sat and watched him write in silence. "You're being moved to a new facility for the remainder of your training. It's inland," Harari exclaimed suddenly.

"Okay," I responded.

I never asked questions I already knew the answer to. My time with Harari was done. I had other areas of myself to tighten up. I wasn't ready to go home.

Later that year, members of Fatah executed twelve Israelis at the 1972 Olympic Games in Munich. The entire thing was televised. Mossad decided that Mike Harari should lead a team of assassins to hunt the terrorists down and execute them one by one. I wasn't involved in that, but it marked a shift in time for me. It made Harari a very important figure within Mossad. However, in July 1973, Mossad agents on a top-secret mission mistakenly assassinated an innocent Moroccan waiter in Lillehammer, Norway, believing him to be a Black September operative. Harari, as the Mossad operations chief, was publicly blamed for overseeing the botched mission that exposed the agency and led to arrests of its agents.

At my new facility, sometime later, a trainer named Eli awoke me one summer day. Blotches of sweat covered my skin, and I stuck to the thin sheets that layered my cot. The crust in my eyes sewed them shut. It broke apart as I forced them open.

"Get up. Meet me by the chicken coop," Eli said before exiting my room.

The facility in the desert held fewer men. It was more specialized, a new tier of responsibility. I didn't ask about it. The sun on that particular day was fierce. I had never seen it so bright. The heat swaddled my body. It was inescapable. I could see Eli by the chicken coops. He stood by a helicopter, holding a machete in his left hand and a coconut in his right.

Eli dropped the machete and the coconut at my feet. Chickens in the coop squawked. My eardrums rang, my brain pounding against the inside of my skull. Eli kneeled. He opened a coop and snatched a chicken by its neck. "Get in the helicopter," he demanded. A pilot wearing sunglasses sat up front. His mustache peeked through the breather port. Eli squeezed in next to me and tossed the chicken into my lap. "Hold onto that," he said. As the helicopter took off and rose, I leaned carefully to gaze down at the land turn to desert. Then we touched down in the sand.

Eli tossed the machete and the coconut out of the chopper. "Make your way back to base," he said.

The helicopter lifted, blades cutting through the air. I shielded my eyes from the onslaught of sand that shot at me, lashing against my back. In a flash, the chopper was high in the sky, a spec in the great blue that hung overhead. I watched what direction it flew. That was my way home. West. I had to move west if I wanted to live. Still holding the chicken, I gripped my hand around its throat and looked in its beady little eyes. It must have been a fucking joke. What use would I have for a chicken in the desert? It had to go.

I moved west into the sun's glowing lens, which sat atop the sandy hills. The stained machete stuck to the palm of my left hand. The hairs of the coconut tickled my right. The dead body of the chicken was slung from my back pocket. I trudged along the sand. Waves of heat danced for me. The heat beat me down to my knees. There was a hill ahead. The sun shone behind it, casting a shadow on its edge. I crawled toward it. The shade felt like ice. I gripped the machete and plunged it into the coconut. A crack lined the shell. I froze. The blade gently slipped out. Droplets of coconut water dripped from the tip. My arms shook as I lifted the coconut and poured its nourishment into my dry mouth. Darkness set over me, and stars sparkled in the sky. I looked for constellations as I lay on my back. I hadn't felt that close to home in a long time.

Thinking of Panama, I stayed awake. I reminisced on my past, and I thought about my future. I had vowed to return an asset for Manuel. He needed me. My country needed me. My youth rested in the stars, millions of miles away. I could only look. My reach was short. It was time to transition. I knew it was. My gaze lingered on the shifting and shimmering life in the space above until the sun arose in the east, and light crept along the sand until it reached my feet.

I couldn't even cook the fucking chicken. It dangled from me like a ballsack. At one point, I gripped it by the base and launched it thirty yards. It crashed into the sand by the beak. I was given it for a reason. I had no choice but to pick it back up and carry it the rest of the journey with me. The air weighed heavy. Gravity tugged at my pants. I couldn't lift my knees. Every step forward caused a shock of pain to ripple along my muscles. The coconut emptied. My piss turned orange. Sweat didn't even come out of me. My hope faltered as I saw the sun dip toward the west once more. My hands were shredded from digging into the sand. I was at an incline, and the peak was close. I wanted to reach it before the darkness set over. "Chucha," I groaned over and over. Every movement forward put me closer to the stars. My vision wavered. The chicken dangled. I looked at the machete in my hand. The blade sliced the rope with ease, and the chicken fell into the sand. I felt on the verge of death; then, everything opened up. A gust of wind blew at the peak. I rolled onto my back. Stars began to sparkle. My breathing steadied. Blood rushed to my head. I pushed myself to my feet and gazed west with dry eyes. In the distance, the floodlights of the training facility shone. I laughed. The machete fell into the sand. It sank half an inch and imprinted its outline. I put my hands behind my head. Home was finally within reach.

Chapter 8
A Gringo's Second Trip to Panama

My second trip to Panama came in April 2024. In the five to six months since my first visit, I spent more time researching Carlos's story. It was all I did. Because I didn't have an income, I couldn't afford to live in my apartment anymore, and I actually went homeless for a brief time before two godsends, Miriam McDonell and Dr. Neel Anand, took me in and let me live in their pool house in Los Angeles. I am forever grateful for them. I would spend my mornings reading and researching in the pool house, and when my friend, Michael Frick, would go to work, he would let me drive to his apartment, where I could write until seven or eight in the evening when he would return home. I spent so much time there that I should have paid him rent. My life was a mess, but I was so engrossed in this project that I didn't care.

My gut told me Carlos lied to me. I could feel it when I sat with him. Although he wore a friendly smile, there was a sense of delusion in his words. I was sure the Noriega narrative written by the wary hands of Washington was false, but I was just as certain that Carlos embellished stories to preserve his legacy. I wrote a draft of the book, and as I suspected, there were many events and incidents I could not prove or corroborate with materials within reach. For instance, Carlos was trained by Mike Harari, who would ultimately become one of Noriega's significant sources of intelligence in the late 1980s. There isn't much documentation with regard to their relationship behind closed doors. Harari had supposedly retired from Mossad by 1988 and engaged in a trade and supply business, which Noriega took advantage of, just as did the United States and many countries in the Middle East. Harari was able to transport weapons all over the world. His connections through Mossad had put him in a position of importance.

"Do you think Harari knew of the invasion before it happened and that's why he left the country a day before the troops came?" I asked Carlos over the phone before my trip.

"Absolutely not," he responded.

After Lillehammer, Mike Harari's past was elusive. I didn't believe he was in the dark about the invasion, but I had zero proof of that, and Carlos himself told me nobody in Noriega's inner circle knew the invasion was coming.

Then there was Omar Torrijos's 1972 constitution, which changed Panama's political landscape. Carlos was in Israel when it was signed. It was a big deal for the Panamanian people. Torrijos had achieved his first major goal. It came at a time when the world wasn't exactly sure how to feel about what was happening in Panama. Torrijos was criticized for seizing power and for using authoritarian methods to remain on the throne. Still, the people of Panama idolized him, even if the constitution gave Torrijos the power to appoint ministers, judges, and public officials. It seemed to have all the makings of a dictator solidifying his power, as it also gave him authority over foreign relations, public administration, and national defense, which replaced traditional political parties with representatives aligned with his revolutionary ideals. I knew I needed to understand the social climate of this time more, especially from the perspective of the poor.

In my research, I also read a lot about a man named Kurt Muse. He had been imprisoned in 1989 for creating anti-Noriega radio transmissions within Panama. When Manuel found out, he ordered the PDF to capture Muse and throw him in a cell. The US Southern Command had no idea at first until people began to wonder where Kurt was. Many sources stated this was the last straw and was what sparked the US invasion of Panama, or as Bush and Reagan titled it, Operation Just Cause. Did I fully believe that? No, I thought their minds had been made up for quite a while before then. Operation Acid Gambit, the operation within an operation, undertaken on December 20, 1989, was undoubtedly a vital part of the invasion for the Americans, as a group of Delta operators extracted Muse from the Carcel Modelo. Kurt's book with John Gilstrap, *Six Minutes to Freedom*, was an informative piece for me to read during my research. I saw this mission as an earned, localized example of American patriotism. That made me realize I needed to speak with Americans who fought in the invasion to understand their story and ensure they were represented in this book. Although they didn't fully understand why they were in Panama, they knew who Noriega was—they had seen his name smeared in international media for years by 1989. So when their commanding officers shipped them south, they did as they were ordered, and most of them were happy to do so.

I was referred to a wonderful man, Colonel James Ruffer. He lived in Las Vegas when we spoke, and he had written several hundred pages of his memoirs, some of which he shared with me. In the late 1980s, he was an officer in the US Air Force Medical Corps, involved in humanitarian care and medical oversight for American hostages at the Modelo prison in Panama. Additionally, he had a role in rescue planning. His work was recognized by Colonel Patrick H. Corbett of the Center for Treaty Affairs, who sent him a Letter of Appreciation that Jim shared with me. Jim said the letter caused tension with Colonel Michael A. McConnell, Jim's superior, and Major Ray Terrill, who were skeptical of Jim's involvement and perceived independence. Jim also told me that "nobody in Washington was speaking with Noriega directly in eighty-nine. Only a handful of individuals within the Southern Command had dialogue." During the invasion, Jim was an integral part of Operation Acid Gambit, and I could tell how important his role was to him and his legacy. He and his family lived in Panama for several years before the invasion. He gave me permission to relay our conversation in the book. "I am an old man who spends his days on the phone talking to those who are still in my life. You can write what I say because it is the truth," he told me. I listened to him recount his memories of his time in Panama. He was not directly involved in conflict during the invasion, but he had experience in conflicts before that, such as Vietnam. Jim and Kurt

Muse were great friends, and they both believed the Panamanian people saw them, and the American military in general, as heroes for ousting Noriega from his throne. I found that to be true among many Panamanian civilians.

I knew I could call Jose if I ever learned something I didn't understand. He was knowledgeable about a lot of things, but when it came to politics and business in Panama, he either had the answer or knew where to find it.

"Simply put," Jose said, "we need to be able to back up every single word. You need to inspire Carlos to give you more controversial information, stuff you can't find online or in a book," Jose said over the phone after reading my draft, stressing just how imperative it was that I return to Panama to fill the gaps in what I had already written.

Carlos was more than happy to continue our interviews, as was Natasha, who became immensely helpful by sending me her own voice recordings of him that she had taken over the months and years. They were in contact with me constantly before I was to arrive one day during the last week of April. Jose and Jack reserved me a hotel room about a mile from Carlos's apartment, so the interviews would take place in his home instead of Jose's.

The night before my flight, Carlos asked me for my flight number. "I will come pick you up at Tocumen," he said.

"I land very early, señor, 7 a.m. I won't ask you to waste your morning," I responded.

Carlos insisted, over and over.

My flight could have been arriving at three in the morning, and Carlos still would have offered to pick me up, so I finally thanked him and accepted his offer. I felt nervous on departure day. There was a feeling in my gut that wouldn't go away. My mind told me to relax, that I had already been down there and done what I was about to do, but I couldn't shake the feeling that this trip would be different. And I was right.

I stepped through the airport doors at 6:45 a.m. to find Carlos behind the wheel of his car and Natasha in the passenger seat. "Welcome, welcome, get in," they yelled with a wave.

I had been trying to learn more Spanish in my free time, so I conversed with them in their native tongue.

"I like that when you are here, you try to speak like a Panamanian. Do not worry; you will learn the more time you spend with us," Carlos told me.

I sat in the middle seat, watching Carlos whizz through lanes as we entered the city. If somebody cut him off, he would yell at them furiously. This happened every five minutes, as every driver tried to cut the other off. Carlos's temper came through the most on the road. He was fiery for a moment, then he would turn to me with a smile and a joke.

The skies were gray, the streets were filled with rush hour traffic, and the stench of exhaust lingered.

"We are going to eat now. Do you like Chinese food?" Carlos asked.

"Yes, of course," I responded.

We arrived at a Chinese restaurant at 7:30 a.m. We were one of two tables. It was a traditionally styled restaurant. The staff all wore black pants, white shirts, and red vests. They rolled food carts around the carpet floor. We sat at a round table and etched our orders onto a slip of paper. I was still nauseous from my redeye, but I did not want to be rude, so I ate what I ordered—dumplings, rice, and fish. Carlos ordered an assortment of food. I thought the quality was good, but Carlos did not. We left close to eight and decided to return to his apartment. Señor Wittgreen lived about two miles from Jose. His neighborhood was nice. There was a park nearby where children would play, and the sounds of the city were muffled enough to experience some silence and solitude. Natasha owned a little green parrot whom she referred to as her *hijo* (son). They were incredibly welcoming and told me to get some rest in their spare bedroom for a couple of hours before we would begin with the questions. But first, a beer. Carlos and I shared a short conversation over a cold one as people made their way to work on the streets below. I wasn't as reserved in my questioning this time around, and Carlos liked that.

"Why weren't you at Noriega's drug trial in Miami?" I asked. "The people Noriega had alleged dealings with were there, but you, the man who was closest to him, was nowhere to be seen. Why?"

"Exactly. Because they knew Manuel was not guilty of drug trafficking. Men like me would have been able to provide evidence to support that. The men they put on the stand to testify against him, like Floyd Carlton, were forced into their testimonies."

Floyd Carlton intrigued me in my research. He was one of the fifteen men used in the Noriega trial. He was a pilot who became involved in drug smuggling during the 1980s when the CIA was employing men like him to transport weapons to Nicaragua. Carlton testified that he and Noriega were in the narco business together during Manuel's drug trial in Miami. But, in the following document uncovered by Jose Hilario Trujillo, it says Noriega's men arrested him in 1985 for drug smuggling and informed the United States. Carlton was facing fifty to ninety years, so prosecutors were able to coerce him, and he lied in US court. This was not my opinion. Floyd Carlton admitted to this years after the trial; he lied to the US government, so he spent only four years in jail and was ultimately released into the witness protection program.

Junio   : El ciudadano panameño FLOYD CARLTON, ·en asocio con la organización dirigida por el narcotraficante colombiano PABLO ESCOBAR GAVIRIA,
introducen desde Colombia grandes cantidades
de cocaína a los Estados Unidos de América,
en compañía del piloto panameño TEOFILO WAT-
SON. En Panamá, es capturado ALBERTO AUDEMAR
FARATAY, ciudadano norteamericano de origen
francés, fugitivo de las autoridades estadounidenses. AUDEMAR FARATAY, representando
a la organización de ESCOBAR GAVIRIA, intentó ejecutar actos de violencia en contra del
grupo de FLOYD CARLTON en Panamá. Ambas organizaciones fueron desarticuladas y AUDEMAR
FARATAY, entregado a la justicia de los Esta
dos Unidos.

En un operativo de la Fuerza Especial Antinarcotráfico llevado a cabo en el Puerto de
Cristobal en el litoral Atlántico del país,
se logró la captura de 65 tanques de 55 galones cada uno de Eter Etílico, que iban co
mo carga de cerveza hacia Buenaventura, Colombia. En el citado operativo, se detuvo
a los ciudadanos colombianos CARLOS GUTIERREZ
y JOSE DIAZ, quienes informaron que éstos tan
ques iban destinados a laboratorios clandestinos del narcotráfico en Colombia.

Agosto   Se logra la captura del avión con matrícula
boliviana CP-1620 , el cual tenía 8 maletas
que contenían 12 kilos de cocaína cada una.
En dicha aprenhensión, fueron arrestados el
ciudadano panameño PEDRO ROGNONI y los pilo
tos bolivianos CARLOS CASTEDO y CARLOS YAMA-
MOTO.

Septiembre: Las Fuerzas de Defensa de Panamá organizó y
llevó a efecto un operativo para erradicar
la presencia de plantaciones de marihuana en
el Archipiélago de las Perlas. La Agencia

*Figure 8.1. Chronology of narco seizures on Panamanian soil
and in Panamanian waters between June and September 1985.*

97

"When did the attitude toward Torrijos change, you know, with the Americans?" I asked, attempting to understand the transition of power better.

"It was mostly the threat of communism, but Torrijos also refused to meet the chief of Southern Command at any point in his life because of the CIA's role in the 1969 coup against him. That angered him greatly, and so he did not care to cater to the gringos unless it was necessary. If he had his way, he would have never dealt with America, and Panama would have been socialist, but that was not reality. He did what they asked, and he did nothing more."

"When you returned home from Israel, things had changed, hadn't they? Communism wasn't the only problem in Central America for the gringos," I blurted out. "The DEA set up shop in Panama. They were recruiting guys like you, asking you for favors because of a new problem—narcotrafficking."

Carlos showed me a framed training certificate he had received from the DEA in 1973. It was a prized possession for him. He had propped it up between pictures of family and a photograph of him shaking hands with Jimmy Carter in the late 1970s. "You should get a little rest before we speak more. I have invited my children over this afternoon to help," Carlos said, pointing me to a room with a made bed and blasting air-conditioning.

I accepted and slept until around noon. When I woke up, a new man was sitting at Carlos's table.

"This is my son, Carlos Jr.," Carlitos said, introducing me.

Incredibly accommodating, Carlos Jr. was a very nice man, constantly smiling, and tried to make conversation, as his English was excellent. He acted as a translator that afternoon as others came to visit.

A bottle of seco was immediately broken out, and a glass was placed before me. I couldn't say no. While in the States, I had missed seco. It didn't give me a hangover, and I could drink it all day without losing steam. It was perfect for those interviews. I whipped out the recording device and placed it in the center of the table.

"I was trusted. I cared deeply for my friends and family. I have been grateful my entire life and have worked hard for those I love. This is who I am," Carlos proudly stated.

As the day went on, we naturally grew drunker. We would often top our glasses off with ice so the water would melt and help keep us balanced in conversation, but by the time Carlos's youngest daughter arrived, we were drunk. She was about my age, and she made it clear that she was confused why someone like me, a gringo who couldn't even speak the language, was interested in writing her father's story. It felt like an inquisition. There were no smiles exchanged. It caught me off-guard, and because Carlos and I had been drinking all day, I was sure she wasn't going to believe whatever I responded with. Still, I explained that I had spent six months of my life couch surfing and incomeless because of how dedicated I was to writing this book. It was the truth, and I wasn't asked any more questions of the same.

I felt in control until Carlos made a joke about kidnapping me. "This man has probably kidnapped hundreds in his lifetime," I thought, and in my highly drunken state, I freaked out, wanting to leave. I had to get myself out of there. Rushing into the bedroom where I had napped, I calmed my breathing. I couldn't just run. I had to stop being a little bitch and get back in the room with my voice recorder.

The evening turned to night, and Carlos's youngest daughter had gone home. We had all lost steam. I recorded hours of great material that day and looked forward to translating and transcribing it from my hotel room. I thanked Carlos and Natasha for a wonderful day, and I told Carlos Jr. it was a pleasure meeting him. He offered to drive me to my hotel, and I accepted.

"What do you mean?" Carlitos suddenly asked. "You are staying here."

My laptop wouldn't connect to the Wi-Fi in their apartment, and I was still shaking from the kidnapping comment earlier. Without doing the transcriptions each night and having a full context of what we had spoken about the day before, I would be unprepared the following day.

"You are not going anywhere," he insisted, stating that they had made the room and prepared for me to be with them for the week. That night, I went to my hotel room anyway, and I called Jose. I felt guilty for leaving, and after a conversation that lasted a few minutes, I realized that I should have taken Carlos up on his offer and stayed. So, the following day, I packed up and returned to Carlos's apartment.

"You are staying this time," he said at breakfast.

"*Si, si. Lo siento*," I responded. Carlitos was very understanding, but it was a learning lesson for me. I was happy not to ruffle any feathers.

"My friend Trujillo is coming for breakfast," Carlos exclaimed, handing me a cup of coffee.

I remembered the name from my first trip to Panama. Carlos spoke highly of him, and from the moment Jose Trujillo stepped through the front door in a combination of neatly pressed cargo pants and a tucked-in sleeveless collared shirt, I understood why. He had come prepared with a briefcase. Carlitos introduced me to him. He sat opposite me at the table and laid his briefcase atop the counter. The first item he slipped out was a copy of his book, *George H. W. Bush vs Manuel Antonio Noriega: centro financiero internacional; narcotráfico invasión*. He signed the back of it for me before Carlos's maid handed us each a plate with eggs and toast, as well as a freshly blended fruit smoothie. That's how we were served breakfast every single day I was there. I flicked through the book. It was written in Spanish, but I felt it was necessary to translate and read it, and I did that some days later.

What Torrijos pulled from the case next was what would come to make a major difference in the validity of this very book. Documents. Hundreds of pages of documents. Trujillo pulled some out and handed them to me for review. They were written in a combination of English and Spanish.

TOP SECRET

UNITED STATES DEPARTMENT OF JUSTICE
DRUG ENFORCEMENT ADMINISTRATION
Washington, D.C. 20537

January 25, 1978

The Honorable
Griffin B. Bell
Attorney General
Department of Justice
Washington, D.C.

Sir:

As agreed at our last meeting on January 23, I am putting into writing the details of the alleged involvement of Moises Torrijos, brother of General Omar Torrijos, in drug trafficking into the United States, to be used in your report to the President.

On July 8, 1971, customs agents at Kennedy Airport arrested two Panamanians who were trying to smuggle 154 pounds of heroin into this country. Subsequent investigations resulted in the arrest of the suspected ring-leader in heroin smuggling, Guillermo Gonzalez, a former bodyguard of Moises Torrijos. No evidence whatever was uncovered to link the latter to this illicit activity.

In October, 1971, the chief of the CIA field station in Panama, Stanley R. Burnett, reported to Washington on Moises Torrijos's connections with the drug smugglers. The relevant information, already known to you, was conveyed to John Ingersoll with a note from the former CIA Director, Richard Helms: "The President is informed. The information may be used in the national interests of the United States".

Mr. Ingersoll personally instructed our agents in the Panama DO to verify the information. No confirmatory evidence was found.

However, on the direct instruction of the former Attorney General, John Mitchell, the information was filed as unimpeachable and led to Moises Torrijos's indictment by a grand jury in the Eastern District of New York in May, 1972, and the issue of a bench warrant for his arrest.

The Drug Enforcement Administration believes that the dubious and unproven character of the available information makes its presentation to General Omar Torrijos at his request undesirable as being potentially damaging to the prestige of the American Executive.

Sincerely,

Peter B. Bensinger
Administrator

ARCHIVADO JUL 5 1980
A 3

TOP SECRET

Figure 8.2. Letter from Peter B. Bensinger, Administrator of the US Drug Enforcement Administration, to Attorney General Griffin Bell, January 25, 1978, detailing allegations of Moises Torrijos's involvement in drug trafficking and the subsequent investigations._repeat of figure 6.1.

102

ULTRASECRETO

Honorable   25 de enero de 1978
Griffin B. Bell
Procurador General
Departamento de Justicia
Washington, D.C.

Señor:

Tal como fué acordado en nuestra última reunión del 23 de enero, le estoy poniendo por escrito los detalles de la supuesta implicación de Moisés Torrijos, hermano del General Omar Torrijos, en el tráfico de drogas en los EE.UU., para que sea usado en su informe al Presidente.

El 8 de julio de 1971, inspectores de aduana del aeropuerto Kennedy detuvieron a dos panameños que estaban tratando de pasar clandestinamente 154 libras de heroína. Investigaciones subsiguientes condujeron al arresto del supuesto cabecilla del contrabando de heroína, Guillermo González, anteriormente guardaespaldas de Moisés Torrijos. Ninguna prueba, de cualquier índole que fuese, pudo descubrirse que pudiera vincular a este último con tal actividad ilegal.

En octubre de 1971, el jefe de la estación de la CIA en Panamá, Stanley R. Burnett, informó a Washington sobre la relación de Moisés Torrijos con los traficantes de drogas. La información pertinente, ya conocida de Ud., fué transmitida a John Ingersoll con una nota del entonces Director de la CIA, Richard Helms,[1] que decía así: "El Presidente está informado. La información puede usarse en aras de los intereses nacionales de los EE.UU.".

El señor Ingersoll personalmente instruyó a nuestros agentes de la Oficina de Drogas de Panamá para que verificase la información. No se encontró prueba alguna que la confirmase.

Sin embargo, siguiendo las instrucciones directas del entonces Procurador General, John Mitchell[2] esta información fue presentada como irrefutable y dió como resultado que Moisés Torrijos fuese acusado por un Jurado[3] en el Distrito Este de Nueva York, en mayo de 1972, y a la expedición de un auto para su detención.

El Departamento para la aplicación de las leyes contra la droga estima que el carácter dudoso y sin evidencia de la información que poseemos, hace que la presentación de ésta al General Omar Torrijos, solicitada por él, no es aconsejable porque sería potencial

Figure 8.2. Spanish-language memorandum dated January 25, 1978, summarizing allegations of Moises Torrijos's involvement in drug trafficking and investigations linking him to smuggling activities.

United States Department of Justice

UNITED STATES ATTORNEY
Eastern District of New York
Federal Building
BROOKLYN, N. Y. 11201

LJS:MGB:ga

June 2, 1980

Donald T. Fox, Esq.
Fox, Glynn & Melamed
299 Park Avenue
New York, New York 10017

Re: United States v. Moises Torrijos Herrera
Docket No.: 72 CR 555

Dear Mr. Fox:

Pursuant to your request I am herewith enclosing copy of the Order of Dismissal in the above referenced case

Very truly yours,

EDWARD R. KORMAN
United States Attorney

By: Marilyn Gainey Barney
Assistant U.S. Attorney
Chief, General Crimes

*Figure 8.3. Letter from US Attorney Edward R. Korman, June 2, 1980,
enclosing the order of dismissal in the case United States v. Moises Torrijos Herrera.*

In paraphrasing what I understood from Carlos's and Trujillo's following conversation, those letters highlighted that Nixon wanted Moises Torrijos served to him on a platter for some bullshit narcotrafficking involving his former bodyguard. Of course, Omar could never give up his brother. This created a problem that did not go away for eight years until Edward Korman threw out the case in 1980 (see figure 8.3), long after Nixon had been publicly humiliated. That first letter explicitly states the US can use this incident as leverage over Panama. I sat by with my recorder, soaking as much in as I could, knowing I wouldn't be able to translate or transcribe until I could get Wi-Fi. The only problem was that I didn't get to leave the apartment by myself, other than once for a brief walk on the Cinta Costera. I was recording blindly in many ways. "Did you know that, at the time of this letter, there was a rumored Nixon administration plot to assassinate Noriega and Torrijos?"

They reminisced on the old days. They made connections between past and present, using the conflict in Israel and Gaza as an example. "America funds one side; someone else funds the other. It is a proxy war, and it is the local people who get demolished."

After a couple of hours, Trujillo went home, but he would return each day with his briefcase, and I would listen to him and Carlos talk about the politics of the past, present, and future. There was even a day when several other men came by who were members of the PDF under Noriega. They chimed in every now and again, but it was Trujillo who looked to be most knowledgeable.

I didn't see Jose or Diego all week. I spoke to Jose on the phone on my last day, telling him that Carlos and I had had productive sessions and that he had introduced me to people who could corroborate his story.

That night, Carlos took me to one of his friend's apartments. When we arrived, Roderick Purcell answered the door. A couple of his friends were seated and eating a stew, which reminded me of a spicier Irish beef stew without the potatoes. After we ate, they invited me over to the couch. Everyone sat down. Roderick asked me to start my recording device. He was the first to speak, telling stories about Carlos from the 1980s when he was just a teenager. Roderick's family was well-regarded in the Panamanian military, especially in the air force, where Roderick's father, Lorenzo Purcell, led the division until 1988. Roderick then stated he was one of the last people to see Noriega alive. As a talented chef, Roderick often cooked meals for Noriega when he was in the hospital. "The dish we ate tonight was something I made for Noriega often," he claimed.

Roderick shifted to the side, and Carlos thanked him for his words.

A man named Flavio spoke next. He and Carlos had known each other since the 1980s. He told how when Carlos was working in insurance one day, a young man came to the office looking for a favor, a loan. "Without a thought, Carlitos handed the man five thousand dollars and did not demand to be reimbursed anytime soon. It was pure generosity," Flavio stated.

It was clear the evening was set up for me. I was the one everybody spoke to. The men were all much younger than Carlos, likely by twenty-five years on average. They cared for him, and that was obvious. Yet again, I got the feeling I was being lied to, but there was sincerity in every anecdote, and I forced myself to believe that it was the truth. It seemed that Carlos was a soldier, but one with morals. Those who loved him, loved him. After everyone had spoken, there was a period when we had some drinks and relaxed. Carlos didn't consume anything, and neither did Natasha, but the rest of the men and I opened a bottle of seco. One of them was scouring YouTube for 1980s rock 'n' roll music videos, blasting songs from Van Halen, Kiss, and Motley Crue at full volume.

"Give me the remote," one of the others said, putting on clips from the movie *Top Gun: Maverick*.

"Tom Cruise is the man," they agreed as scenes of American jets dropping bombs on foreign soil flashed before them. I found it to be slightly ironic. We left around eleven that night, and Roderick brought us outside while the others stayed. I believe the others were planning to go to a club to meet some women. I thanked them for their hospitality and for contributing to the book.

Carlos and I had a drink when we got home. Natasha went to bed. It was close to midnight. Carlitos turned on the TV, and the first channel that popped up was showing the film *Scarface* (1983).

It was one of the many scenes where Al Pacino's Tony Montana is snorting a line of cocaine. Carlos turned to me, waved his finger, and in English with his thick, Panamanian accent, said, "You see? Very, very bad." Carlos vehemently denied involvement in drug smuggling. He didn't like it when I brought up the narco trafficking allegations against Noriega. He claimed there was no evidence and the testimonies and stories people tell are inaccurate.

"Racketeering, drug smuggling, money laundering. This is what Noriega was accused of," I reminded Carlos.

"The gringos knew him. They knew where his office was. There was no need for an invasion," he responded. Carlos would not give up his friend, even to me.

Carlos, Natasha, and Carlos Jr. drove me to the airport the following day. Before I left, Carlos gifted me a bottle of Pisco and some coffee beans, both from Peru. I felt grateful for his hospitality. He went out of his way to ensure I was comfortable. His escapades around the world had made him very culturally intelligent, and I could see how his trained and learned abilities as an intelligence asset had shaped his life.

When I returned to the United States, I jumped right into the recordings and spent weeks translating and transcribing, highlighting new information, and figuring out where it fell in the timeline of Carlos's life. After almost a year of working on the book, I had written another draft, and it was clear I had uncovered some information that would help shift the narrative that had been set in stone for decades.

Chapter 9
An Inmate Escapes Coiba Island

The phone on my bedside table rang loud with a vibration. The wood shook. The woman in my bed groaned, turning to face the window. "Hello?" I said.

"Get over here," Manuel said, calling me to his home.

When I arrived, there were dozens of journalists outside. Photographers snapped pictures of me as I stepped out of my car. The flashes blinded me. "Put the fucking cameras away," I yelled, covering my eyes. The men and women stepped aside. The pathway leading to Manuel's residence revealed itself.

"Beautiful day, isn't it, Mr. Wittgreen?" a gringo voice bellowed from the group.

As I closed my hand to a fist to knock on the door, I turned to find a *Newsday* jockey from Washington smirking at me. I wanted to smash his camera in front of the world, but I didn't give him the time of day.

Noriega's maid let me into his home. A Nicaraguan. She was beautiful. Her petite body led me right to him. He sat at a table in his kitchen, drinking a cup of coffee and reading the *New York Times*. The headline read "A Look Behind Nixon's Presidency."

Nixon was relentless with my country. He never quite trusted our people enough to run our own affairs. Manuel set the paper down when he saw me. "Carlitos, would you like a cup of coffee?" he asked. "I had the beans sent from a friend in Peru."

While Noriega's maid brewed my cup, Manuel and I sat and talked. The smell of Peru wafted through the home.

"Those journalists outside . . . they've been out there for forty-five minutes looking to speak with me," he said.

"About what?" I asked.

"Whatever I will give them an answer for—the Cubans sending airport workers to Grenada, my thoughts about Watergate, anything."

I was hearing more about Grenada by the month. The nation had started to express anti-imperialist rhetoric through its new leader ,Maurice Bishop, and his New Jewel Movement. They were going through changes just like we were. The Americans needed their land, too. "Assholes," I said.

"It is what it is. How's business?"

In the seventies, I had started working with various casino commissions in Panama. It was my way of making extra income. I did this with a few different ventures, and they brought me money. Cockfighting, insurance, car imports, gambling, fighting and training . . . I was multi-faceted when it came to income. It all came naturally to me. The relationships I made through military and government gave me a leg up in the world. However, as successful as I became, I was an intelligence officer first. "Business is good," I responded.

People wanted to do business with men like me. At this time, many casinos were coming to Panama, and they brought with them domestic and foreign gamblers. Many of the owners were first-timers, and so they needed a local who knew the landscape to help their business stay free from criminals. It was common for me to see establishments getting robbed.

Noriega leaned back and set the paper down on the table. He whistled, and his maid left the kitchen. The chatter of reporters outside rang in the air. "Can you go out to Coiba Island and check on things for me?" Manuel asked. "Sheldon Reyher visits Panama next week. He's our new correspondent in the DEA."

I understood the importance. The DEA was investing in people and facilities in Panama. After 1972, every two years, Noriega would have a new contact in the DEA to collaborate with. Reyher was our agent until '76. Whenever the DEA came to Panama, Noriega was the man they came to see.

```
Todo el trabajo realizado por la Fuerza Especial Antinarcotrá-
fico de Panamá, ha sido coordinado con la agencia Federal del DEA,
a través de los siguientes agentes:

   -   1972  -  1974    Edward Heath
   -   1974  -  1976    Sledon E. Reyher
   -   1976  -  1978    M.C. Farland
   -   1978  -  1980    Arthur Sedillo
   -   1980  -  1982    Leonard Williams
   -   1982  -  1984    James Bramble
   -   1984  -  1986    Thomas Telles
```

Figure 9.1. List of DEA attachés between 1972 and 1986.

"I can be on Coiba by the morning," I responded.

"You see those reporters outside? They treat my words like an iceberg. They show 30 percent of the truth, and the other 70 percent is a dramatized narrative. It will never be as it seems."

I knew the flight to Coiba would be rough in the morning, so I vowed to take it easy that night. There was some business I had to tend to at a casino by Tocumen Airport in Don Bosco. The sun was covered by clouds as I arrived. The cool grip of the casino door sent a shiver up my spine. A waft of warm air circumnavigated me as I entered.

"Carlos," a voice bellowed. It was the owner. It's been too long to remember, but he was a fat bastard, so I remember him as La Ballerna (the Whale). He had a dirty gold ring on each finger.

"Which machine was it?" I asked.

"Come this way," La Ballena responded, pointing his overgrown finger at a row of slots.

The casino was new. It had an American design. Every casino I visited during that time had inspirations from the gringos or the Chinese. The business was a good sign.

La Ballerna hyperventilated with every step. "Right here," he said.

I hunkered down. A thin injection into the side of the machine was visible. Only a power tool could have done it.

"We don't know how, but he robbed us," La Ballerna said.

"You remember what this guy looked like?" I asked.

"He was small, Venezuelan, I think."

"Install cameras like I told you to. You'll make my job a lot easier," I stated. I put my hands on my hips and scanned the casino floor. The constant ringing of slot machines and coins clinking together thumped in my head. "Okay, I'm leaving now," I said as I started walking toward the exit.

La Ballerna stepped forward. The tremors ran up and along the bones in my legs. "Wait, there's something else," he yelled out.

I turned and saw him reaching into his pants pocket. He ripped out a twenty-dollar bill. He pinched it at either end and held it out far from his chest.

"What of it?" I said.

"It's fake, señor," he responded. I ripped the currency from his fingers and held it to the light. There was no transparency. It felt heavy compared to normal currency. It was a fake.

"I had to call the bank to make sure I was right. How can I stop this?"

"I'll look into it," I said as I shoved the bill into my pocket. "Now, I have to leave, Ballerna. See you soon."

"Don't you want to stay for a drink? I have premium seco."

I woke up at the casino twelve hours later. It was 6:00 a.m. Luckily, Tocumen Airport was closed because my helicopter left at 6:15 a.m. The clothes I wore stank of liquor. My eyes were crusted together. I didn't open them once the entire ride. Wind from the propellers rustled my hair. My ears were covered by soft muffs. Chucha, fucking La Ballerna could drink like a fish. His pit was endless. I opened my eyes to the sensation of descending. The veins in my eyes stung from the salty ocean air. In my gaze was the rainforest island of Coiba. Sandbanks lit up the shoreline, and crystal-clear waves crashed. Two armed guards wearing black T-shirts and dark-green pants patrolled the outer banks of the forest with machine guns. A slew of ragged prisoners shifted in the sand behind them with their heads held low. The chopper touched down, and I puked out the side.

Guards eyed me up as I was escorted around the island. I was the superior of everyone on that rock. "That's Noriega's man," the whispers echoed. Everyone was on their best behavior, even the dirty prisoners locked in their cells. I was led right to the warden's office.

Domingo was his name. He stood patiently behind his desk, waiting for me. "Buenas, Carlos," he said with a smile. The skin on his hand felt like old leather. There were calices ribbed along his palm. His overgrown nails had dirt in them.

"Sit down," I told him.

He took a seat behind his desk. I sat opposite.

"You can relax. I'm just here to see how things are going on the island," I said.

"Can I get you anything to drink?"

"Chucha, no." My headache returned. I squinted my eyes and rubbed my temples. Fucking Ballerna.

"Can I get you some aspirin?" Domingo asked.

I shook my head.

"There is something I should show you, señor," he stated.

I opened my eyes.

Domingo leaned forward with a picture laid out on the desk before me. It was of a bald man with ancient Peruvian tattoos on his neck. I had never seen him before. "This is Santiago Pereira.

He has been a prisoner here since 1970. As you can see, his file is sizeable."

"What did he do?" I asked.

"He's a murderer, a thief, and a conspirator against the government."

"An Arnulfista?"

"Yes."

"What about him?"

"He's been missing for a week," Domingo said.

Coiba was the largest island prison in Central America, the largest I had seen, anyway. A foolish man would think he could cross the waters to the mainland for freedom. I knew a desperate man would do the same. There was a chance the sea had already taken him. However, the island was big. He could have been surviving off its natural resources. Still, I knew we had to find him. I knew Noriega would not have been pleased to find out a prisoner roamed free on Coiba while the DEA was in his presence. "Have you checked the whole island?"

"Yes, señor. We did not find him, but we heard rumor of a seaplane landing."

"You're saying he was picked up?"

"Possibly, señor."

"Show me his cell," I demanded.

Prisoners grinned at me as I passed by their cells. They leaned against the bars and pressed their faces between the gaps. Their chipped, rotten, yellow teeth stank. Dirt covered their frail bodies. Shit and piss stained the floors. It was animalist, but those men were animals. Innocence never existed in Coiba. I found the darkest of humanity to run supreme on the island.

"This is it," Domingo said as he stopped and pointed at a cell with three men inside.

"Let me in," I said.

Domingo's hand shook as he slotted the key into the door. I stepped inside and put my hands on my hips. Each of the three men was in his twenties. A constant drip of water fell and corroded the stone floor.

"Santiago Pereira . . . where is he?" I asked.

The fuckers didn't even look me in the eye.

I stepped closer, slamming my feet down. "I'm going to ask you again. Where is Santiago?"

"We don't know," one of them said.

"When was the last time you saw him?"

"Last week. Just after the sunset. We all came back to our cells. Santiago stayed outside fishing with Lucas, and then he never came back," said the same man.

"Let's go."

Enemies of the state populated Coiba. There were several generations of criminals. Some were in cells for fighting against a government that had long since existed. The island itself was a visual paradise, but I knew that beneath it lay the graves of thousands. Executions, disease, murder . . . all of it existed on the island. Noriega had informed me that Torrijos was under pressure from the Comision Interamericana de Derechos Humanos (CIDH, Inter-American Court of Human Rights) to fix problems at the prison. That organization had a particular interest in our involvement in government and civil affairs. I agreed with the CIDH that a change was needed. The institution needed more structure.

Walking along the outer banks of the island, I felt a sense of unease. I couldn't see land from where I stood. The ocean seemed to extend forever. I wondered how somebody could land a plane and get away unseen. What purpose would they have had? None of the criminals on the island were particularly special, not special enough for an escape that grandiose. I snapped back to reality as Domingo pointed toward an inmate by the shore. He held onto a makeshift wooden rod with a flimsy line cast into the sea.

"Somebody from the National Guard is here to speak with you," Domingo yelled out.

Lucas dug his rod into the sand. "Hola, señor," Lucas mumbled.

"Carlos has some questions about Santiago's disappearance. He is not somebody you want to lie to," Domingo stated.

"Did a plane come for him?" I asked.

"They were Colombian drug smugglers. Santiago worked for them. I think he worked out a deal to get himself off the island," Lucas said.

"Smuggling drugs?"

"Si, yes."

"Did you know about this, Domingo?"

"It is a new problem," Domingo responded.

Just as Noriega had forewarned, drug smugglers were starting to pass through Panama before heading north. I would have never suspected Coiba to be a point on the journey, but it was clear to me that my world had a new climate, and I would need to adapt. Coiba was a big island with little security. I felt good about our work on Coiba. Prisoners were given more freedom there than in any other encampment. They could roam, fish, cook, and farm. It was self-governance in my eyes. I have been to prison before, and I would have killed for those conditions.

Manuel and Torrijos had been invited to Washington on short notice. Congress wanted the pair of them to speak about the heightening issue of narcotrafficking in the Caribbean. Noriega was seen as an expert in the area. I would have to inform him about Coiba when he returned.

It was nice having a break for a few days. I worked like a dog. I had several children at this point, and I always made sure they were taken care of before I spent money on myself. I was lucky to have a lot of money for a young man in those times. I fought cocks every night, feeling a flow of winning and losing like waves crashing on Coiba. I had met a new lover, and there were days spent lying in bed, drinking, fucking; it was perfect.

I stumbled out of a taverna on Via Argentina one afternoon, thinking of this woman. Noriega was coming home from Washington that night. A pair of sunglasses rested over my eyes. I started walking to my first love's apartment a few blocks away. The traffic raged. My eyesight was blurred by the afternoon light. A payphone shimmered like a mirage. I stumbled to it and dialed.

"This better be the right number," I mumbled to myself as the dial tone rang over and over. It was the right number. I was invited over. When I arrived, my lady was naked in bed, waiting for me, the sheets barely covering her smooth body. After hours spent in bed, I poured my last glass of wine and picked up the phone that hung on the wall.

"Did you install those cameras?" I asked.

"Yes, señor."

"Good, I'm stopping by on my way to the airport."

My lady wasn't happy to see me leave, but I told her I would see her soon. Manuel was returning, and I had information for him, but first, I would stop for a drink and a conversation. A waft of cigarette smoke smacked me in the face as I entered the casino by the airport. Several dozen people roamed the floor. Some sat at blackjack tables and smoked cigars, and others sank back alcoholic drinks at slot machines. In the corners of the space, I saw cameras. Little red lights shone by their lenses. La Ballerna stood by the cashier station, speaking with a gringo. More and more were showing up in places I had never seen before.

I had a few drinks until it was time for me to go to the airport. Noriega's flight was landing any minute. I was parked outside the terminal, listening to the radio. One of Torrijos's recent speeches echoed over the speakers. "Our people are poor and need to be fed first," he roared. Omar was a man who seemed to put the less fortunate first. I admired him for it, even if I didn't truly know the man. Manuel knew him. I'd hear stories through the grapevine.

Torrijos was just socialist enough to piss off the Americans but capitalist enough to work with them. His speeches were a big deal.

I saw Manuel exit through the doors accompanied by two servicemen. "I'll see both of you at my house," Noriega said to his guards before they climbed into a black car parked just behind mine.

"It's good to see you, my friend," Manuel said as he climbed into my vehicle.

"How was the flight?"

"Chucha, long . . . we stopped in Miami. Omar is still there."

"Coiba lost one of its prisoners. Nobody can find him. He had known dealings with Colombian drug traffickers. I think they are using Panamanian islands to stop before flying to America."

"I know all about it; that is why Reyher is coming. Do not worry," he responded.

"What's going to happen?" I asked.

"In some cities like New York and Miami, it is more common for teenagers to do drugs than to not. The demand is there, and so the supply will follow," Noriega said. "When I was in Washington, I met with John Bartels, the administrator of the DEA. He wants this trade coming out of Colombia to become a major focus, a collaborative effort between our governments. This industry will bring with it violence, counterfeit currency schemes, and political chaos. Bartels wants dozens of our men to fly to Washington for training on the matter."

There was an entire industry out there that nobody knew anything about. The Americans got their intelligence from us and our neighbors. I could walk into any room and be treated with respect; a gringo never could have. They needed us. I'd come to learn that quickly. That trip to Washington was the first step. We had bright minds in Panama. Our generation was the first to have been educated and trained by the DEA. We were the first to be fed the lie that we were working alongside the Americans, not for them.

We made it back to Noriega's house. We ate and drank, refusing to speak of work while we enjoyed each other's company. We were brothers-in-law, after all, and every so often, we wanted to keep each other up-to-date on the family. A rain shower was unleashed outside the doors of that warm home. We sat in silence after hours of laughter. Manuel sighed and removed a sealed envelope from one of his cupboards. He sliced the envelope open with a knife and slid out a letter. "More gratitude. The Americans need us now more than ever," Manuel said.

I hadn't yet seen what an international narcotic ring would look like. Manuel, as usual, could see the road ten miles ahead. I trusted him implicitly. Torrijos paid less attention to these issues than Manuel. Omar still cared more about domestic issues. It was a big reason why the Americans directed all their needs to Noriega. Manuel understood it was the gringo hand that fed us.

On that night, I didn't give a shit about any of that. Noriega and I drank until two in the morning before he fell asleep on his sofa. I sat in an armchair opposite, with a cool glass in hand, mind wandering until warm rays of light accompanied the rising sun. It eventually hit me that I was going to America and I didn't know when I would be returning. I trusted things would work out for me in Washington and hoped we could exist there as their people did in Panama. I took pride in the work that I did, all of it. I joined the DEA, and everything changed.

Chapter 10
Washington, DC

I always understood there were tiers to intelligence, and I was a foot soldier in many ways, not the chess master. I would learn of something, and I would report it. Within our military, I saw new positions open that focused entirely on collaborating with the DEA. In the 1970s, men like Nivaldo Madrinan and Luis Quiel started popping up, and as the 1980s came crashing in, the two grew more important. Their sole job was to work with the DEA. It became common all over Central and South America, but we were the most important. The DEA had requested that a large group of Panamanians fly to DC for training. There, we would learn about what was really happening and how we could help keep the peace. I was excited. I had watched Westerns growing up with my father. He was an avid Hollywood film lover.

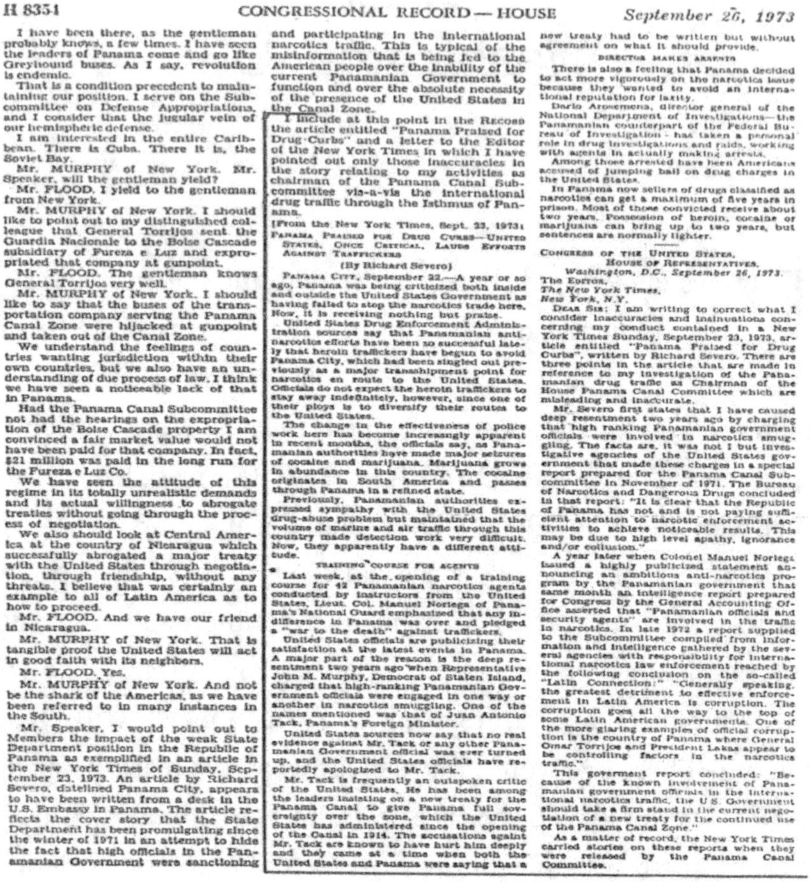

H 8354 CONGRESSIONAL RECORD — HOUSE September 26, 1973

I have been there, as the gentleman probably knows, a few times. I have seen the leaders of Panama come and go like Greyhound buses. As I say, revolution is endemic.

That is a condition precedent to maintaining our position. I serve on the Subcommittee on Defense Appropriations, and I consider that the jugular vein of our hemispheric defense.

I am interested in the entire Caribbean. There is Cuba. There it is, the Soviet Bay.

Mr. MURPHY of New York. Mr. Speaker, will the gentleman yield?

Mr. FLOOD. I yield to the gentleman from New York.

Mr. MURPHY of New York. I should like to point out to my distinguished colleague that General Torrijos sent the Guardia Nacionale to the Boise Cascade subsidiary of Fureza e Luz and expropriated that company at gunpoint.

Mr. FLOOD. The gentleman knows General Torrijos very well.

Mr. MURPHY of New York. I should like to say that the buses of the transportation company serving the Panama Canal Zone were hijacked at gunpoint and taken out of the Canal Zone.

We understand the feelings of countries wanting jurisdiction within their own countries, but we also have an understanding of due process of law. I think we have seen a noticeable lack of that in Panama.

Had the Panama Canal Subcommittee not had the hearings on the expropriation of the Boise Cascade property I am convinced a fair market value would not have been paid for that company. In fact, $21 million was paid in the long run for the Fureza e Luz Co.

We have seen the attitude of this regime in its totally unrealistic demands and its actual willingness to abrogate treaties without going through the process of negotiation.

We also should look at Central America at the country of Nicaragua which successfully abrogated a major treaty with the United States through negotiation, through friendship, without any threats. I believe that was certainly an example to all of Latin America as to how to proceed.

Mr. FLOOD. And we have our friend in Nicaragua.

Mr. MURPHY of New York. That is tangible proof the United States will act in good faith with its neighbors.

Mr. FLOOD. Yes.

Mr. MURPHY of New York. And not be the shark of the Americas, as we have been referred to in many instances in the South.

Mr. Speaker, I would point out to Members the impact of the weak State Department position in the Republic of Panama as exemplified in an article in the New York Times of Sunday, September 23, 1973. An article by Richard Severo, datelined Panama City, appears to have been written from a desk in the U.S. Embassy in Panama. The article reflects the cover story that the State Department has been promulgating since the winter of 1971 in an attempt to hide the fact that high officials in the Panamanian Government were sanctioning and participating in the international narcotics traffic. This is typical of the misinformation that is being fed to the American people over the inability of the current Panamanian Government to function and over the absolute necessity of the presence of the United States in the Canal Zone.

I include at this point in the RECORD the article entitled "Panama Praised for Drug Curbs" and a letter to the Editor of the New York Times in which I have pointed out only those inaccuracies in the story relating to my activities as chairman of the Panama Canal Subcommittee vis-a-vis the international drug traffic through the Isthmus of Panama.

[From the New York Times, Sept. 23, 1973]

PANAMA PRAISED FOR DRUG CURBS—UNITED STATES, ONCE CRITICAL, LAUDS EFFORTS AGAINST TRAFFICKERS

(By Richard Severo)

PANAMA CITY, September 22.—A year or so ago, Panama was being criticized both inside and outside the United States Government as having failed to stop the narcotics trade here. Now, it is receiving nothing but praise.

United States Drug Enforcement Administration sources say that Panamanian anti-narcotics efforts have been so successful lately that heroin traffickers have begun to avoid Panama City, which had been singled out previously as a major transshipment point for narcotics en route to the United States. Officials do not expect the heroin traffickers to stay away indefinitely, however, since one of their ploys is to diversify their routes to the United States.

The change in the effectiveness of police work here has become increasingly apparent in recent months, the officials say, as Panamanian authorities have made major seizures of cocaine and marijuana. Marijuana grows in abundance in this country. The cocaine originates in South America and passes through Panama in a refined state.

Previously, Panamanian authorities expressed sympathy with the United States drug-abuse problem but maintained that the volume of marine and air traffic through this country made detection work very difficult. Now, they apparently have a different attitude.

TRAINING COURSE FOR AGENTS

Last week, at the opening of a training course for 42 Panamanian narcotics agents conducted by instructors from the United States, Lieut. Col. Manuel Noriega of Panama's National Guard emphasized that any indifference in Panama was over and pledged a "war to the death" against traffickers.

United States officials are publicizing their satisfaction at the latest events in Panama. A major part of the reason is the deep resentment two years ago when Representative John M. Murphy, Democrat of Staten Island, charged that high-ranking Panamanian Government officials were engaged in one way or another in narcotics smuggling. One of the names mentioned was that of Juan Antonio Tack, Panama's Foreign Minister.

United States sources now say that no real evidence against Mr. Tack or any other Panamanian Government official was ever turned up, and the United States officials have reportedly apologized to Mr. Tack.

Mr. Tack is frequently an outspoken critic of the United States. He has been among the leaders insisting on a new treaty for the Panama Canal to give Panama full sovereignty over the zone, which the United States has administered since the opening of the Canal in 1914. The accusations against Mr. Tack are known to have hurt him deeply and they came at a time when both the United States and Panama were saying that a new treaty had to be written but without agreement on what it should provide.

DIRECTOR MAKES ARRESTS

There is also a feeling that Panama decided to act more vigorously on the narcotics issue because they wanted to avoid an international reputation for laxity.

Dario Arosemena, director general of the National Department of Investigations—the Panamanian counterpart of the Federal Bureau of Investigation - has taken a personal role in drug investigations and raids, working with agents in actually making arrests.

Among those arrested have been Americans accused of jumping bail on drug charges in the United States.

In Panama now sellers of drugs classified as narcotics can get a maximum of five years in prison. Most of those convicted receive about two years. Possession of heroin, cocaine or marijuana can bring up to two years, but sentences are normally lighter.

CONGRESS OF THE UNITED STATES,
HOUSE OF REPRESENTATIVES,
Washington, D.C., September 26, 1973.

The EDITOR,
The New York Times,
New York, N.Y.

DEAR SIR: I am writing to correct what I consider inaccuracies and insinuations concerning my conduct contained in a New York Times Sunday, September 23, 1973, article entitled "Panama Praised for Drug Curbs", written by Richard Severo. There are three points in the article that are made in reference to my investigation of the Panamanian drug traffic as Chairman of the House Panama Canal Committee which are misleading and inaccurate.

Mr. Severo first states that I have caused deep resentment two years ago by charging that high ranking Panamanian government officials were involved in narcotics smuggling. The facts are, it was not I but investigative agencies of the United States government that made these charges in a special report prepared for the Panama Canal Subcommittee in November of 1971. The Bureau of Narcotics and Dangerous Drugs concluded in that report: "It is clear that the Republic of Panama has not and is not paying sufficient attention to narcotic enforcement activities to achieve noticeable results. This may be due to high level apathy, ignorance and/or collusion."

A year later when Colonel Manuel Noriega issued a highly publicized statement announcing an ambitious anti-narcotics program by the Panamanian government that same month an intelligence report prepared for Congress by the General Accounting Office asserted that "Panamanian officials and security agents" are involved in the traffic in narcotics. In late 1972 a report supplied to the Subcommittee compiled from information and intelligence gathered by the several agencies with responsibility for international narcotics law enforcement reached by the following conclusion on the so-called "Latin Connection:" "Generally speaking, the greatest detriment to effective enforcement in Latin America is corruption. The corruption goes all the way to the top of some Latin American governments. One of the more glaring examples of official corruption is the country of Panama where General Omar Torrijos and President Lakas appear to be controlling factors in the narcotics traffic."

This goverment report concluded: "Because of the known involvement of Panamanian government officials in the international narcotics traffic, the U.S. Government should take a firm stand in the current negotiation of a new treaty for the continued use of the Panama Canal Zone."

As a matter of record, the New York Times carried stories on these reports when they were released by the Panama Canal Committee.

Figure 10.1. Congressional Record, September 26, 1973, H 8354, submissions by Representative John Murphy, New York: "Panama Praised for Drug Curbs" and a letter to the editor, both from the New York Times.

The Right Hand Man

Mr. Severo then implies that I identified Panama's Foreign Minister Juan Antonio Tack as being involved in the narcotics traffic. The facts are, the allegations against Mr. Tack were made by BNDD officers in the Republic of Panama on February 23, 1972, during a subcommittee briefing in that country. Tack became so incensed he had three BNDD agents expelled from the country on 24 hours notice. Senor Tack's name originally arose during a briefing for Members of the Panama Canal Committee by Customs agents on a case that reached into the highest levels of Panamanian officialdom including Moises Torrijos, the brother of Panama's dictator and Foreign Minister Tack. One of the expelled BNDD agents testified before me in Executive Session and confirmed not only that he had told the committee of Minister Tack's involvement, but that he had been forced to sign a letter to Mr. Tack *written by the State Department* denying that he had so informed the committee. Inasmuch as the State Department has had a historic policy of frequently ignoring or denying the involvement of high ranking officials of friendly governments in the narcotics traffic it is not difficult to determine the source of Mr. Severo's information for his article.

All of which leads to the third and most mischievous statement in the article which claims that U.S. sources say that no real evidence against Mr. Torrijos or any other Panamanian government official was ever turned up. The facts are that Joaquin Him Gonzalez, a high ranking Panamanian official and notorious smuggler was arrested in the Canal Zone by U.S. authorities on February 6, 1971. Within two weeks he was brought to Dallas, Texas, for his active participation in the drug market and tried for conspiracy. Him Gonzalez was international transit chief at Panama's Tocumen Airport and he used his high position to protect shipments of drugs to the United States. He was accused on this occasion of sending to Dallas somewhat over a million dollars worth of heroin. Gonzalez was a Torrijos protege and this relationship was made clear when the Panamanian Government mobilized all its resources, something it had not done until that point, for the offender to be returned to Panama. Reports in the press cited the angry outburst and outraged protest the Panamanian government—led by Juan Tack—over the arrest of Gonzalez.

The rupture became so great over the arrest of this high ranking Panamanian official the Attorney General of the United States was forced to dispatch a personal envoy to Panama to calm the situation down and write a letter of apology to Panama's President Lakas. Of even more significance, John Ingersoll testified before the Panama Canal Subcommittee in Executive Session that because of State Department pressure over the arrest of Him Gonzalez there would never again be a Panamanian official arrested for narcotics by U.S. narcotic enforcement agencies. And this is just one of the documented cases of official Panamanian involvement in the drug traffic.

I believe Mr. Severo did make one correct observation when he claimed that Panama finally decided to act more vigorously against the narcotic traffic because they wanted to avoid an international reputation for laxity. I am convinced that the reason this has come about, if indeed it has, is due to the efforts of the House Panama Canal Committee in exposing the fact of "high level apathy, ignorance and/or collusion" on the part of the government of the Republic of Panama in international drug running.

Sincerely,

John M. Murphy,
Member of Congress.

Mr. FLOOD. The gentlemen are very kind to me. I am sure they will have an audience. I hope I do as well.

Mr. ASHBROOK. Mr. Speaker, I firmly support the exceptional, statesman's-like address delivered here today by my colleague from the neighboring State of Pennsylvania, Dan Flood.

When it comes to the subject of the Panama Canal Zone and the Americas—nay, the free world's stake—in that vital, strategic real estate, the House has always been able to rely on Dan to "tell it like it is." Today, he did just that.

I recall that only a few months ago when Dan Flood and Phil Crane appeared on the TV program, "The Advocates" that he made the point, concerning Soviet presence in the Caribbean, that their submarines zipped in and out of Cuba with the frequency of Greyhound buses.

And in his colorful fashion he underscored the crucial importance of the canal by contrasting its proximity to Red Cuba, which sits astride the vital sealanes between South and North America, by stating that one could stand on Cuba's shores and spit a mouthful of Bicardi rum into the waters of the canal.

As a postscript to the above comments, I might add that the results of the followup poll conducted by the TV program, taken among 12,000 persons on the question, "Should the United States give up the Canal Zone?" show that 87 percent voted "No."

Mr. FLOOD's remarks today, which I urge all of my colleagues to read, points out that the overthrow of the Marxist government in Chile is the first major setback for the world revolutionary movement since the Spanish War of 1936-39.

Information received by the House Committee on Internal Security at hearings held in Miami last October revealed that the late Salvador Allende, then President of Chile and then a senator was the leader of the Chilean delegation which attended the infamous Havana Conference—popularly known as the Tricontinental Conference—of January 1966. Without question this gathering, representing 83 groups from 3 continents, brought together every leading Communist, radical, revolutionary, and every other leftwing luminary worth his Marxist salt from all quarters of the globe. The Kremlin supported this meeting—even at the expense of bypassing its own line—organizations—the orthodox Communist parties.

Allende, who reportedly said he would fight the recent military coup to the very end—but took his own life instead, returned to Chile after the Havana Conference and headed up the Conference's branch office in Santiago de Chile hence giving it a quasi-legal status. He was an official of the Chilean Government at this time.

Chile, in short, was being "Cubanized" as one committee witness related. Noteworthy is the fact that the largest nation in South America, Brazil, had 15 persons in the Chilean Embassy while Castro's Embassy had 48. Moreover, Luis Fernandez Ona, a top intelligence officer in

the Red Cuban Embassy is married to Beatriz Allende, daughter of the late President. Not to be overlooked is the fact that Castro, having blown up the Bolivan takeover operation attempted by Che Guevara, his former Cabinet officer, was not unmindful of the fact that Chile has over 2,000 miles of common border while Peru, Argentina and Bolivia. Nor was he unaware of the fact that U.S. strategic raw materials from these and other nations pass through the Panama Canal.

Mr. Speaker, to relinquish the canal to the left wing—tilting Panamian Government, is, in effect, sever the Americas in half. It is—in the national and in the hemispheric interests that such a calamity does not come to pass.

If, as Dan Flood has stated, the Canal is easily accessible to Red Cuba, the geopolitical reality of the situation in the Caribbean—keeping in mind the abortive Cubanization of Chile and of Bolivia and the unlimited support afforded Castro by Brezhnev—it is well within the realm of rational speculation that the Cuban dictator has every intention of Cubanizing the canal.

As in the case of the canal which links this country with her friends in South America, I would sincerely hope that the aisle dividing Republicans and Democrats in this House would provide the political, bipartisan path through which all of my colleagues may rise in support of Dan Flood's legislation.

Mr. CRANE. Mr. Speaker, I would like to commend my distinguished colleague from Pennsylvania (Mr. Flood) for taking this special order to again call attention to a very serious matter to all of us, the future of American sovereignty in the Canal Zone and the latest threat to that sovereignty.

The departure of Omar Torrijos from the Republic of Panama only days before the overthrow of the Allende regime in Chile is, as Mr. Flood indicated, very significant in viewing our role in the Canal Zone.

But Torrijos' flight follows the pattern of earlier rulers of Panama. His 5 years as dictator established a longevity record for rulers of Panama since the end of World War II.

I would like to share with my colleagues a portion of the transcript of "The Advocates" program of last spring in which the subject of American sovereignty in the Canal Zone was debated:

If we gave up the Canal Zone, we would be entrusting the security of the Canal to one of the most unstable countries in the Western Hemisphere. Consider the political upheaval just since World War II.

Enrique Jimenez became President under a new constitution. He served until the elections of 1948 which were declared a fraud, and was succeeded by Daniel Chanis. Police chief, Jose Ramon forced Chanis to resign and Roberto Chiari was declared President.

The Supreme Court voided Chiari's appointment, and Arnulfo Arias took office. Police chief Remon pressured Arias out of office and Alcibiades Arosemena in. He served about a year until Remon himself was elected President in 1952. Remon was assassinated in 1955 and replaced by Jose Remon Guizado who was a suspect in the assassination. Ricardo Arias served out his term. Ernesto de la

Before I left for America, Noriega sat me down and gripped both sides of my face with sheer power. "Have fun," he said, slapping me. He had been there many times. "The DEA is very powerful, almost as powerful as the CIA or FBI. Do a good job, and you'll benefit," he said.

The CIA had an interest in Panama for decades. During World War 2, the canal opened America up to threats. The CIA had a lot of friends in Panama because of this. We provided the Americans with Galeta Island, a base for US electronic surveillance that intercepted communications across the hemisphere. As the years passed, more spies stepped foot on Panamanian land. It was a haven for espionage with the CIA right at its center. If the DEA were going to become just as integral in our affairs, I knew I would have to create a positive relationship.

My flight's departure time was nearing. Washington awaited me.

Noriega looked at the clock. "Can you believe the gringos are still trying to put Moises Torrijos away?" he said.

"What is going on?" I asked.

The radio played softly.

He shook his head. "They're trying to create leverage over Omar."

He was right, as usual. The Americans were growing frustrated with Omar. It was clear he had his own interests in mind and the American interest came second. That was what we needed, but I knew better than to think the Americans would not still put pressure on us.

Noriega switched off the radio. He lit up a cigar and leaned back. "Tell Bartels I said hello," he exclaimed with a grin.

I stepped off the plane in Washington, DC, on a hot summer day. The sun felt different there. The city had a unique smell, too, an amalgamation of urbanity that resulted in a strangely satisfying stench. It was like gasoline. I was culturally entranced. A yellow cab picked me up at the airport and took me to the address the DEA had provided. My eyes were glued to the window, watching everything I passed. At first, the neighborhoods were poverty stricken. I could see the White House in the distance from one trash-ridden street. Gringos in fine suits populated the city the closer we got to our destination. Buildings had chrome windows, like mirrors, warping the reflection of the cab into various shapes and sizes as we drove down a bustling road.

The driver smoked a cigarette and fiddled with the radio. Rock music sparked, and he bobbed his head, leaning back and holding the wheel with one hand. "Where you from, man?" he asked.

"Panama," I responded.

"Panama? Is that where the, uh, the canal is?"

"Yes."

"Yeah, man. I've heard of Panama. Right on."

The asshole wasn't paying attention to where he was going. My fist tightened. I could feel the bones in my hand crack. I knew better than to start a fight in a foreign country.

The windows slid down. The cabbie stuck his arm outside. "Well, this is it, amigo," he said as the car rolled to a halt.

I exited the vehicle. It sped off. I lingered in its exhaust with my eyes gazing toward the top of the gray structure. Everything felt bigger, louder. I entered the building confidently. I told the receptionist who I was and what I was there for. My eyes scanned the room. Other Panamanians sat waiting.

Loud, thumping footsteps echoed. All of us Panamanians lifted our heads and turned our gaze to the receptionist, where a man, who I will call Agent Gannon, stopped to whisper to her. I could see my reflection in the shine of his briefcase. "You can all follow me," he exclaimed.

We arose in unison. I let the others walk ahead of me so I could stand at the back of the pack.

Agent Gannon stopped by the entrance to a lecture-style classroom. "Take a seat," he said over and over as we new agents spilled into the room. The door closed behind us. I sat right at the top of the class, just in front of the empty whiteboard. Gannon stepped out of sight.

He was swiftly replaced by an equally tall and slender man wearing an identical suit. He snapped his fingers, and a projector sparked from the back of the classroom. A map of Central America lit up the board. "My name is Agent McFarland. Some of you may have already heard of me. I'm an agent of the DEA, and I'm one of the men responsible for communicating with your military," he said confidently. McFarland carefully paced back and forth, scanning the room. "You all know why you're here, but none of you know yet the magnitude of this problem. As you can see behind me, this is Central America. Right here is Panama, and this little part of Panama that connects to Colombia is the Darien Gap, a hot zone of dangerous activity. . . . The Darien is so dangerous that when the Pan-American Highway was being built, they had to stop. Men were picked off by predators, machinery malfunctioned in the rain and mud. . . . They just left it as is and never returned to excavate the forest. . . . Nowadays, nobody really monitors this area."

McFarland gestured to the projectionist, and the slide changed to images of laboratories. Some of them were pristine, some filthy. All of them were crime sites, taped off, and under investigation. "These are cocaine labs we seized in Bolivia and Peru. That's where cocaine leaves are grown, so that's where a lot of these labs used to be until these guys started to branch out. Now, Colombia is the hotspot," McFarland exclaimed before the slide changed again. Images of glass jars stacked together in a never-ending line glowed at the top of the class. "This is ethyl ether, critical for refining cocaine hydrochloride. This stuff is not easy to get."

At the time, cocaine was not something I heard about often. Yes, there were people like rock stars and even world leaders who did it prominently, but regular civilians would not have had easy access. What I learned in that lecture hall was that a small problem had gotten bigger.

"Our intelligence has informed us that large quantities of ethyl ether pass through the canal frequently. These shipments of ethyl ether come from all over the world. The cocaine is manufactured onsite in South America and then transported through Panama's waterways and airways."

The projector whirred. I could hear its fan spinning during moments of silence. McFarland snapped his fingers, and the slide changed one more time. An image of a one-hundred-dollar bill flashed on the screen. It cast a green hue onto our wide-eyed faces. "This is what everyone is after. Plain and simple, only this bill is a fake," he said. The image zoomed in. The color of the bill was washed upon closer inspection as if it had gotten stuck in a washing machine. "While you are in Washington, you are going to be educated on the narco trade and the counterfeit currency scheme that stems from it, and you're going to be given instructions for protocol moving forward."

The projector fell silent, and the light dimmed. We sat in darkness until the overhead bulbs sparked and cast artificial rays onto us. The door at the back of the room opened. The silhouette of a man stood in the archway. McFarland beckoned. The man walked slowly down the aisle of steps. He was a stocky man with gray hair and reading glasses. His eyes were magnified in the lenses. "Everyone, welcome Mr. John Bartels, the administrator of the DEA," McFarland exclaimed.

Bartels put his hands behind his back and smiled. I could see the reflection of the overhead lights sparkled in his glasses. "I wanted to stop by on behalf of the DEA and welcome you all to Washington, DC. You should all enjoy your time in the United States. I know for many of you, this is your first visit. Please let me know if there's anything I can do for you during your stay. Oh, and just make sure to stay away from Eleventh Street and U Street.

There's a heap of women over there, but a lot of thugs, too," the administrator joked.

I wasn't afraid of anyone.

Just before the bell rang, Bartels cleared his throat and said, "Remember, this isn't just for the safety of our nations but is for the entire world."

My time in Washington was eye-opening. I saw the magnitude of the problem ahead and how, every year, it would get worse. In the sixties, narcotrafficking was small, an industry that could fly under the radar for many governments. The growing cartels in South America realized they could print money, both literally and metaphorically. Most of the currency they created funded drug operations. The two often ran hand in hand. It was a major issue for the United States.

This program in DC was like school, and I was never an academic like my brother, Gaspar. There were tests, assignments, and even field trips to various monuments and historical sites in Washington. We had fun when we could. Washington was filled with women of all delegations. We were Latin men with foreign tongues. It made us popular.

Still, my mind would often wander back to Panama. I never felt more Panamanian than I did when I left. I was a representative of my nation. Every evening, I would call home and do my rounds. Noriega was always first. He'd fill me in on what was happening at home. He and Torrijos were working on a grand plan to transfer ownership of the canal back into our hands. I didn't yet know how possible that truly was, but I knew it was Omar's priority.

"They are open to conversation, but they will not part with it easily. We need a more agreeable president in Washington to finish this," Noriega expressed.

Manuel was careful with what we spoke of over the phone. We knew the CIA tapped many of Omar's devices, and there was a chance ours were, too. We were men with knowledge, and they were organizations created to harvest information men like us would have.

"The gringos are already on thin ice with Omar over his brother, Moises," Manuel said. "That fucking judge Edward Korman in New York received false, coerced testimonies from Joaquin Gonzalez and Rafael Ricard. They are looking for any reason not to trust Torrijos," Manuel said with an exhale.

Torrijos wasn't always the calm, cool, and collected man that I would see behind a podium. He needed Manuel to stabilize him and provide him with information that would create a path forward for Omar.

One day in class, the bell rang, and Gannon held us for a few minutes. "The United Nations are in town, so there'll be no class tomorrow," he said.

A rumble started in the room. We had been slaving away at our research, and a break felt earned. A chatter muttered from ear to ear. Womanizing and drinking were on our minds. I could practically hear the bottles popping.

"Don't do anything stupid. We'll hear about it, trust me," Gannon said before exiting the room.

As I rushed out into the hallway, McFarland stood by the door and gestured for me to stop. "Carlos Wittgreen?" he asked.

"Yes," I responded.

He handed me a yellow envelope, a smile pinned to his face. "You're Noriega's brother-in-law, aren't you?"

"Yes."

"I don't know what we'd do without him. Tell him I was asking for him."

I arrived at the bar alongside one of the other students. Everyone from the class was at this one bar on Eleventh Street and U Street. Pitchers of American beer flowed, and shots of Tennessee bourbon appeared in my hand every twenty minutes. None of us were well-behaved. We were animals set free for one night in the American capital. We felt protected like we meant something to not only the United States but also to the world. We were told we were solving a problem.

"Carlos!" my friend yelled from across the bar.

I shoved through a horde of people to find mi amigo sitting with two women in fine dress suits. One was a blonde, like the soldiers' wives in the zone, and the other was a redhead.

"This is Carlos, the guy I was talking about," he said.

I kissed both of their hands. The scent of fruit lingered in my nose long after.

"Where are you from?" the redhead asked.

"Panama," I responded, leaning in close.

She smiled.

"What're you so dressed up for?" I asked.

The bar door suddenly opened, and a strand of light struck me in the eye. Four men entered in suits. Two white, two black, none American. They had pins on their chests.

"First round's on me!" one of them yelled.

The redhead grabbed my arm, and I turned to her. "We're with the UN," she said.

We sat with them for the next two hours. I wanted the blonde, but the redhead was more interested in me.

"Can you get me a drink?" she drunkenly asked.

"Sure, what do you want?" I responded.

"Whatever you're having," she said, refusing to break eye contact.

Four men sat at the bar to the left of me. It was the same four who had come in yelling. They swayed back and forth in their stools.

I leaned on the counter and beckoned for the bartender to approach. "Give me two beers . . . Budweiser," I yelled.

The bartender nodded and walked to a cooler at the other end.

I looked to the suited drunkard by my side. The pin on his chest represented a Ugandan flag. He grunted. His eyes struggled to stay open. He rose to his feet and wobbled, barely grasping the bar with his dry fingertips. His hand grabbed the zipper and pulled it down slowly. Before I could blink, he had whipped his dick out and started pissing against the wood. Splashes of urine sprayed onto his shoes.

I jumped to my right. "Chucha! What the fuck?" I yelled out loud.

The Ugandan tilted his head to look at me, piss still streaming from his tip like a fucking firehose. "What's your problem?" he mumbled.

The bartender returned and screamed bloody murder.

The Ugandan didn't flinch an inch. He just kept pissing and pissing.

"Put your fucking dick away. We're not in Africa," I screamed at him.

"I'm in the fucking UN, asshole," he responded.

I clenched my fist. My heart thumped. I pummeled him right in the cheek. He fell into his friends, dick out and piss flying everywhere. Bar patrons stopped their conversations. All heads turned to face me.

The Ugandan dragged himself to his feet. I slammed my hand onto his shoulder and shoved him back onto the barstool. "You're going to put your dick back in your pants, you're going to apologize to the bartender, and then you're going to pay for my beers. You understand?"

There were few thoughts behind his glazed eyes. He nodded in understanding anyway. His cheek was bright red. He handed the bartender two dollars.

"They tip in America, you know," I said.

The Ugandan's hand shook as he reached back into his pocket and pulled out two more dollars.

I walked right back to my table, and I drank until I couldn't. We were berated for the fight, but it was brief and inconsequential.

In my final days, an impressive skyline lit up against a red backdrop. I had never seen the sun so gargantuan. A slew of yellow cabs lined the sidewalk and honked loudly, targeting our large group, foreigners they could swindle for a few extra dollars. I stood there, admiring the view, until someone put his hand on me from behind.

"Good evening, Carlos. How'd you like the tour?" Agent Sedillo asked.

"American history is fascinating," I responded.

He shook my hand and led me to his blacked-out car. A personal driver sat up front. Sedillo and I sat in the back. There were miles of traffic. It took us forever to get where we were going. "I heard good things about you," Sedillo stated.

I heard those words a lot. Noriega was the man; everybody knew it. I stood by his side, not for status but out of loyalty. That was respected in more circles than my own. The DEA knew me to be capable and brighter than the rest. They wanted to make a statement.

"This whole thing is only getting worse. We wish we had nipped this in the bud years ago."

"It is a problem that requires many hands," I responded.

The DEA was still a relatively new organization. It had kinks that needed to be worked out. I always felt agents who performed duties for the DEA were pioneers in a way. Until that point, the United States cared more for the suppression of communism and Marxist ideals. It was the Cold War, after all, covert, rooted in intellect, even if the United States would still fund nationalist and capitalist politicians, per the National Security Doctrine. The narcotrade was different. It was a new war for everyone, especially America. This required them to communicate and collaborate constantly with us. There was an agreement on both of our sides. We Panamanians are a trusting people; contracts were implemented with the shake of a hand. I made that handshake, and I expected to be treated equally.

Yet again, I returned to Panama a more culturally enhanced man. I viewed my own country differently. I noticed cracks in the foundation that I otherwise would not have recognized, should I have spread my wings and left the nest. When I made it home, Noriega attended a secret meeting with George Bush. Regarding the words spoken in those rooms, I didn't know the extent of what was said. Yet an invitation to the dinner table often came with a tasked responsibility. I hoped Manuel could find a way to appease everyone. Our people deserved more than what they had.

My children were the first people I wanted to see at home. None of them had left Panama yet. I cherished the time I spent with them. Work consumed my days, but at heart, I was a family man. I've had many wives and many children. I have felt cohesion with all of them. I was able to get significant rest before my phone rang one day.

"Balboa Taverna, one hour," Noriega said.

When I arrived at the bar, Noriega was surrounded by a dozen men and two dozen women. All the high-ranking officials were there—Jose Melo, Paredes del Rio, Diaz Herrera, men whose intentions I wish were known earlier.

Noriega saw me enter, his eyes lit up wider than mine. "Carlitos, back from America! Come over here!" he yelled. "Come, come, take a seat next to Señor Purcell."

Alberto Purcell was a good man, a military man who one day became head of our air force. He was the man who flew Noriega to Cuba for the CIA in order to negotiate the trade of CIA spies; I was too young and inexperienced to be able to join. Alberto sat next to Colonel Jose Melo. My friend Jose Trujillo was there, too. He was younger than all of us.

The crowd of men hollered loudly like Mongolian tribesmen, ready to tear down a village. Droplets of beer sprayed as men slammed their glasses down on the hardwood tables. Women caressed their arms and shoulders. "Settle down," Noriega said as he waved his hand, laughing. Our parties always drew women. Our parties quickly got out of hand.

Under Torrijos, society in Panama was becoming stable. I felt the independence of our decisions, but the Americans lingered around us. Their troops sat in bases considered to be American soil, less than five kilometers from where I slept.

It was not long after this that I found myself alone with Manuel after a trip to Washington to meet with CIA Director George Bush.

"The CIA will help us plant bombs in the Canal Zone to help us speed up negotiations for the canal. If we can prove the Panamanian presence would make for smoother operations, we can get it back. Bush is pro-canal."

Considering the way things turned out in the end, I find that is what people believe least, yet it's something Noriega stood by right up until he died. Amongst men like me, it's well-known how it all started and how it ended. Noriega even told us all in his memoir that Bush wanted to help at first, but as time went on, the relationship quickly soured and became personal. I do not know much of what was said behind closed doors, but back in the mid-seventies, I was happy to hear the daily news of national progress.

But my mind still wandered back to that taverna on Via Argentina. Women surrounded us. Music reverberated through the walls and vibrated at the soles of our feet. The tables shook. Glasses fell over, and wine spilled along the wood and dripped to the planks. We felt pride in our blood. We would have to deal with guys like Peter Bensinger, John Poindexter, Oliver North, and countless other high-ranking American officials, but it was Bush who put fear into me the most over all those years. His hatred for Manuel became palpable. I knew Noriega was capable of cradling the relationship. Yet, there was a feeling in my gut that, one day, push would come to shove, and Bush and Noriega would butt heads on the international stage.

Chapter 11
La Bodeguita

A wave of clapping showered over the strategy room. Torrijos stood before us with a smile, Noriega by his side. We had had a good month. Few smugglers had evaded us. "Excellent work," Omar praised. I stood alongside DENI [Panama's National Department of Investigations]and G-2 men who collaborated with the DEA. We were proud of ourselves. I never took my time for granted. It was an honor, in many ways, to feel I was doing something with my life. The problem was clear. The drug trade brought with it many issues—safety, political, and environmental—but it was under control. The collaboration improved our relationship with the United States. It felt like they respected us.

"As you've noticed, the quantities of narcotics seized have been steadily increasing month over month. This means the Medellin Cartel is expanding operations," Noriega said, handing out pieces of paper to everyone.

The Right Hand Man

CRONOLOGIA DE UNA LUCHA

RESUMEN CRONOLOGICO

I.- Década de 1970 a 1980

A comienzos de la década de los años 70, la cocaína y la marihuana, se convierten en la droga de mayor producción y consumo, especialmente en el mayor mercado de consumo que son los Estados Unidos de América.

Durante la década de 1970 a 1980, en ese entonces, la Guardia Nacional de Panamá, decomisó en diversos casos un total de 293.384 gramos de cocaína y 2,215.868.2 gramos de marihuana.

De igual manera, fueron deportados por casos de drogas, 201 personas de diversas nacionalidades a diferentes países de los cuales, 46 personas fugitivas de delitos de drogas en los Estados Unidos de América fueron entregadas por las autoridades panameñas a las autoridades federales norteamericanas.

Entre los casos sobresalientes en la citada década, cabe señalar los siguientes:

Figure 11.1. Chronological summary of narco seizures between 1970 and 1980.

I.-   AÑO 1971 .

JULIO

Durante la Administración del Presidente RICHARD NIXON, Inspectores de Aduana del Aeropuerto Internacional JOHN F.KENNEDY, detuvieron a los ciudadanos panameños GUILLERMO GONZALEZ y RAFAEL RICHARD en posesión de dos maletas que contenian 154 libras de heroína. Investigaciones subsiguientes al arresto, señalaron que GUILLERMO GONZALEZ en una ocasión había sido guardaespaldas del Señor MOISES TORRIJOS h., hermano del General OMAR TORRIJOS H., situación esta que fue aprovechada por los detractores del proceso panameño como RICHARD HELMS, quien fungía en la época como Director de la CIA y fue tratado de mentiroso en el Senado norteamericano y JOHN MITCHELL, temido consejero de la administración NIXON, que por sus mentiras ante el Senado y por su participación conspicua en la conjura de Watergate fue condenado a cumplir pena de prisión, que desataron una campaña de infundios canallescos en contra del Señor MOISES TORRIHOS H., quien era Embajador de Panamá en España, el General OMAR TORRIJOS HERRERA, el Ministro de Relaciones Exteriores de Panamá, Licenciado JUAN ANTONIO TACK y otros funcionarios del gobierno revolucionario panameño. A pesar de que las investigaciones del Departamento de Justicia de los Estados Unidos de América, demostraron feha-

Figure 11.2. Chronological summary of narco seizures in 1971.

141

II   AÑO 1976

SEPTIEMBRE   Unidades de narcóticos del Ministerio de Hacienda y Te
                  soro, arrestaron al ciudadano colombiano ALVARO SUAREZ,
                  quien llegó en el Vuelo No.976 de BRANIFF INTERNATIONAL
                  procedente de Colombia y encontrado en una maleta de su
                  propiedad, la cantidad de 12 envoltorios de cocaína.

III   AÑO 1977

AGOSTO   El norteamericano DONALD POMERLOY ROBERTS a su arribo
                  a Panamá procedente de Lima, Perú, fue detenido por
                  autoridades panameñas antinarcotráficos en el Aeropuer
                  to Internacional de Tocumen, incantándosele 3 kilos de
                  cocaína que estaba oculta en una maleta de doble fondo.

SEPTIEMBRE   TERESA MEATRIZ ALBORNOZ GUTIERREZ, ciudadana colombiana,
                  fue detenida en el Aeropuerto Internacional de Tocumen
                  procedente del Perú, incautandose 3 kilos de cocaína con
                  destino a el Canadá.

DICIEMBRE   Unidades de narcóticos panameñas arrestaron al norteame
                  ricano SHULER PHILLIPHS COX Jr. en el Aeropuerto Inter-
                  nacional de Tocumen decomisandose 460 gramos de cocaína
                  que trató de introducir al país en el interior de un ra
                  dio-cassette y en los tacones de sus calzados.

Figure 11.3. Chronological summary of narco seizures in September
1976 and August, September, and December 1977.

IV   AÑO 1978

ENERO

La colombiana MARINA LUCILA MAZZINI DE PAREJA, fué detenida por autoridades panameñas en el Aeropuerto Internacional de Tocumen al momento de su arribo de Medellín, Colombia decomisandosele un kilo de cocaína que traía en una maleta de doble fondo.

FEBRERO

Unidades de narcóticos de Panamá, detuvieron a los ciudadanos norteamericanos MICHAEL EDWARD MC. MILLAN y WILLINSTON MADISON COX, cuando trataron de introducir al territorio nacional 9 envoltorios con cocaína ocultados en el interior de 2 tanques de oxigeno para buzos. La droga provenía de Cali, Colombia.

JOHN ARCHER NEAL, británico, fué arrestado en el Aeropuerto Internacional de Tocumen al momento de su arribo de Lima, Perú, decomisandosele una maleta que contenía 140 gramos de cocaína.

MARZO

Por requerimiento formal de la Agencia Regional del DEA en Panamá a cargo del Agente Especial ARTHUR M. SEDILLO, fué deportada y entregada a las autoridades legales de los Estados Unidos de América, la ciudadana Estadounidense PATRICIA ANN BEAUSANG, quien fué arrestada por agentes panameños por estar relacionada directamente con el tráfico de estupefacientes.

Autoridades panameñas arrestaron a los colombianos DAVID SCHUMACKER BULA, CARLOS PERREIRA CAMARENA y AGUSTIN BERNIER, fugitivos de la justicia norteamericana a quienes se les entregó a través de la Oficina de la Agencia del DEA en Panamá a las autoridades de los Estados Unidos de América.

La ciudadana canadiense CLAUDE VALEQUETTE fué arrestada en el Aeropuerto Internacional de Tocumen al momento de su arribo procedente del Perú decomisandosele un kilo de cocaína.

Figure 11.4. Chronological summary of narco
seizures between January and March 1978.

Torrijos reclaimed our attention. The room fell silent. He seemed uneasy at the time. It was difficult for me to know what was going on at a high level. I was trusted by Torrijos, but a man needed to keep things secret. I would never dare ask. "Every day we get closer to being the country we can be," Torrijos stated to finish his speech. Our government wasn't like most others. We had a de facto leader in Torrijos, so political communication filtered through our military arm. We G-2 men wore many hats— spy, diplomat, businessman. We could be whoever we wanted to be as long as we served our nation.

PROTOCOL FOR MARITIME SEIZURES
Step One:
The DEA provides intelligence to G-2.
Step Two:
G-2 conveys Panama's decision to the Ministry of Foreign Affairs and the DEA.
Step Three:
The US embassy assesses G-2's decision, then submits a formal diplomatic request to the Ministry of Foreign Affairs.
Step Four:
The Ministry of Foreign Affairs confirms decision and handles formal documentation while G-2 and DEA handle the operations.

Figure 11.5. US and Panamanian protocol
for maritime narco seizures.

"Meeting dismissed," Noriega exclaimed. "Carlitos, walk with me."

The hallways were filled with agents and National Guardsmen. Men rushed back and forth, in and out of doors, holding stacks of documents. Noriega held his tongue. It was clear he had something to tell me. He knew that every set of ears we walked by was open. Manuel was an important man. Everyone in that corridor would have killed to know what he knew.

"Close the door behind you," he said as he swiftly turned into an office.

Sounds muffled as I enclosed us in the room.

"Omar is very close to working out a deal to bring the canal back into our hands," Noriega told me.

"Do you think the Americans will actually give it to us?"

"It is possible if we play the situation exactly right."

"What does that mean?"

"Jimmy Carter is a humanitarian. He's going to be looking to make big civil statements. It's important we take advantage of this because a man like Carter does not serve two terms."

"If that happens, this will bring a lot of wealth into our country."

The more I earned, the more I gave away to my friends and family. I was charitable. The values my father instilled in me at a young age made me grateful for my newfound wealth as a man. It was easy come, easy go. I spent my money on a variety of things—cockfighting, gambling, women, booze, weapons, animals. I had no spending filter. Manuel and I would often go on micro-vacations around the country. We rented beach houses and invited dozens of our generals and foreign politicians to blow off steam for a few days. Chucha, I jet-skied with the shah of Iran's wife off Contadora Island in the summer of 1979. There were many stories of good times, most of which I could never prove, but it was during this period of my life that I was dragged into issues much larger than I had ever dealt with.

G-2 was the heartbeat of the National Guard. It pumped life into Panama. I served Manuel first, but I was constantly reminded that the DEA and Americans needed our help and that was the priority. Noriega always had something to deal with. If he didn't know how to blow off steam, the man would have exploded. He carried the weight of an entire nation on his back.

We made plans to drink later that evening with my family. My parents had traveled to the city from Chiriqui. They wanted to see everyone—Gaspar, Muneca, Manuel, and me. They had grown older, but they could hold their own when it came to celebrating.

Before we left to meet the family, Manuel removed a stack of files from a drawer on the desk. "The DEA is becoming very concerned about Cuba. Ever since my first trip for the CIA in 1971, things have gotten more tense because of narcotrafficking. We have been asked for our help."

I leaned over to get a better look at the DEA files.

"The Americans have been trying to gather intelligence from Cuba for years. Ever since Castro came to power, they have constantly attempted to implement a deep web of spies on their home soil. Of course, Castro knows this, and it is not a worry. However, the narcotrafficking trade brings with it new challenges. Smugglers are creating routes between Cuba and Florida. They are discovering where they will and won't be seen. Cuba is out of sight, the only place where the Americans don't have any power."

"How does Castro feel about this?"

"He knows he has to cooperate sometimes. That is why the DEA is asking us to find some information. They know that only we can get what they need."

I'd come to learn things that would chill my bones until the day I die. I was told there was a fishing village not far from Havana that underwent a devastating slaughter from a boat at sea armed with machine guns. Mothers, children, many died horrible deaths at the hands of Comandante Villa, a Galician man hired by the CIA to take care of this guerrilla problem in Cuba. So this man went to those fishing communities and, without remorse, opened fire on them from the sea. Villa slaughtered innocent Cubans while on CIA payroll. He was eventually captured and held captive by Castro. Immediately, the CIA came to us and asked for a favor—to set Comandante Villa free and back out into the world. I was sickened by it. We sent some of our talented men to negotiate, but all returned empty-handed. It was only Manuel who could get the job done.

"You know, while I sat with Castro, right before he agreed to set Villa free, he asked me why I was working for the CIA, and I paused for a moment. I then told him that it was the only way to keep things stable. It was then he gave me the real answer—fear. But fear can be squelched. There is not a plane that lands in Cuba that Castro does not know about. That is true fear."

Noriega showed me a letter from Peter Bensinger. The administrator of the DEA communicated directly with Manuel and, essentially, only Manuel, at least about secret, volatile matters that needed to be squelched or contained. He expressed gratitude for us, a true smiling American. The ask was for us to deliver information regarding narcoterrorism. Bensinger understood that Cuba was a blind spot for them. We had access to it. Noriega and Castro were close. They were military strongmen, leading their nation during the Cold War. Trust was not common. Their politics may have differed, but on the grand stage, that didn't matter for us. Those men knew how to take action and keep control.

"There have been arrangements made with one of our contacts at *Granma*, the leading newspaper of Castro's communist party. They think that you are a journalist from Panama. You will find out what you can."

I was exhausted walking onto that plane. It was a commercial flight. Every fucking seat was occupied. Cigarette smoke hung just below my nostrils. My eyes watered from the stench. Young children screamed and wailed for their mothers. No amount of alcohol could put me to sleep. I thought about my children the whole flight. Life moved quickly. My children were growing older by the day. I made as much time as I could for them. My father once told me that a great man needed to have a legacy. They each excelled in their own lives.

Havana impressed me immediately. The first thing I noticed was the cars. Everyone drove a vehicle manufactured in the 1950s and 1960s. My cabby drove me along the shore. My eyes had already seen so much, yet everything new excited me. My face stuck to the glass, looking out at the markets, old cigar rollers, and finally, the Hilton Hotel. That building was a piece of history. I was a young man when Castro began his revolution. He took it home in the penthouse of that hotel and used it as a base of operations during the insurgence. It was symbolic. I was always fond of Fidel. I found him to be a man with principles, unrelenting in his desire to do what he saw fit. In Cuba, I was not Carlos Wittgreen, intelligence officer for Noriega's G-2; I was Carlos Wittgreen, a foreign journalist. *Chucha pendejo* . . .

The Cuban women caught my eye almost immediately. I instantly knew this would be a place I would want to return to many times. The work I was undertaking brought with it social challenges. I had to walk a fine line when speaking with anybody; it didn't matter who they were. The DEA paid me, and they gave me orders that I followed through on; the wrong person could catch wind of that. It was important that I stayed vigilant, even if my gaze washed over every woman who crossed my line of sight.

I leaned over my hotel room's balcony railing, watching the sky turn from amber-red to darkness. The soft glistening of city lights glowed before me. Honking cars and yelling men sounded from the streets below. I closed the balcony doors and sat on the edge of the bed. It seemed that every camera in the world was pointed at Cuba during that time. I lay in my bed, staring up at the light pink ceiling, pondering over these thoughts until there was a knock at my door. I looked through the peephole. A young Cuban man, no older than twenty-one, stood on the other side holding an envelope.

"Mr. Wittgreen?" the young man asked as I opened the door.

"Yes?" I responded.

"This is for you, señor." He handed it to me and then scurried off.

I opened the envelope. It was my journalist badge. Chucha, I had no idea how to act. Gaspar was the one who knew how to use his words; I was the brawn. I understood how the body worked and what someone could say without saying it. Yet journalists were a different breed. They looked between the lines, where I would tear the lines apart.

The event itself was electric. Cubans were loud, passionate people. They were just like us. Castro himself was in attendance. There was a reception afterward where the journalists could gather to collect statements. I got myself together, and I walked there. Women eyed me on the streets. I was different. The men cowered. They could smell the blood on my knuckles. I was clearly no journalist, even if a thin notepad sat in my pocket alongside a pen. If anything happened to me, Manuel would take care of it, and I knew that.

"Carlos Wittgreen, a journalist from Panama," I said as I handed my ID to one of the guards outside the event.

"He's a guest of *Granma*," the guard told his buddy before letting me through.

I immediately entered into a hallway with a red carpet stretching seventy feet and a dozen rooms on either side. Cubans shot out of doors and stumbled into each other. I maneuvered my way toward the music. Pairs of eyes followed me. Gazes were brought to my journalist badge. My strength came in use. Men failed to scatter; I had to push through them. Each room on my right and left had a different atmosphere and a unique theme. On my left, one of them had red-leather sofas encircling the room. Old Cuban men sat in them and watched three young ladies in the center dance naked. To my right, I heard the sounds of squealing roosters. I clung to the door frame and peered in. Two cocks slashed at each other. Blood spurted all over the shoes of the audience, who crouched in a circle and waved pesos like fans. I walked as close to the action as possible.

The man next to me held cash. His eyes were focused on the ring until his rooster lost and he threw his cash into the air. "Fuck!" he yelled, before turning to me and pointing at my badge. "A journalist?"

"Yes, from Panama," I responded.

"What's your name?" he inquired.

"Carlos."

"Chucha! What are the odds? My name is Carlos, too. Carlos Sarmiento."

"You don't sound Cuban," I exclaimed.

"I'm from Costa Rica, but I spend a lot of time here," he responded.

Sarmiento was an interesting man. He said he was a businessman. I took a liking to him instantly. Our shared love of cockfighting began as our foundation. Two Cuban women strutted on by. They turned their heads at an angle and smiled at us. We stood still. "Sir, a drink?" A waiter asked, suddenly appearing. I almost had a heart attack. My mind was elsewhere. The waiter held a tray of glasses of rum with ice. I grabbed one, and Sarmiento did the same. We entered a grand banquet hall where a band of caballeros played instruments like the saxophone, guitar, and violin.

"What brings you to Cuba?" I asked.

"I have business here," he responded.

"Business? You know this is a communist country?"

"Not for everyone."

The music stopped. Murmurs in the crowd fell to silence. Sarmiento placed his hands on his hips. A Rolex sat on his shaven wrist. There was something off about him, but I liked the man. My gaze drew to the stage where the band stood. From behind a curtain, Fidel Castro stepped in, and the audience was captivated. It was like seeing a rock star. Every woman in the room wanted to fuck him. Every man wished he held his presence. Castro's guards were scattered around the hall. There must have been twenty people for every soldier. Fidel couldn't have been more relaxed. He exuded power. There were probably a dozen men like me in that room, spies. The CIA and DEA were so desperate for Cuban information that they threw shit at the wall, hoping some would stick. The country was an enigma to the Americans.

"I will make this brief so as to not interrupt the celebrations," Castro said. "Your support is the reason this country's fire burns hot and bright. Please, enjoy the festivities."

Over the course of the evening, I met with many Cubans. It was a party, after all, and so I made sure to have some fun. I could feel the presence of someone lingering behind me. Sarmiento, next to me, stopped mid-speech. His eyes shot wide open, and he clasped his drink with two hands and pinned his lips shut.

"Another journalist," a familiar voice boomed.

Goosebumps popped along my arms and legs. My neck creaked as I turned. Standing before me, cigar in mouth, dressed in his forest green military uniform and cap, was Fidel Castro. Burning embers crackled. His sharp eyes squinted. He reached out his hand, and I shook it. The words were held captive in my mouth.

"Come, walk with me," Castro said.

I strolled alongside Fidel through hordes of people.

He removed two cigars from his breast pocket and handed one to me. "What brings you to Cuba?" he asked.

"I'm here to learn about your culture," I responded.

Fidel lit my cigar. The flame burned blue. Smoke appeared before my eyes. "Who better to learn the culture from than me?" Castro exclaimed, firing up his cigar.

My hand slipped into my pocket. The tips of my fingers were perspiring. I gripped my notepad.

Castro looked down at the empty pages. "The truth is, Cuba is not perfect. No nation is perfect. There are some problems in this country. . . . You are here because of one," he said.

"What problem?"

"You tell me."

Fidel's presence was larger than life. I had met many important men in my day—presidents, senators, celebrities. None of them felt as powerful as Castro.

"Noriega has spoken of you, Señor Wittgreen. I know the DEA has asked you to come here to gather information, so I will give you what you need. Now, I am more interested in getting to know the man behind the name. There are endless amounts of liquor, beautiful women, and cockfighting 24/7."

Castro was not perfect. Nobody was. Yet he was smarter than most, and that was obvious. Intelligence was like a game of Chinese whispers. Facts and figures would often change from ear to ear. It was partially my responsibility to discern what was important and what wasn't. When it came to Fidel, I trusted what he said. He clearly knew more than he would divulge, but he was a master at giving just enough. It was not that I had any interest in the American agenda, anyways. What they required of me was to provide information about narcotrafficking between Colombia, Cuba, and America. I would oblige for the check and the letter of gratitude.

Fidel and I finished our cigars, enjoyed the night, and I eventually went back to my hotel in the early hours of the morning. I lay in my bed, processing my conversation with him. The man sat in a unique position in history. He successfully opposed the giant that was America. He was a dictator. Many died in poverty under his rule, yet he was passionate, a genuine lover of his people and country. Cuba was his home. He ruled it with an iron fist because outside influence would destroy what he knew his nation to be. He understood that the battle he fought was ideological. It was relatable for me. After the Spanish-American War, the United States occupied Cuba for several years, clinging to it, investing as much as it could into the nation, and squeezing it dry of its resources. Cuba got it worse than we did, being so close to Miami. Fidel liberated his people from Batista's grasp.

We met the following day at La Bodeguita del Medio in Havana. Castro was one of the owners. It was a fine establishment. The food was incredible, and the dancers beautiful, a highlight of Havana. I was told that Ernest Hemingway used to drink there. He sat at the edge of the bar and spoke tongues to beautiful women. I walked along the red-leather stools by the bar;

Castro sat at a small wooden table. A fat cigar hung from his lips, grinning at the beautiful, barely dressed women who danced before him. "Carlos, come, sit," he yelled out.

I sat next to Fidel. A waiter with a box of cigars approached. He leaned to me, presenting the selection inches from my face. I could smell the variations of tobacco. The stench would rest in my nostrils for weeks. I picked the biggest one and sat upright.

"What do you think of this place?" Castro asked me.

"I could spend days here," I responded.

Fidel stood up. "I thought as much. . . . Waiter, two mojitos!" Castro yelled out. "The mojitos here are legendary," he said.

The waiter returned with our drinks. Water dripped down the rim of the glasses. The mint must have been picked that morning. The rum was exquisite. It was the greatest mojito I had ever tasted.

"How do you like Cuba?"

"It is like a second home," I responded.

"La Bodeguita is special to me. I have been involved for years. It is like a home. . . . I believe you and I can open one in Panama," he said.

"I would be honored, Señor Castro."

"I can provide you with dancers, singers, chefs, waiters . . . everything you need to keep the integrity of this place."

"Thank you, señor."

"Give Manuel my best," he said.

The DEA needed all the help it could get, so it worked with people like me and Fidel—soldiers, killers, ready to be a martyr for a cause bigger than capitalism. The gringos had unlimited resources and no choice but to work with us. Yes, we did some things under their protection that the world should not know, but my crimes were nothing compared to what the DEA was doing to keep people like us silent after we had served our purpose. Nobody trusted a gringo. The DEA agents had no charm in Central or South America. They were told what we wanted to tell them and nothing else.

I was good at what I did, not only because I was trained by the best but also because I sat in circles of men who could not be touched without an international conflict erupting. I had a reason to be on the payroll. The Cold War still garnered the majority of the world's attention, but narcotrafficking was on the rise. In the mid-1970s, Pablo Escobar entered the cocaine trade, laying the groundwork for what would become the Medellín Cartel a few years later. Central America was going through its greatest period of change since the invasion of the Spanish, and I was at the heart of it. I felt like I could do whatever I wanted. I opened La Bodeguita del Medio in Panama City not long after my trip to Cuba. I would return to Havana many times. The women, the cigars, the food, the cockfighting, it was a paradise with no influence from the outside world.

"What do you have for us?" a DEA agent asked over the phone.

"I am faxing everything over now."

"Good work. Did you learn anything else?" he asked.

"Nothing."

Business was booming. I was a busy man who never stood still. I enjoyed that very much. Life was meant to be lived. The experience gave me pleasure. It had nothing to do with the money or the power that came with the work I did. It was about fulfillment. My father had always instilled in me great values. "Family over fortune," he taught me. There were many men in my line of work who disregarded statements like these, but many of them did not make it far. It was people like that who ultimately became submissive and turned against us.

I knew every nation had to hold hands with the United States in one way or another, but we did so with professionalism. We gave far more than we asked. I had nothing but optimism. Yet, for every step forward, there was always something that would drag us back. Internal power struggles ruptured the National Guard, G-2, and our government. Torrijos was our leader. Manuel was our operator. The two worked symbiotically.

Bombs soon detonated in the Canal Zone. Car bombs. The incident became the focal point of media in Panama and the United States. Torrijos's words became very clear. "If the US holds onto the zone, violence and instability will follow." I agreed with Omar's words. We needed to prove that the canal would be safer in our hands. Manuel played a game of political chess. I saw the letters the DEA sent him. Peter Bensinger, the man at the very top, personally congratulated Noriega for just about every seizure. G-2 was vital. I was vital. They kissed our asses. Whenever DEA guys would come to visit us, they brought smiles and gifts. We presented our nation as a playground for them. They could do whatever they wanted.

"The signing of this treaty will be the single most important event in our nation's history. The window of opportunity is so small that even I still struggle to believe the chance is real," Torrijos said.

Omar was a smart man. The American government had already been out to get him since 1968. The CIA wanted him out. They founded coups against him. Omar could never trust a gringo, not really. The issue with his brother, Moises, had been bubbling for years. At that time, Moises had been appointed Panama's ambassador to Spain, but due to the gringo grip, Omar was forced to drag Moises from his post and instead replace him with their other brother, Hugo. Washington openly demanded Omar give up Moises so he could finally be detained in the United States for his alleged crimes. Omar did not comply.

The conversations Manuel and Torrijos had regarding that whole phenomenon have washed away in the waves of history. Jimmy Carter and Omar Torrijos signed the Canal treaty at the Pan-American Union Building in 1977. The canal would finally belong to us. We would have to wait twenty-three years for it to transfer into our hands, but the deal had been made, and I saw it with my own eyes. Yet the internal power struggles began there, and they didn't stop until the Americans invaded us twelve years later. Panama was a nation held inside a snow globe that the gringos could shake at any moment. There were men among us who took advantage of our situation. These men tainted our image and attracted unwanted attention from Washington.

CANAL 3-4 ROE

POR NICHOLAS DANILOFF

RECIBIDO MAR 27 1978

WASHINGTON, MARZO 4 (UPI) -- UN ALTO OFICIAL DE LA GUARDIA NACIONAL DE PANAMA, SOSPECHOSO DE ESTAR MEZCLADO EN EL TRAFICO DE ESTUPEFACIENTES A ESTADOS UNIDOS, APARENTEMENTE OBTUVO INMUNIDAD PARA SUS ACTIVIDADES PORQUE EL GOBERNANTE PANAMEÑO, GENERAL OMAR TORRIJOS, LO CONSIDERABA VITAL PARA MANTENERSE EN EL PODER. UN INFORME DEL SENADO AGREGA QUE EL MISMO OFICIAL, DETUVO DURANTE DOS SEMANAS AL GOBERNANTE PANAMEÑO, RECLUYENDOLO SECRETAMENTE.

LA CONCLUSION EMERGE DE LAS REUNIONES A PUERTAS CERRADAS DEL SENADO LOS DIAS 21 Y 22 DE FEBRERO, PARA CONOCER LAS PERSISTENTES ACUSACIONES DE QUE ALTOS FUNCIONARIOS DEL GOBIERNO DE PANAMA ESTABAN COMPROMETIDOS EN DELITOS DE DROGAS.

UNA TRANSCRIPCION EXPURGADA DE LAS INFORMACIONES RECIBIDAS POR EL SENADO Y PUBLICADAS A ULTIMA HORA DE AYER, INDICAN QUE DESDE 1973 LOS FUNCIONARIOS NO IDENTIFICADOS COMENZARON A COOPERAR CON LAS AUTORIDADES ESTADOUNIDENSES PARA FRENAR EL FLUJO DE NARCOTICOS DESDE PANAMA.

LAS TRANSCRIPCIONES REVELAN ADEMAS, QUE LAS AUTORIDADES DE ESTADOS UNIDOS POSEIAN EVIDENCIAS DIGNAS DE CREDITO DE QUE HUGO TORRIJOS, HERMANO DEL GOBERNANTE PANAMEÑO, PODIA ESTAR ENVUELTO EN LOS DELITOS. PERO ESAS EVIDENCIAS NO SON TAN FUERTES COMO LAS QUE EXISTEN EN CONTRA DE MOISES TORRIJOS, OTRO HERMANO DEL GENERAL OMAR TORRIJOS.

LA SESION SECRETA, CONVOCADA POR LA INSISTENCIA DEL SENADOR ROBERT DOLE, PARA DILUCIDAR LAS PERSISTENTES ACUSACIONES DEL TRAFICO DE DROGAS REALIZADO POR ALTOS FUNCIONARIOS PANAMEÑOS, REVELO ALGUNOS ANTECEDENTES DE UN EVENTUAL PROYECTO DURANTE EL GOBIERNO DEL PRESIDENTE RICHARD NIXON, PARA ASESINAR A UN OFICIAL DE LAS FUERZAS ARMADAS PANAMEÑAS.

PERO LA PARTE DE LA TRANSCRIPCION QUE ALUDE A LA INMOVILIZACION TOTAL DEL OFICIAL PANAMEÑO, ESTA TAN EXPURGADA, QUE LOS PRINCIPALES DETALLES SE MANTIENEN EN LA OSCURIDAD.

SIN EMBARGO, UN INFORME EMITIDO LA SEMANA PASADA POR LA COMISION DE INTELIGENCIA DEL SENADO, ESTABLECE QUE LA OPCION DEL ASESINATO NUNCA LLEGO A PONERSE EN MARCHA Y UNA INVESTIGACION HECHA EN 1975 POR EL DEPARTAMENTO DE JUSTICIA, SEÑALA QUE JAMAS SE REALIZO NINGUNA ACCION ILEGAL EN ESE PUNTO.

Figure 11.6. First page of Spanish-language report referencing US Senate Intelligence Committee discussions about Panamanian officials, including Manuel Noriega and Moises Torrijos, and alleged involvement in drug trafficking.

FUENTES AL TANTO DE LO OCURRIDO, HAN SUGERIDO QUE EL OFICIAL
PANAMEÑO QUE AL PARECER GOZABA DE INMUNIDAD ESPECIAL, PUDO SER EL
CORONEL MANUEL ANTONIO NORIEGA, JEFE DE LOS SERVICIOS DE INTELIGENCIA
DE PANAMÁ.

DE ACUERDO CON LAS TRANSCRIPCIONES, EL SENADOR BIRCH BAYH,
PRESIDENTE DE LA COMISION DE INTELIGENCIA DEL SENADO, DIJO QUE SE
PUDO INICIAR UNA QUERELLA EN CONTRA DE UN OFICIAL DE LA GUARDIA
NACIONAL POR TRÁFICO DE DROGAS.

"CREO QUE LA MEJOR ACCIÓN EN EL CASO EN CUESTIÓN, PUDO TOMARSE
CONTRA UN OFICIAL DE LA GUARDIA NACIONAL. PERO AQUÍ, NUEVAMENTE, CREO
QUE NO TENEMOS EVIDENCIAS SUFICIENTES, DE LA CLASE QUE HARÍAN POSIBLE
ALCANZAR UNA SANCIÓN EN SU CONTRA EN ÉSTE PAÍS".

"HAY UNA TREMENDA CANTIDAD DE HUMO EN ESTE CASO, POR LO MENOS EN
LO QUE SE REFIERE AL OFICIAL DE LA GUARDIA", DIJO BAYH. SI SE ME PIDE
QUE DIGA MÁS, DIRÉ QUE ES UNA IMPORTANTE FIGURA EN LA GUARDIA. SIN
PROCURAR DISCULPAR EL POCO DESEO DEL GENERAL TORRIJOS PARA PONER EL
MARTILLO ENCIMA DE ÉL, LA CONCLUSIÓN GENERAL ES QUE FUE RELUCTANTE A
HACERLO PORQUE NECESITABA SU APOYO PARA MANTENER SU BASE DE PODER."

LAS TRANSCRIPCIONES SEÑALAN TAMBIÉN QUE UN PANAMEÑO RECIENTEMENTE
EXILIADO DE SU PAÍS, DONDE TRABAJÓ PARA LOS SERVICIOS DE INTELIGENCIA
DE PANAMÁ, DECLARÓ QUE EL CORONEL NORIEGA DETUVO AL GENERAL OMAR
TORRIJOS EN 1976 Y LO MANTUVO DETENIDO EN SECRETO DURANTE DOS SEMANAS
CUANDO TORRIJOS AMENAZÓ CON ENTRAR A LA ZONA DEL CANAL PARA DISPARAR
SUS PISTOLAS.

LAS REUNIONES SECRETAS CONFIRMARON LA SEMANA PASADA EL INFORME DE
LA COMISIÓN DE INTELIGENCIA DEL SENADO DE QUE ESTADOS UNIDOS NO TENÍA
EVIDENCIAS NI CARGOS CONTRA OMAR TORRIJOS.

UN GRAN JURADO DE NUEVA YORK ORDENÓ EL 16 DE MAYO DE 1972, EL
PROCESAMIENTO DE MOISÉS TORRIJOS, POR TRÁFICO DE HEROINA, PERO LA
CASA BLANCA Y EL DEPARTAMENTO DE ESTADO, DISCRETAMENTE INFORMARON AL
GOBIERNO DE PANAMÁ CUANDO SE INTENTÓ DETENERLO EN DICIEMBRE DE 1972.

MOISÉS TORRIJOS, QUIEN HA NEGADO TERMINANTEMENTE SU VINCULACIÓN
CON EL CASO, FUE RETIRADO ESTA SEMANA COMO EMBAJADOR DE PANAMÁ EN
ESPAÑA Y SERÁ REEMPLAZADO POR U HERMANO HUGO TORRIJOS, ACTUAL JEFE
DE LOS CASINOS NACIONALES DE PANAMÁ.

UPI 03-04 91059 AZ6

Figure 11.7. *Continuation of the report, March 4, 1978, detailing Senate transcripts on Panamanian officials linked to narcotics trafficking, and reference to a Nixon-era plan to target a Panamanian officer, which Carlos believed was Noriega.*

In many ways, I had become Panama's liaison to Cuba. I was there constantly. Everybody in Havana knew my name. I would come to create businesses in Cuba that I would operate with friends. Caza y Pesca. A true enterprise. Manuel and I made a lot of money in Cuba. His relationship with Castro was one of his strongest. Noriega would often provide Castro with Panamanian passports for Cuban spies. They would give us information for us to use with the DEA. We all used the relationship we had with each other to the best of our advantage, some more than others. We learned that in Washington, the Senate Intelligence Committee had held closed hearings about us (see figures 11.6 and 11.7). Manuel was suspected of running drugs. Baseless claims. They knew he was indispensable to Torrijos. There were rumors that the White House quietly tipped off Noriega before the arrest of Moises Torrijos. There were some conversations I was not involved in. I cannot speak to them. But Manuel got his hands on these Senate transcripts. He kept them, collected them, and then they ended up in Torrijos's hands. The years went by with plenty of ups and downs. Men I admired greatly died, women I loved vanished, the fog of collaboration fizzled away, and dangers that lay on the road ahead became clear.

Chapter 12
Operation Tigre

In 1979, the United States called us asking for a favor. The shah of Iran and his family were in need of refuge after being ousted from their throne. The gringos were the ones who had put his family into that seat in the first place. I could see the gears moving in Manuel's head. This was a great opportunity for us to not only show our loyalty but to also provide solace to a representative of the most impressive modern dynasty in recent history. We knew the American government backed Mohammed Reza and was staunchly against the man who overthrew him, Ayatollah Ruhollah Khomeini. Before Reza came to us, he had been in exile in the United States, but as a move in the recent Iran hostage crisis, the gringos were forced to let him go, and so we took him. I knew Torrijos understood the value of this, especially considering the fragility of our new relationship with America post-treaty. They were watching our every move.

The shah arrived on December 15, 1979, and it was a glorious day for us. The man was infamous; the news that looped on my radio often spoke of him. The gringos would come to say that Torrijos was agitated by the shah and his family, but that was not true. We were honored. The Iranian government consistently asked us to extradite him, and we did not. If we truly did not want the man in our nation, he would have been exiled instantly. However, we knew the hostage crisis was a major issue for Carter, and we would learn just how devastating the aftermath of it would be for them and for us. Yet, when I saw Shah Reza and his wife, Farah Pahlavi, step off their plane alongside a slew of security guards, a smile stuck to my face, and it did not falter until the couple left for Egypt one year later.

"Shah Reza, it is an honor," Torrijos said with a smile.

"The honor is ours," the shah responded.

Farah Pahlavi was one of the most beautiful women I had ever seen in my life. Manuel and I knew our soldiers would gawk, so we never overwhelmed them with our military presence. They were taken to Contadora Island, where they could live peacefully, knowing they were protected by some of our finest men. I had many opportunities to visit the island and be in their presence. It looked like they were enjoying their time there. Our men on patrol boats would often catch a glimpse of Farah jet skiing across crystal-blue waters. She was something else; I was lucky to be in circles where I could hear their words. We loved them; we all did.

There was a group of us on Contadora one day. The sun was setting. The amber light projected across the darkening sky. It was gorgeous; the shah seemed to be entranced. Our chatter did not take his attention from the rippling waters, and not even his wife's gentle arm strokes could break his focus. "People use the word *dynasty* when they speak of my name, yet there is just me and my father," the shah said. "I think of him a lot these days. I wonder how he would deal with the situation that I now face. We are different. The government declared him shah in 1925; he was popular, necessary. My people want nothing to do with me."

"These men are misguided, and they do not speak for the nation, my love," Farah responded.

"They are extremists."

Our problems didn't seem so big when we were in the presence of the shah and his family. We had our own issues to deal with at the time. The narcotrade was enhanced in 1978, and by 1979, the industry was booming. More smugglers than ever before were actively crossing our waterways and airways. We were doing as much as we could, but it was clear the issue was a lack of collaboration. It was common for our units to catch wind of a smuggler ship or plane passing through us, but we would have no idea whom to call in our neighboring countries to seize it. The anti-narcotrade was siloed, and so we knew that something had to be done. After some time going back and forth with the DEA, a decision was finally made to get all of us into one room.

It was Friday, May 18, 1979, when I realized the gravity of the situation at hand. I remember the meeting clearly. We were told to be there at 09:00 hours sharp. A slew of gringos flew down for the event. The importance was clear to us. We gathered in the Yellow Hall of G-2 Command, the air thick with the usual mix of smoke and tension. Noriega and Torrijos shook hands with Colonel Walter Sears, a retired US Navy officer now representing the DEA. Sears took his place at the head of the table and flicked through a series of documents laid out between us.

"Is everybody who needs to be here, here?" Special Agent McFarland yelled out. At that time, he was serving as Walter's interpreter, though I always knew that Sears understood more Spanish than he let on. He was smarter than most of the men who came to us.

Five minutes of mindless chatter ended when one of the G-2 officers asked the obvious question: "What exactly is this about?"

The room fell into silence. Sears cleared his throat, taking the stage. "The job is simple but critical: identify, report, and coordinate rapid responses every time a suspect aircraft enters your airspace," he said.

The role was clear, but there were unanswered questions on our end. We didn't have a problem identifying threats; the issue was collaboration.

"Let's be clear; you want us to tip you off so you can catch these men when they land, correct?" Noriega clarified.

"Yes. Your proposed liaison officer would ensure an immediate alert to G-2 Command, preventing traffickers from slipping through unnoticed," McFarland said.

"There is a lot of land between our countries," Torrijos stated.

"That is why Operation Tigre will not just consist of our two nations. I have spent months traveling North and Central America. Mexico, Belize, Guatemala, El Salvador, Colombia, and Costa Rica have already agreed to participate. They are now part of COCESNA, and more Latin American and Caribbean nations are expected to follow," Sears exclaimed. He further laid out the problem for us: for years, drug traffickers had been outpacing law enforcement, staying one step ahead at every turn. But Operation Tigre, he claimed, would turn the tables.

The concept was straightforward—constant monitoring. It wasn't anything new for us, but the increased collaboration would make our work more worthwhile. We learned that the FAA, in collaboration with EPIC-DEA [El Paso Intelligence Center-DEA], would track every aircraft suspected of drug-running from takeoff to landing. The moment a plane was flagged, it would be followed by air and radar, ensuring it had nowhere to hide. The goal was to intercept these aircraft the moment they touched the ground.

"I propose that Luis Quiel be your liaison officer to coordinate between the FAA and G-2," Sears said. "He has impressed the right men in the right rooms in Washington."

Our eyes moved to Quiel, who looked to be honored to take on the role. His dedicated work for us never went unnoticed. He was trusted to perform stressful duties that the rest of us either didn't want or weren't skilled enough for.

"I accept," Luis stated.

"Quiel will immediately report any unauthorized aircraft entering our airspace. The moment one is detected, whether within our territory or approaching from abroad, G-2 Command needs to be informed to prevent unsanctioned landings," McFarland said.

The meeting was quick and painless. It was obvious what we needed to do, and so we joined the highly classified Operation Tigre.

ARCHIVADO

PANAMA,VIERNES 18 de MAYO de 1979.-

AL   : COMANDO DEL G-2
VIA   : Secretaría del G-2
DEL
ASUNTO   : ENTREVISTA DEL DEA-FAA-EPIC-G-2.
                        SOBRE " OPERACION TIGRE ".

RECIBIDO MAYO 2/2 1979

MI CORONEL:

PERMITOME PRESENTARLE INFORME SOBRE LO TRATADO EN LA
ENTREVISTA " DEA - G-2 ", SOBRE " OPERACION TIGRE ".

09:00 HORAS.- EN ENTREVISTA SOSTENIDA EN EL SALON AMARILLO, DEL
G-2, CON EL COMANDO DEL G-2., EL CORONEL (RETIRA-
DO DE LA MARINA NORTEAMERICANA), WALTER SEARS,
DEL DEA., EN REPRESENTACION DEL DEA-FAA Y EPIC Y
TENIENDO COMO INTERPRETE AL AGENTE ESPECIAL DEL
DEA REGIONAL-PANAMA, MC.FARLAND., PROPUSO LA PARTI-
CIPACION DE PANAMA EN EL NUEVO PROGRAMA DE LUCHA
CONTRA LOS NARCOTRAFICANTES, DENOMINADO " OPERACION
TIGRE ", DE CLASIFICACION CONFIDENCIAL.
EL CORONEL WALTER SEARS MANIFESTO QUE MEXICO,BELICE,
GUATEMALA, EL SALVADOR, COLOMBIA Y COSTA RICA, YA
HABIAN ACEPTADO INTEGRARSE A LA OPERACION TIGRE,
FORMANDO PARTE DE " COCESNA " Y QUE ESPERABAN QUE
LOS DEMAS PAISES LATINOAMERICANOS Y DEL CARIBE TAM-
BIEN SE INTEGRARAN.
ANTES LOS NARCOTRAFICANTES NOS LLEVABAN UN PASO ADE-
LANTE PERO CON ESTE NUEVO PLAN NOSOTROS LE SALIAMOS
ADELANTE. EL PLAN CONSISTE EN MANTENER INFORMADA A
TODAS LAS AGENCIAS PARTICIPANTES, A TRAVES DE LA
FAA, CON LA COLABORACION DE EPIC-DEA, SOBRE EL MO-
VIMIENTO CONSTANTE DE TODOS LOS AVIONES QUE ESTAN I-
DENTIFICADOS EN EL USO DEL TRANSPORTE DE DROGAS Y
NARCOTRAFICANTES. DESDE EL MOMENTO EN QUE UN AVION
SALE, DE DONDE SALGA, ES RASTREADO Y SEGUIDO, EN EL
AIRE Y POR EL AIRE, HASTA QUE ATERRIZE, DONDE ATE-
RRIZE. SE REQUIERE UN OFICIAL DE ENLACE Y COORDINA-
DOR ENTRE LA FAA Y SU AGENCIA (G-2).

Figure 12.1. Operation Tigre meeting memo 1.

169

Ø9:Ø5 HORAS.- A PREGUNTA FORMULADA POR EL COMANDO DEL G-2, EL
CORONEL " SEARS " MANIFESTO QUE LA LABOR DEL O-
FICIAL DE ENLACE CONSISTIRIA EN COMUNICAR DE IN-
MEDIATO AL COMANDO DEL G-2 SOBRE CUALQUIER AVION
DETECTADO DENTRO DEL TERRITORIO NACIONAL O QUE
ESTE EN VUELO DEL EXTERIOR HACIA PANAMA Y SUPLIR
A LA FAA CON LOS PLANES DE VUELOS DE LOS AVIONES
IDENTIFICADOS COMO USADO PARA EL TRANSPORTE DE
DROGAS Y DE NARCOTRAFICANTES, YA SEAN QUE ENTREN
O SALGAN DEL PAIS, POR TOCUMEN, PAITILLA O POR
DAVID, CHIRIQUI, ETC.ETC.
QUE PANAMA, POR SU POSICION GEOGRAFICA Y PASO
OBLIGADO PARA ESCALA, GASEAR, TRANSITO, ETC.,
ERA UN LUGAR ESPECIAL PARA ESTE TIPO DE TRABAJO.

EL COMANDO DEL G-2 LE COMUNICO Y/O DIJO AL CORO-
NEL " SEARS ", QUE CONTARA CON EL APOYO DE PANA-
MA SOBRE LA OPERACION TIGRE, QUE ESTABAMOS DE A-
CUERDO Y QUE YA HABIA SELECCIONADO A UN AGENTE
DEL G-2 PARA QUE SE OCUPARA DEL ENLACE Y COORDI-
NACION, MENCIONANDO AL INSPECTOR, LUIS QUIEL.

EL AGENTE ESPECIAL, MC.FARLAND, DEL DEA REGIONAL-
PANAMA, DIJO QUE EL PROXIMO LUNES 21 DE MAYO LO
PUSIERAMOS EN CONTACTO CON EL AGENTE ESPECIAL,
ARTHUR M. SEDILLO, ENCARGADO DEL DEA REGIONAL-PA-
NAMA, PARA DARLE INSTRUCCIONES AL RESPECTO, A FIN
DE INICIAR LA LABOR DE DETECCION E INMOBILIZACION
DE LOS AVIONES Y DE LOS NARCOTRAFICANTES QUE PA-
SEN POR PANAMA.

Figure 12.2. Operation Tigre meeting memo 2.

Luis was doing incredible work for us while I sat alongside Manuel, who worked tirelessly with Torrijos to implement real change in Panama as we geared up for the return of the canal twenty years from that point. It was a period of relatively good standing with the gringos. Us taking the shah and his wife in while Carter dealt with the hostages in Iran was something they did not overlook, even if their media made us sound sinister in our decision to house the vulnerable former leader. This favor, combined with the consistent seizures of drug shipments, seemed to create a new, sustainable way forward for our government and military. It felt like there could be trust.

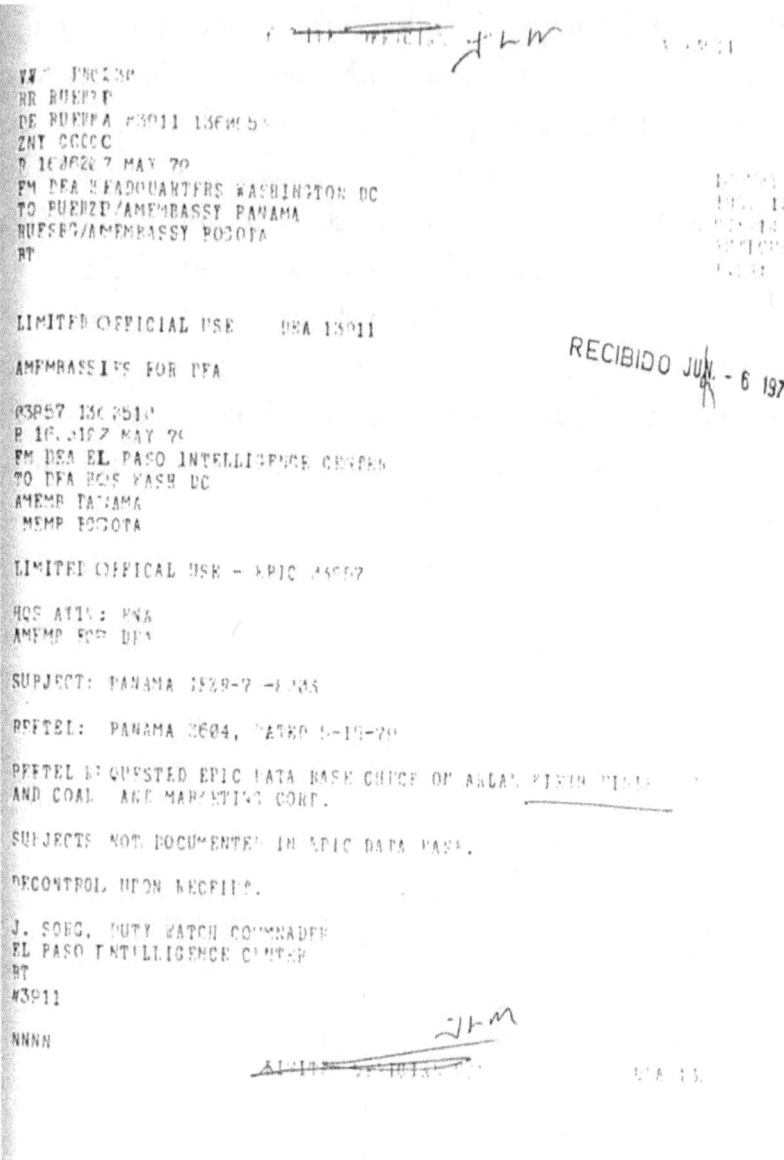

Figure 12.3. DEA cable, May 1979, from El Paso Intelligence Center to Washington and Panama, referencing Panamanian subjects in the EPIC (El Paso Intelligence Center) database and narcotics investigations.

UNITED STATES DEPARTMENT OF JUSTICE
DRUG ENFORCEMENT ADMINISTRATION

30 APRIL 1979

DEA-04-#5,

TENIENTE CORONEL
MANUEL A. NORIEGA
G-2 DEL ESTADO MAYOR
GUARDIA NACIONAL
E. S. D.

CORONEL NORIEGA:

OUR SAN JUAN, PUERTO RICO D.E.A. OFFICE HAS NOTIFIED US
THAT THEY HAVE RECEIVED INFORMATION INDICATING THAT D.E.A.
FUGITIVE COLOMBIAN NATIONAL JOHNNY JOSE DACCARET-GHIA,
D.E.A. NADDIS NUMBER 398262 WAS MAKING FREQUENT TRIPS
FROM COLOMBIA TO PANAMA. IF THIS INDIVIDUAL IS LOCATED
IN PANAMA WE WOULD APPRECIATE IT IF YOU COULD HAVE HIM
ARRESTED AND EXPELED TO PUERTO RICO WHERE HE WILL BE
PROSECUTED AS CO-CONSPIRATOR FOR SMUGGLING 5,000 POUNDS
OF MARIHUANA INTO THAT JURISDICTION. ATTACHED TO THIS
MEMORANDUM IS A PHOTOGRAPH OF DACCARET AND HIS ARREST
WARRANT.

IF HE IS LOCATED AND ARRESTED AND YOU AGREE TO HAVE HIM
EXPELLED TO PUERTO RICO OUR OFFICE WILL FINANCE TRANSPOR-
TATION AND RELATED EXPENSES FOR HIM AND TWO PANAMANIAN
OFFICIAL ESCORTS.

SUBSEQUENT TO RECEIVING THE ABOVE INFORMATION FROM PUERTO
RICO, WE RECEIVED A CABLE "BOGOTA 4236" INFORMING US
THAT THEY HAD LEARNED THAT DACCARET IS PLANNING TO
TRAVEL TO PANAMA AROUND THE MIDDLE OF MAY, 1979 TO TAKE
CARE OF FINANCIAL MATTERS.

JOHNNY JOSE DACCARET-GHIA ALIAS SILVA ALIAS FABIAN DAKARE
IS A WHITE MALE, 6'2" TALL, 205 POUNDS, BLACK HAIR, BROWN
EYES, COLOMBIAN PASSPORT NUMBER M435048; CEDULA NUMBER
7.447.301 AND COLOMBIAN DRIVER'S LICENSE 240720. HE WAS
BORN MAY 11, 1946 IN BARRANQUILLA, COLOMBIA AND LISTS
HIS ADDRESS IN COLOMBIA AT CARRERA 49, NUMBER 86-16,
BARRANQUILLA, COLOMBIA. HIS PARENTS JOSE AND ZOILA RESIDE
AT CARRERA 53, NUMBER 54-63, BARRANQUILLA.

SINCERELY,

ARTHUR M. SEDILLO
SPECIAL AGENT IN CHARGE
DRUG ENFORCEMENT ADMINISTRATION

Figure 12.4. DEA letter, April 30, 1979, from Special Agent Arthur M. Sedillo to Colonel Manuel A. Noriega, requesting his help in arresting and expelling a Colombian fugitive to Puerto Rico for prosecution, with DEA covering transport and expenses.

PANAMA,MIERCOLES 16 de MAYO de 1979.—

AL   : COMANDO DEL G-2

VIA   : Secretaría del G-2

DEL

ASUNTO   : REQUERIMIENTO DEL DEA
                    SOBRE DETENIDO.

ARCHIVADO MAYO 2 5 1979

DEL: 16 de MAYO, 79.—

DEA — 5 — No. 9.   RECIBIDO MAY/19 1979

CORONEL NORIEGA:

HACEMOS,REFERENCIA AL MEMORANDUM ADJUNTO, FECHADO EL 3Ø DE ABRIL,
DE 1979, EN LA QUE SE LE PIDIO A VUESTRA OFICINA REFERENTE A LAS
ACTIVIDADES DEL NARCOTRAFICANTE, JOHNNY JOSE DACCARETT GHIAS,
COLOMBIANO.
PEDIMOS A USTED QUE SEA EXPULSADO A LOS ESTADOS UNIDOS, A LA MAYOR
BREVEDAD POSIBLE. SERIA ACOMPAÑADO POR UN AGENTE DEL DEA Y UN OFI-
CIAL DEL GOBIERNO PANAMEÑO, A MIAMI, FLORIDA.

GRACIAS POR SU AYUDA.

ARTHUR M. SEDILLO
DEA

— MI CORONEL: ALFREDO BOTELLO (DEL DENI) Y JULIAN RUIZ
(DE HACIENDA), IRAN DE ESCOLTA.

Figure 12.5. Spanish-language DEA memorandum, dated May 16, 1979, addressed to Colonel Manuel Noriega, following up on an earlier request and asking for the prompt expulsion of a Colombian trafficker to the United States, with thanks for Noriega's assistance and arrangements for DEA and Panamanian escorts to Miami.

I was in the room when Noriega received a call from the shah.

"President of Egypt, Anwar Sadat, has granted me asylum in Cairo. I believe it is time for me to go," he told Noriega.

There was a lot of false information circulating about the shah's decision to leave Panama after such a short time in refuge on Contadora. The rumors were about Torrijos and his apparent decision to comply with Iran's extradition request, but I never thought this was true.

It was March 23, 1980. I stood alongside Noriega, Torrijos, and a small team of men as we parted ways with the shah and his wife. There were tears. I did not want them to leave, but I, of course, understood they needed to be as close to home as possible. The shah could not bear the distance.

The shah approached me and shook my hand. "Thank you for your hospitality. You please take care of these men," he said before moving on to the next man. It was warm that day.

Chapter 13
A Gringo's Uncertainty

The Trujillo documents weighed heavy on my mind. Within them, there was a claim in expurgated US Senate Intelligence Committee transcripts (see figures 11.6 and 11.7) that Omar Torrijos was once detained for two weeks by Manuel Noriega after Torrijos threatened to enter the Canal Zone with guns drawn. I asked around Carlos's circle, and nobody believed it, so I am not sure of the validity of that statement. Still, it exists in an expurgated transcript, and if true, opposes what Carlos told me of the relationship between Torrijos and Noriega during the canal treaty negotiations. Carlos's story was amazing, so rich with vivid imagery, and the themes popped like fireworks. Still, I had to trust my instincts, and I didn't fully believe Carlitos. His story was almost too clean, too perfect. It was time to contest Carlos, and to do that, I needed to go deeper. This meant going above and beyond, not just reading textbooks published by some historians from the comfort of their home offices. Jose was the first to say we should negotiate a deal for Trujillo's documents to be used in this book. That was where the truth lay. I had written another draft that I felt was as accurate as I could make it with the information I had, but those letters were the golden goose. I wondered if they touched on any conspiracy theories people talk about when Omar Torrijos's or Manuel Noriega's name is brought up, like the plane crash or the canal bombing campaign supposedly planned by the CIA to push the canal out of American hands. Those letters were from men I could research—Bensinger, Bartels, Sedillo, Bramble, Driver, Telles. Their names were imprinted on those documents, and they very clearly showed gratitude for the work Manuel Noriega was doing on behalf of their organizations. That correspondence contained proof that never became public. Noriega kept them for a reason, and when he was taken during the invasion, he handed them over to Trujillo. Making information like that available would muddy the already murky waters between the truth and the narrative we know of Noriega. In my research, it became obvious to me that, after the canal treaty was signed between Carter and Torrijos, everything opened up between the two nations, and favors began flying.

"Do you remember the Contra affair?" I asked Carlos during one of our interviews.

"Of course. I lived it. When Oliver North came to us in '84 asking for our help training Contras and ending their war in Nicaragua for them and Noriega said no, I sensed a shift."

"How close were you to all of it?"

"I was the one who first trained the Sandinistas. They were good people. The Contras were animals. We wanted nothing to do with them. And our good standing with the Somozas before their fall was also important to us, too. But still, we liked the

Sandinistas. The Americans knew these things, and they expected us to burn our bridge and build a new one for them."

"They found their ways. That is well-documented. People like Gary Webb have faced the consequences for talking about it," I stated, projecting my own worries.

"After the outrage created by the Contra scandal, things were different. Even though the favors from the DEA kept coming, the sentiment of gratitude was not shared in Washington. Bush had bad blood with Noriega, and the international disgrace of the Contra affair proved to be the greatest embarrassment for the American government since Watergate. Anybody with a brain could have seen what was to happen next. Blame needed to be shifted."

"And what was it like specifically for you?"

"Well, the DEA, DENI, and G-2 worked together seamlessly until 1986. I spent much of that time serving ourselves by serving the gringos. Favors soon became asked discreetly, and trusted men like me would get a phone call. Flying money, weapons, soldiers, I did it all for the Americans, just like many others. I flew weapons and money for the Contras. I flew to El Salvador; I transported many weapons, bundles of cash, and supplies for enemies of Soviet-influenced militia."

"In 1986, the narrative changed," I said. "The Americans were no longer fighting a war on Communism; they were fighting a war on drugs, weren't they?"

"We had been fighting a war on drugs for over a decade at that point. But, when the favors stopped coming in '86, I knew a fresh narrative would be created and we would be targeted. Bush already had it out for Noriega. Panama was a transit hub for the narcotrade. All it would take was a clever headline in the *Washington Post*, and Panama would become the next Colombia. Yes, advantages were taken, and I do not wish to speak about those. . . . We were sitting ducks, and no amount of favors could change what was to come over the following years."

I became more intrigued by a character Carlitos had told me about named Carlos Sarmiento. His dealings in Cuba and Panama made me curious about how the whole narcotrade between Columbia, Cuba, and the United States worked. Carlitos had a lot of knowledge on the subject. He was treated like a king in Cuba, and he had wealthy friends in Miami. I spoke with them over the phone, as well as individuals in Spain and Mexico. Sarmiento's name came up a couple of times when I spoke to the Cubans.

"This Carlos Sarmiento, who exactly was he?" I asked.

"He wouldn't be in any of Trujillo's documents. He was a businessman. I was very good friends with him until he betrayed me."

"What did he do?"

"He once supported me in tough times. He made a lot of money with the banks in Panama, and I knew him to be generous, and he was. Then, a few years before the invasion, he got into trouble with the CIA and DEA. He had connections to smuggling. He was the financier, the launderer. He tried to feed me to the lions, but I was too smart."

Panama has had a status as a tax haven and financial hub for a long time. The Americans sparked this, creating a place to store their funds from operations in Central and South America. Panamanian businessmen were among the best in the world, and still are in certain industries. However, by the 1980s, many cases of illicit finances were intentionally routed through the country due to cracks in the relatively new financial system. Laundering money was something I knew little of, but it was clear why this clandestine activity happened there. The Panamanian banking hub was new, liberal, and being taken advantage of by everyone, from the Americans to the Colombians. I believe it was created for the Americans as a way to keep their money out of America and avoid paying taxes. It did not take a genius to understand the chain of events that ultimately led to the Panama Papers. People took advantage of the system too much. Criminals. Money launderers. Major corporations, some we all know and use their products daily. Many were guilty. Many still are.

"We knew that people were taking advantage of our financial system. That is why Noriega imposed Law 23 in 1983, which required transparency for foreign individuals bringing large amounts of money into Panama," I was told.

"How well did you know Florencio Flores?" I asked Carlitos.

"Ah, si, mi amigo Chito. I knew him. I knew his character. He was a product of Nicaraguan military training. He became commander of the National Guard after Torrijos tragically passed, although he did not want this responsibility of Commander."

"And that's why Paredes stepped in?"

"You ask me questions you already know the fucking answer to! Yes, Paredes stepped in, and then the role rightfully became Manuel's soon after."

"Did Noriega have secret tapes of George Bush that he used as leverage?" I asked.

"Secret tapes? No, not that I know of. We had contacts in the White House and Pentagon that would share these details with Manuel. We knew they planned to take many of our leaders out. Very undemocratic behavior. . . . Yet Manuel had honor. He died with all of his secrets," Carlos responded.

I was particularly interested in learning about the alleged tapes. The conspiracy goes something like this: Noriega had recorded Bush during meetings while Bush was the director of the CIA. Noriega claimed that, in 1976, Bush even agreed to plant bombs in the Canal Zone to speed up negotiations for ownership of the Panama Canal, insinuating that, at one point, Bush was pro-Panama, and Noriega could use that against him. Given the 180-degree turn Bush would take in the 1980s, I didn't think this was something I could ever prove.

"I want to ask you something, Carlos."

"Yes?"

"Did the CIA assassinate Torrijos?"

"Torrijos died in a plane crash," Señor Wittgreen responded.

"Did Noriega do it?"

"I just fucking told you the truth."

"People witnessed it. Some said they saw the plane explode in mid-air," I countered, citing a piece of text I read in R. M. Koster's *In the Time of the Tyrants*.

"That's not how it happened."

"It's suspicious, don't you think?"

"His plane crashed into the side of a mountain. Marta . . . I was there; I saw the wreckage," Carlos said.

"I still can't understand it," I said. "The Americans tried to oust him from the day Omar took the lead. They first tried to get him through his brother, but that didn't work out. Edward Korman was forced to dismiss those charges in 1980. Eight years spent on that case. Why? All the while, there are reports of bombings in the Canal Zone and rumors of secret meetings between guys in the National Guard and the CIA to take Torrijos out from the inside. Nobody knows what's true or what isn't, but Omar's relationship with America worsens. People close to him are suspected of conspiracies, and they're exiled or killed. Torrijos was never the Americans' ideal choice. So, then, when 1981 comes around and Torrijos mysteriously dies in a plane crash, it seems to me like they finally got him. Or maybe it was Manuel." I caught my breath, awaiting a strike to the nose or for Carlos to gouge my eyes out.

"Cholito Adames," Carlos muttered softly.

"What?"

"Cholito Adames . . . that was the name of the pilot," he said as he leaned back into the cushion before following with a monologue that transported my mind and soul back decades. "He flew members of our government frequently, even Manuel and me. He was a fine pilot. On this day, Cholito's wife had given birth. The baby was born in the early hours of the morning, and Cholito, being a proud father, was by the side of his amor. Torrijos received word that same morning that he had to fly to the other end of the country for a meeting. He called Cholito and told him to be on the runway within the hour. Cholito did not want to go, but what could he say to the man? He could say nothing, and both he and his wife knew it. He arrived at the plane late, Torrijos was unhappy, and they rushed to get into the air. The winds seemed to pick up just as the bird took off. Cholito was experienced, but his mind was elsewhere. It wasn't long before the plane crashed into Marta Hill. It was devastating. I was called to the crash site. I saw the remains with my own eyes."

"Be that as it may," I said, "Trujillo's documents prove the DEA was asking you for favors while the flames were still burning at the crash site. I'm sure the CIA was, too. You said yourself that you and men you knew were taking advantage of that goodwill— weapons trafficking, drugs—even if you didn't explicitly say it. Really, I am just not naive enough to believe the Americans ever cared about who led the country. I think they wanted somebody in there who could and would do more for them, and that man was Noriega."

I think Carlos liked that I showed him strength and contested his words. Guys like him were gangsters back in the day. They would do business deals poolside with plates of powder. Naked prostitutes swarmed them like sharks. They were gangsters. These men, like Carlitos, were also expert liars, just as Richard Koster had warned. Still, I was hooked, entranced by the words of a man once so powerful that the world's largest intelligence agencies needed him. I know how devious this man was. I just couldn't get him to provide me the details. He would have never told me how many he killed and for what reason or how much money passed through Noriega's office from Medellin and sent to Miami. There were many parts of this history that I could not corroborate in general. Those conspiracies, the ones that people talk about the most, were the areas where the information feels unattainable. However, that did not stop me from trying.

I knew I had a great story, one that was truthful in many, many ways, but I wanted the full picture. So I found an old journalist in Panama named Ruben Murgas, about whom I had heard a rumor. "He was the last Panamanian to interview Noriega on home soil before the invasion," Ciro Noriega, Manuel's brother, once told me. I messaged Ruben back and forth one day, and he agreed to help me, claiming he had lived the history himself. However, when I reached out the next day, he had forgotten who I was and what we had spoken about. Alzheimer's seemed to be corroding his memory, a tale as old as time. It became obvious that the truth was whittling away just like Ruben's mind. There were fewer and fewer men who could tell the story. Unfortunately, Murgas was not a viable lead, and I wished him well. Still, I kept an open ear, hoping to hear something that somebody shouldn't have said, while Carlitos continued to present his story to me with unmistakable vigor and passion in each word.

Chapter 14
Terror on a Trade Route

I stood by a team of military officials on a dirt road beneath Marta as shards of metal scattered the base. The airplane's tail was still intact. It jutted out from the rock. I wore sunglasses. The man I served was dead. It was silent. A thin layer of mist hung just above the trees. We were all in disbelief. A cleaning crew showed up and got to work gathering whatever remains they could find. Everything had to remain secret until a public announcement could be made. "*Chucha madre*, what a tragedy," I said to myself over and over.

Instability immediately ruptured the Panama National Guard. It was chaos behind closed doors and in the streets. There was no direction, no leader. Torrijos was our general. I watched as Colonel Florencio Flores assumed Torrijos's role but not with the support he needed. The National Guard was not fully aligned with this vision, and neither was I. Manuel was still the eyes and ears of intelligence. "We're seeing people's true colors," Noriega told me. He was right. It was chaos. We still had to move forward as usual, working with the DEA while also tending to our own problems. The Guard split before me, just as it did after the 1968 coup. Nobody knew which direction to take the country in.

I never saw Florencio as the man to make those decisions. Ruben Dario Paredes del Rio replaced him within only a few months. I thought Ruben, on paper, was balanced. He was trained at the top military academy in Nicaragua, and he was raised in poverty with only an innate drive to succeed, propelling him through the ranks. I respected that about him. Yet I knew he lacked vision, unlike Noriega, who had nothing but plans. His meetings in Washington and his dealings with the CIA and DEA built the foundation of a general who would be an ally in Central America. It was obvious what was going to happen.

"Be patient, Carlos. Balance will be restored," Noriega said.

Paredes del Rio had a strong connection to Nicaragua. It was his home for many years, and he held a place in his heart for its wonderful people. In 1978, a civil war sparked; I heard about it in the news every day.

Manuel was most knowledgeable about these affairs. "The head of Nicaragua, Anastasio Somoza, has found himself in trouble," he told me. I learned much about Somoza and his family dynasty through Manuel. "He had led with a true iron fist for many years; the same with his father and his father before him. Somoza was someone with whom our leaders had a stable relationship. The United States supported the family."

During the early days of the Sandinista conflict with the Somozas, Omar Torrijos offered the services of the National Guard to the United States to help resolve the issue before the war became too extreme. I went in 1977 and 1978, and I trained Somoza followers. They were under my instruction. Everything I had learned from my days of training was instilled in them. I knew the United States had backed Somoza's government for decades, and Panama was so close that it was likely it would call on allies. But it did not matter; the Sandinistas overthrew the government in 1979. Their new enemies, the Contras, were animalistic. I trained Sandinistas, I liked Sandinistas, but the US government wanted us to help the fucking hyenas. They needed us to solve their problems.

"The Nicaragua Triangle is a threat to the Americans," Omar said. "They fear that the rise of socialism in Cuba, Nicaragua, and Grenada will open them up to risk. There is a consolidation of socialism across very, very important areas in the Caribbean and Central America, and the United States will be determined to maintain its grip of the Western Hemisphere. This is the Monroe Doctrine at work."

After Torrijos died in that plane crash, the sentiment I felt from America was different. The United States wanted our help even more. CIA presence in Panama heightened. The intelligence we provided was vital to them. Anything we could share about Cuba, Nicaragua, or Grenada was well received. Because of our position, physically, politically, and financially, we found ourselves at the epicenter of the problems in Central America. We catered to the intelligence agents who came to us for help. We threw parties and presented them to as many women as they wanted. The CIA would return to Langley, and then the DEA would pop its head up and ask us for more favors. It was a fucking revolving door. Yet the narco climate was hot. Maritime seizures had become common for us. I saw more illicit products than I ever thought I would. We would stop freighters in the canal and search them. I was paid for my efforts, but I was proud of the work I was doing.

The early 1980s were tumultuous. To the southeast, Colombia produced cocaine at a nearly unstoppable rate. Ships, planes, submarines—they left in the night and hoped our navy wouldn't find them. To the northwest, a civil war raged. The CIA was everywhere and always moving. The DEA set just as many eyes on us. Intelligence passed through all our hands. Because we were the closest to Colombia, we bore the brunt of the responsibility. We would often receive letters from a DEA agent like Tomas Telles, making us aware of a fugitive on the run that we would be expected to locate, capture, and extradite. We had recently intercepted the Colombian-flagged vessel *Doña Elenita* near the San Blas archipelago. She was carrying twelve tons of marijuana intended for the US market. It was the job of Inspector Luis Quiel to communicate on our behalf.

U.S. Departn. t of Justice

Drug Enforcement Administration

PCO-86-06

Panama 19 de Marzo de 1986

Inspector Luis A. Quiel
Oficina de Coordinacion y
  Enlace Internacional
Comandancia de las Fuerzas de Defensa
E. S. D.

Estimado Inspector:

El dia 19 de Marzo del presente ano, La Corte Federal de Lafaye e, Louisiana expidio la orden Federal de Arresto numero 84-60056-f contra el ciudadano Colombiano Alberto MEJIA-A. por violacion las leyes Federales de narcoticos de los Estados Unidos.

El cuidadano Colombiano Alberto MEJIA-A. estaba enredado y fue acusado por la corte Federal de los Estados Unidos en la captur. de 1,197 libras de cocaina en New Iberia, Louisiana el 20 de Mayo 1982.

La Corte Federal ha formulado cargos contra MEJIA-A. por violacion de los siguientes articulos del Codigo Penal Criminal de los Estados Unidos de Norteamerica:

(1) Articulo 21 U.S.C. 841 (A)(1) - Posesion de cocaina con intencion de distribuirla

(2) Articulo 21 U.S.C. 846 - Conspiracion para poseer y distribuir cocaina

(3) Articulo 21 U.S.C. 952(a) - Importacion ilegal de substancias controladas

El ciudadano Alberto MEJIA-A. es actualmente fugitivo de la Justicia penal norteamericana. En la eventualidad que la presencia de este fugitivo se logre detectar en la Republica de Panama, le solicitamos la cooperacion de las autoridades competentes Panamenas para arrestar a este narcotraficante y ponerlo a disposicion de los tribunales para que responda a los cargos que se le emputan por trafico internacional de estupefacientes.

*Figure 14.1. DEA memo, March 19, 1986, to Inspector Luis A. Quiel
requesting Panama's help to locate and arrest a Colombian fugitive.*

"Carlos, I need you to bring four fugitives to Tocumen. Telles will be there to meet you and make the transfer. Agent Leonard Williams is waiting for them in the States," Quiel said.

I wore many hats for many people, but when Noriega came knocking, I dropped everything. He didn't expect that of me, but he was my truest friend, and I would always help a friend if he came to me in need. One morning, I awoke to a ringing phone and a pounding brain.

My wife lay next to me. She covered her ears with the pillow. "Answer it, Carlos," she begged.

Chucha, the phone felt like rocks. I lifted it to my ear and heard the voice of my friend on the other line.

"Carlitos, buenas. I need you to meet me at the airstrip one hour earlier than we agreed," Manuel said.

I put myself together, splashing water on my dry face and brushing my teeth. My mouth smelled like cigars and tequila. No amount of toothpaste could rid me of that feeling. I kissed mi amor goodbye and drove right to the airport.

Manuel stood by a transport plane about the size of a Beechwood Super King. A fat Cuban cigar hung between his lips, and a smile struck his face when he saw me step out of my vehicle. "Good morning, mi amigo," he yelled with his arms in the air. He banged on the side of the plane.

Two men stumbled out. They wore American jeans and leather jackets. The pilot then sauntered down the steps in his pristine uniform, stretched out by a gut that hung over his belt.

"This is Sergio. He'll be the pilot today, and these two dogs are Patricio and Martino. The cargo is already packed. They will meet you at the airstrip. Fly undetected, or someone on the ground may try to take you down," Noriega instructed.

"We need to get going," the pilot said.

"I have to meet with Paredes, Diaz, and President Espriella in the city. Chucha, what a pain in the ass," Manuel said. "Safe flight, mi amigo." Manuel put his hand on my shoulder and turned to my crew. "Carlos is in charge. You do what he says," Noriega yelled.

The men nodded in unison. They entered the jet and took their seats. Manuel made me a better soldier, a more interesting man, someone with a purpose and mission.

"When you return, we will celebrate," he said to me before I stepped onto the plane. The door shut behind me, and I took my seat. I looked through my window. Manuel stood by my car, lighting up a cigar and leaning against the vehicle. We locked eyes, and he grabbed his balls and stuck out his tongue.

The bird flew. Clouds hung high in the air. We passed through them and burst out into the great wide blue. I sat as far back as I could. I could hear the weapons clanking in storage below my feet. They rustled against each other with every movement of the plane. Two rows ahead of me, Patrico and Martino drank Balboas. "Have you got another one?" I asked.

Patrick reached his hand into his bag and pulled out a can. He tossed it to me.

I cracked the seal, and foam sprayed on my lap. It had gone off. The liquid tasted stale, as if the beer had been sitting in the hot sun for days. "What the fuck is this?" I yelled out.

"Beggers can't be choosers," Martino responded with a laugh.

"Look out the window," Patricio said, pointing at a mountain beneath us. "That's Marta, where Torrijos crashed."

"Chucha, what a tragedy," Martino stated before drinking from his can.

"Did you know him well, Señor Wittgreen?" Patricio asked me.

"Si, yes, I did. He was a good man. He cared deeply for this country and our people. I respected him for that."

"Can I ask you something, señor?" Patricio inquired.

"What is it?"

"Do you think the gringos got him?"

I grabbed Martino by the collar and dragged him close. The stench of cigars and tequila wafted from my mouth into his nose. His eyes squinted. "If one more fucking sound comes out of your mouth, I'll shove a grenade in it when we reach Nicaragua."

Martino's eyes were wide. His breathing was sharp and heavy. He trembled in my arms. I let go and pushed him against the wall of the jet, shaking my head and tossing my beer to the back of the plane.

I sauntered down the aisle and entered the cockpit. Sergio had his hands gripped to the wheel. Through the windshield, an onslaught of white clouds rolled just beneath us, and a wondrous blue sky sat above. Being a pilot interested me, but I didn't have the discipline. "How long until we're there?" I asked Sergio.

"Thirty minutes," he responded. He had sweat forming on his forehead. Little droplets bubbled up and rolled down to his nose. He was obese; I was surprised his gut didn't get in the way of the wheel. His breathing was slow and uneven. I decided to leave the cockpit and give him some space.

Martino and Patricio sat upright when they saw me approach. I sat behind their row and leaned back in my seat. They each coughed the phlegm clear from their throats, shifting around, trying to get comfortable.

"Who are we even giving these guns to?" Patricio piped up.

"The Contras."

My gaze moved to the clouds beyond the window. They had risen closer to the jet. I leaned against the pane, eyes an inch from the Plexiglas.

"Do you feel that?" Martino asked, standing up from his seat.

Silence. We all held our breaths, listening closely.

A bang erupted, and the jet turned left, knocking Martino off his feet. He crashed atop Patricio and knocked the beer from his hand. "What the fuck?" Patricio yelled. The jet suddenly leaned right. I hit my head against the window, and Martino fell into the aisle. We descended further into the clouds. The golden rays from the sun vanished, and darkness fell upon the interior.

I looked at the cockpit. The door swung left to right. The pilot's hands were not on the wheel. He gripped his own throat, breathing sharp and fast.

"Quick, the pilot!" I screamed.

We rushed to the cockpit. I grabbed hold of Sergio. His face was beet-red, and sweat rushed down to his collar, soaking it. "Sergio, look at me!" I yelled, pulling his face in my direction. The nose of the plane dipped another inch. We all stumbled against the pilot's chair. A slew of flickering bulbs and buttons lit up the dashboard. My beating brain looked for an answer. "Sergio, what the fuck are you doing?" I said as I slapped his fat cheek.

The pilot's arm slowly rose into the air. His dry and crusted mouth opened, lips attempting to pull the words from his vocabulary. He shook violently as I grabbed hold of his shoulders. There was nothing behind his eyes; they stared into mine with no substance of reality.

"What's wrong with him?" Martino asked.

I slapped Sergio once more. "What's wrong with you?" I screamed into his ear. The clouds thickened. I could see nothing but cotton white. A feeling in my gut rose with the continuous drop.

Patricio rushed alongside me and stuck his fingers on Sergio's neck under his jaw. "His heart is beating fast," he said.

I felt like throwing up, but I had too much to live for. I wouldn't go like Torrijos. "Wake the fuck up, cabron! We're twenty minutes away. Stay awake!" I yelled, shaking him, slapping him, screaming in his ear.

Martino breathed heavily. Patricio held one shoulder, and I held the other.

The pilot's hands loosely gripped the wheel. His eyelids fluttered as his pupils dilated and contracted with every strand of light that broke through the clouds. Sergio breathed through his nostrils. "My . . . my medicine," he mumbled.

"Where is it?" I asked.

The pilot could barely open his mouth.

"Chucha . . . just look around for his medicine. Check all these drawers and boxes," I told Martino. Tools and manuals flew across the floor of the jet as the soldier rifled his way through them.

Patrico and I locked eyes. His were wide, chest pumping with the pace of his icy breaths. "I can't believe I'm going to die smuggling guns to a fucking country I'm not even from," he wailed.

My hand lifted from Sergio's shoulder. I smacked Patricio right across his trembling face. "Shut the fuck up and keep him awake," I demanded. My neck creaked as I turned to watch Martino rummage through every cubby in the plane. A beer can fell off a seat and rolled all the way down to hit my boot. When I lifted my head, we broke through the clouds, and a green landscape lit up my sight. It was the Indio Maíz Biological Reserve, a far-spanning rainforest, home to creatures just as deadly as the Darien. "Up, Sergio," I said, grasping his hands and pulling the wheel back. The floor tilted in the opposite direction. The nose faced the clouds.

Martino stumbled into the back of the plane and knocked into a cupboard. The top door swung open, and two life jackets fell onto him.

"How far to the airstrip?" I yelled at Sergio.

"Ten . . . kilometros."

Bullets of sweat slid down his cheeks and dripped to the floor. I thought about my parents, my sisters, Gaspar. . . . The runway was so close but so far. Sergio slipped between light and dark. Patricio pulled him back into existence with every skipped breath. The air chilled. Shivers ran along my skin. I wished I had fucked one last time. The thought barreled around my brain. I thought about all of the men I wanted to fight, people who deserved beatings. I thought about my legacy and how I would be remembered. The CIA wouldn't send flowers. I was just another asset delivering weapons on its behalf. I might as well have not existed.

"Señor Wittgreen, look!" Martino exclaimed as he charged up the aisle, finger-pointing toward the windshield.

I could see an airstrip shimmering in the distance. It lay in the middle of a forest, surrounded by mystery. A series of armored vehicles stretched along the end of the runway. "Sergio, Sergio!" I yelled, slapping him awake once more. The sound of guns rattling filled the air as the pilot's eyes slowly opened. I grabbed his face and turned it to mine. "Land us safely, and we will get you help," I told him.

Sergio's hands wrapped tighter around the wheel. The nose dipped. We shifted forward. A screech sounded as the wheels jutted out from the belly of the plane. We clung to whatever we could, bending our knees, bracing for whatever impact was to come. My heart beat fast. A million memories rushed over. The landing zone became clear. I took a deep breath. The wheels skidded on impact. Sergio groaned, tensing his muscles as he steered straight. The vehicles grew larger and more defined. I saw dozens of bodies appear. One man in a camouflaged military uniform stood in the direct center of them all. Our pace lowered, and the engines roared.

"Wait, what is this?" Martino yelled. He held an EpiPen in his right hand. I wanted nothing more than to smack him.

The jet rolled to a halt. Through the windshield, I watched as the Nicaraguan soldiers surrounded the plane. I ripped the EpiPen from Martino's hand and jabbed it into Sergio's arm. He gasped for air, then took a long, deep breath. "You fuckers," he mumbled lowly.

A slew of men in camouflage uniforms stood before the doorway as I walked down the steps. A man in a commander's uniform walked out from the group to meet me halfway. The caballero's gaze moved to meet the plane. "Where are the weapons?" he asked.

I whistled.

Martino and Patricio scurried down the steps, skin as white as a ghost, eyes wide and bloodshot.

"What's wrong with your men?" the soldier asked me.

"It was a rough flight."

Patricio and Martino unloaded the guns from the plane.

"God bless America," I said.

The flight home was smooth. It was a steady course back to Panama City. The light of the country sparkled in the night as we drifted over them. I leaned against the window, just staring down at it all. A beer can rolled along the aisle and stopped at my boot. I sighed. My fingers wrapped around the can, and I cracked it slowly. Stale beer had never tasted so good.

The months went by fast. The struggle within the National Guard was inspected closely by the CIA. They needed to make sure that we were acting in their interests. At that time, they operated like political bowling bumpers. We had to stay in our lane, no matter how wide or narrow. Our country had a bad reputation for authoritarianism post–political shift. There were men among us who craved power.

One night, Manuel had sectioned off the top floor of a restaurant in the heart of the city. My car screeched to a halt by a cracked curb, right in front of a mural of our people from the 1903 War of Independence, which was painted on the side of the building. Two armed soldiers stood by the entrance. They nodded as I entered and sauntered up the many stairs. A gentle, amber light shone onto me as I stepped inside to a party. Everybody with a name in politics was there.

Manuel sat smoking a cigar at the head of a table. Two men and six women sat in the other chairs. They all had full glasses in front of them. His eyes lit up when he saw me. "Carlos, come, come!" he yelled out.

A brunette with wide hips and brown, glistening eyes touched my arm as I sat next to Manuel. "Carlos, meet Aria," he said. Aria brushed her hand over my ear. Her fingertips gently scratched my skin. A waitress approached and set a glass of seco down before me. Manuel gestured to it with a grin. I drank it all in one gulp.

"Have you seen Diaz Herrera?"

"No, señor."

"Chucha, he's the only one who didn't come."

Even then, I could tell Noriega knew who would turn on him. I look back, and there were dozens in that room alone who whispered with Washington and switched sides. People were promised things. I was never approached. The CIA knew better than to do that. Sure, my name would get dragged into the headlines a couple of times, but they knew I would go to the grave defending my friend. The rest of those *culebras* in that room, the motherfuckers who became cowards when the heat rose, they were no better than the gringos.

"Two days ago, Communism was the biggest problem in the world. Yesterday, narcotics. And today, a war in Nicaragua. Who knows what tomorrow will bring?" Manuel said.

"They should stay out of business that is not theirs," I stated.

"The CIA is not too happy with me," he said. "I supplied Leopoldo Galtieri with Exocet missiles for their efforts in the Falklands. The same missiles recently took down the HMS *Sheffield*, which was on picket duty protecting the British fleet when it came under attack. It is a war that is bound to end shortly."

"The Americans have asked me to reopen the School of the Americas," Manuel continued. "I had to remind them of the Canal treaty, which explicitly stated the school was to close. It is not Panamanian responsibility to promote American education. It has only been five years, and they are already trying to take back the canal. . . . That's what all of this is really about, Carlos."

We were at the heart of all of it, and Noriega was the nucleus. The Americans tugged on our leash when we misbehaved, but the leash loosened as the gringos realized we were their only ally in Central America capable of extinguishing their fires. All our goodwill put us in a position of true importance. Manuel became our leader in 1983. Paredes could have never led the people as general of the military or as the president. He retired from the National Guard, and he was arrested swiftly afterward. We let him go after a short time. He later took one last swipe at Manuel by running for president, even after we warned him not to. It was in his own best interest. He lost, to no surprise. Manuel Noriega was the only man capable, and I was his right hand.

"Intelligence is our only tool to maintain Panama's autonomy while our allies and global superpowers use us," Manuel said.

I felt a change in 1983, just as I had felt a change in 1968. The tides were turning, and the current beneath us swashed and swayed from the ever-moving political climate. I felt safe. I could do whatever I wanted, and I was determined to provide for my children, mi amor, my family, and my friends. It was never about the riches. It wasn't even about the power. It was about deviation and a genuine love for experience. I knew that everything I did made a contribution to the history of my nation. So, when one of my first missions under new leadership was to collaborate with the gringos on Operation Thunder, a joint effort focused on eradicating illegal drug plantations in the Pearl Archipelago, known for marijuana cultivation, I put on my boots, and I served. Over the next several years, we seized an incredible amount of narcotics for the DEA while we supplied the CIA with intelligence about our neighbors in exchange for a long, loose leash.

De igual manera, en coordinación con el Agente Es pecial LEONARD WILLIAM a cargo de la Oficina del DEA en Panamá en la época, se logra la captura de nueve na ves con bandera panameña en aguas internacionales con contrabando de drogas, incautandose 48,000 libras de marihuana. Fueron deportadas 21 personas de las cuales seis eran fugitivos en el territorio continental norte americano por delitos de drogas y entregados a las au toridades legales pertinentes de los Estados Unidos.

IV.-Año 1982

En el año de 1982, la lucha antidroga, logró en Panamá, el decomiso de 543,834 gramos de cocaína y 320, 254.4 gramos de marihuana; deportó y entregó a 16 delin cuentes por casos de drogas a las autoridades legales de diferentes países, de los cuales 4 fugitivos fueron entregados a los Estados Unidos de América.

En aguas internacionales y previa autorización del Gobierno panameño, son apresadas por el Servicio de Guar dacostas estadounidense, trece barcos con bandera paname ña, decomizandose 503,500 libras de marihuana con desti no al territorio continental norteamericano.

Septiembre: La lancha patrullera "LIGIA ELENA" de Opera ciones Marinas de la Guardia Nacional de Pa namá, capturó en el Archipiélago de San Blas, la embarcación de bandera colombiana "DOÑA RUMBO, que transportaba en sus bodegas, un cargamento de 500 kilos de cocaína. En la caputra fueron arrestadas 11 personas de las cuales 8 eran de nacionalidad colombiana y 3 panameños. Las investigaciones pertinentes determinaron que la droga provenía de Colombia con destino a los centros de consumo en los Estados Unidos de América.

Figure 14.2. Chronological summary of narco seizures and arrests in 1982, primarily in September of that year.

V.- Año 1983

Enero : Un Guardacostas de la Marina Nacional de las
Fuerzas de Defensa de Panamá, capturó a la
altura del Archipiélago de San Blas, el yate
de placer de bandera norteamericana "BLUE WA
TER", donde fue decomisada la cantidad de
25,875 libras de marihuana procedente de Colombia. La tripulación del citado yate esta
ba compuesta por ciudadanos de nacionalidad
colombiana y cubana.

En ese mismo mes, en una revisión de rutina
de las Fuerzas de Defensa, fue detectado un
cargamento de marihuana entre la carga de ca
fé que transportaba el barco de bandera pana
meña "HANOOVER", el cual procedía de Colombia. El cargamento incautado consistía de
125.000 libras de dicha droga, la cual tenía
como destino final los Estados Unidos de Amé
rica.

Abril : Basados primordialmente en informaciones su-
ministradas por la Oficina de Narcóticos de
las Fuerzas de Defensa de Panamá a las Agencias Federales de Estados Unidos del DEA y
Aduanas, las autoridades norteamericanas decomisaron en la localidad de Fort Lauderdale,
Estado de la Florida, la suma de $5.5 millo
nes de dólares en efectivo, 61.4 libras de
cocaína y una aeronave Learjet. Todo lo in
cautado tenía relación directa con el ciuda
dano norteamericano de origen cubano RAMON
MILLIAN RODRIGUEZ.

Agosto : Se realizó conjuntamente con la Agencia del
DEA una observación aérea de las de "PEDRO
GONZALES" y "SAN MIGUEL", ubicadas en el Ar

Figure 14.3. Chronological summary of narco seizures and arrests in January, April, and August 1983, between January and August. (See figure 14.4 for a continuation of August 1983.)

203

hipiélago de las Perlas en el litoral Pacífico pana-
emño, donde se logra detectar la existencia de plantaciones de marihuana. Posteriormente, se dió inicio a un operativo de destrucción llamado "OPERACION
TRUENO", en donde exitosamente se llegó a destruir
1,075, 000 libras de marihuana en la Isla de "PEDRO
GONZALEZ" y 650.000 libras de marihuana en la Isla
de "SAN MIGUEL".

Durante el año de 1983, fueron incautados 66,535 gramos de cocaína y 850.196.9 gramos de marihuana; deportados 51 delincuentes
por delitos de drogas, 9 de los cuales eran fugitivos de la justicia
norteamericana, siendo entregados a los Estados Unidos de América en
coordinación con el Agente del DEA JAMES BRAMBLE. Con la debida autorización del Gobierno panameño, los Guardacostas estadounidenses
procedieron a capturar 8 naves con bandera panameña decomisandose
238.700 libras de marihuana.

VI.- AÑO 1984

ABRIL

La Oficina de Narcóticos de Colón, reportó la existen
cia de gran cantidad de Eter Etílico que había llegado
a la Zona Libre procedente de Alemania en tránsito por
Panamá con destino a puertos colombianos.

Basados en los reportes periódicos que efectuaban los
Agentes del Equipo Antinarcotráfico de Panamá, durante
los controles efectivos que se realizaban a través de
las costas panameñas, las Fuerzas de Defensa de Panamá,
presentó a los Agentes del DEA, diferentes muestras
del material químico que había sido detectado en tráfi
co no normal por el Canal de Panamá.

En base a esta información sobre precursores químicos,
las autoridades federales del DEA, concluyen que el
éter etílico y la acetona eran la nueva modalidad utilizada por los centros técnicos de la mafia del narcotráfico, quienes empezaron a utilizar estos químicos
para aumentar la pureza de la pasta básica de cocaína,
ahorrando al mismo tiempo gran cantidad de materia pri
ma.

*Figure 14.4. Chronological summary of narco seizures and arrests in April 1984
and a continuation of those in figure 14.3 for August in 1983 and 1984.*

The praise was nice but never a motivating factor in my efforts. We were becoming stronger by the day. Noriega implemented Law 20, which integrated the police, air force, navy, and military battalions under a single command. The National Guard was no longer there, and what took its place was the Panama Defense Forces, the PDF. We were taking a step up from the foundation Torrijos had built for our people. Manuel wanted to take our sovereignty to the next level.

On October 25, 1983, I attended a cock fight tournament just outside the city. Men had come from all over Central and South America with their roosters. I had become a name to know. Media stations wanted me to give statements about the sport. I watched as my roosters shredded their opposition under lights. The men around me were part of the elite. They had money to spend.

It was exhilarating until the news began to spread. "The Americans have invaded Grenada."

I rushed to the nearest television. The story was everywhere. "Codenamed Operation Urgent Fury, the United States has sent 7,600 troops to the 344-square-kilometer island after Prime Minister Maurice Bishop was assassinated and the radical General Hudson Austin took his post." I learned that the United States used Jamaican and Barbadian soldiers to fill a number of troops. The gringos needed Grenada for its sea and air ports, just like us, and it justified its invasion through the Monroe Doctrine. Whether intentional or not, we got the message.

Chapter 15
The Million-Dollar Bounty

Gaspar stood to my right, my parents to my left. Gaspar wore a sleek navy suit with polished brown shoes. My mother wore her church dress. It was bright red. My father's cap shaded the sun from his tired eyes. The rays beat down on us. Our gaze was brought to the main stage.

I saw Felicidad in the corner of my eye.

"There you are," Muneca yelled out. She wore her best dress. "When does the speech start?" she asked me.

"*Tranquilo*. You spend enough time with your husband," I responded.

She slapped my arm. She was a good woman and a wonderful wife to Manuel.

Gaspar spoke softly with my mother as he helped her stand upright. My father and I joked around. Everyone suddenly went silent. Noriega stepped onto the stage. Hands were thrown into the air, and people cheered. I whistled using my fingers. He knew how to captivate a crowd, especially when there was civil unrest brewing. We were facing problems in our government due to upcoming elections.

There was a party after the speech that I attended with my family. Muneca pushed her way through the crowd to get to Manuel. I approached Noriega alongside Gaspar and my parents. A smile struck his face. He kissed the cheeks of my family. "Gaspar, look at you!" he yelled out, squeezing my brother so tight that I worried his eyes would pop out. "You should be very proud of your young diplomat. Our European ambassadors are very important," he said to my parents.

"How about that laboratory explosion in Lima?" Gaspar mentioned. It was a disaster, one that showed us the devastation a poorly run narco lab could result in. Labs had been popping up all over South America. Ladronas set up shop in Panama, but we would catch them easily. They knew better than to fuck with us; most of them did, anyways. The PDF did regular scans of our nation from the air and sea. The prominent cooks were in Colombia, working for Escobar. The Medellin Cartel's operation had become so vast that if it were a company, it would have been listed on the Nasdaq.

"*El cocinero viejo*, Ricardo Alvarez Calderon. The world is better off," I said.

Captura y Destrucción del Mayor Contrabando de Éter Etílico

La cocaína (metilbenzoilecgomina), es un alcaloide que se extrae las hojas de coca (erytroxtylon coca) planta que se cultiva principalmente en los Andes peruanos y bolivianos.

La coca es una planta de antiguo cultivo en Sud América, pero es aún poco conocida por la ciencia moderna. La botánica general, ecología, distribución geográfica y arqueología de la coca se encuentran todavía en discusión. La hoja de coca ha jugado un rol importante en la vida de los nativos de Sud América por miles de años. Su uso masticatorio persiste hoy en día en muchas partes de los Andes y de la Cuenca Amazónica.

La cocaína cuyo aislamiento se le atribuye a Albert Niemann de la Universidad de Gottingen quien además le dió su nombre y características químicas, ha sido posteriormente estudiada por múltiples investigadores científicos.

Ante el extraordinario aumento de demanda del alcaloide en los mercados de consumo, ha aumentado notablemente el cultivo de la planta, en forma lícita y, principalmente, clandestina. La hoja de coca es cosechada a mano y para obtener un kilo de Pasta Básica de Cocaína, se usa hojas de coca en una cantidad que varía de 200 a 250 kilos, la cual es macerada en las llamadas "pozas" que son recipientes con paredes de cemento o cilindros metálicos resistentes a los ácidos. Se requiere ácido sulfúrico, kerosene, carbonato de calcio.

Figure 15.1. DEA-style explanatory report titled "Captura y Destrucción del Mayor Contrabando de Éter Etílico" (Capture and Destruction of the Largest Ethyl Ether Smuggling Company), providing background on coca cultivation, the history and chemistry of cocaine, and clandestine processing methods, prepared in connection with a major seizure of ethyl ether used in cocaine production.

We were busier than ever. There were elections coming up that year. They would be our first in sixteen years. I almost lost my sanity when I was told the Democratic Opposition Alliance was backing Arnulfo Arias for another shot at the throne. Arias was staunchly against everything I stood for. He had been ousted by men like me, and he never forgot. He was an old, angry man who wanted the good old days to return. To my surprise, he had support. Our friend Nicolás Ardito Barletta was his opposition. He was with the Democratic Revolutionary Party, and he was a good man. Before the PDF, the National Guard looked favorably on Barletta, who had been vice president of the World Bank in Panama. He was a very well-known economist in the 1970s, a trusted advisor for Omar Torrijos, and a key figure in the financial planning of the city and its future.

Manuel and I were meeting Barletta for lunch one afternoon. Election day was approaching, and we wanted to check in. Manuel's eyes scanned the floral room. It was moderately busy. I could tell something was off that day. I had assumed it was because of the accusations against him. Publications in the United States began openly questioning Manuel's motives.

"The National Endowment for Democracy and the American Institute for Free Labor Development donated twenty thousand dollars to Barletta's campaign," Manuel said.

The Democratic Revolutionary Party was backed by the Americans. They didn't want Arias on the throne, and they made that clear to us. Still, the American interest didn't stop the American media from nailing Manuel to the cross.

"There's a storm brewing, Carlitos," Noriega stated.

"Señor?"

"The Americans . . . they have placed a bounty on my head."

"I will find out who," I told him.

"It doesn't matter who. It's a million dollars. Any man with a cock and balls and a gun would kill me for that much money."

"That won't happen, señor. I will make sure of it." My eyes scanned the crowd. "Any one of those motherfuckers could pull the trigger," I thought to myself, "Panamanians, Americans, Mexicans, Colombians." . . . One million dollars was a lot of money just to kill one man. Noriega was made of flesh and bone.

"The world is changing, Carlitos. There is less integrity in humanity. I spent years of my life trafficking weapons, money, cash . . . all for the fucking gringos."

Barletta entered holding a copy of *La Prensa*, the most recent edition. He set it on the table before shaking our hands and taking a seat. The headline was about him. Most of them were at the time. Our man dominated the media. Nobody wanted to hear a thing from Arias. We told Barletta we would continue to support him. Our presence was strong. The PDF controlled most aspects of our nation.

I stayed vigilant, but I couldn't always be with Manuel. I had my own duties to attend to, and he had enough problems of his own, problems that nobody would ever know about. There were many issues flaring in Central America at the time. I strategized with Luis Quiel to find and expel narco fugitives hiding out in Panama. It was common for our nation to attract that kind of man.

James Benson, second secretary at the US Embassy, was in communication with our narco unit often. Between Benson and Tomas Telles, our mailbox was never empty.

U.S. Depart.   of Justice

Drug Enforcement Administration

84/60

Panamá, 17 de Julio de 1984

Inspector Luis A. Quiel
Oficina de Coordinación y
    Enlace Internacional
Comandancia de la Fuerzas de Defensa
E. S. D.

Estimado Inspector:

Referencia nuestra conversación el 16 de Julio de 1984, el DEA y la oficina del Fiscalía del Distrito de Miami quisiera, con el apoyo de las Fuerzas Armadas de Panamá, obtener la expulsión del narco-traficante profugo que se encuentra actualmente en la Republica de Panamá.

La oficina del DEA que se encuentra en Miami, Florida, nos han avisado que Oscar Alfonso CARDONA-Donato, ciudano Colombiano, nacido el 1 de Agosto de 1944 tiene pedido la captura por tráfico de estupificientes (cocaína) con una fianza de dos milliones de dólares por el Corte Federal del Distrito de Miami.

Quedemos ya agradecido por el apollo y ayuda brindado por su oficina en este caso.

Atentamente,

THOMAS M. TELLES
Agregado del DEA

TMT:jl

Figure 15.2. DEA letter dated July 17, 1984, from Attaché Thomas M. Telles in Panama to Inspector Luis A. Quiel, thanking Panamanian authorities and requesting assistance with the expulsion of Colombian trafficker Oscar Alfonso Cardona-Donato, wanted in Miami on cocaine charges with a two-million-dollar bond.

EMBASSY OF THE
UNITED STATES OF AMERICA

Panamá, R.P.

15 de agosto de 1984

Inspector Luis Quiel
Fuerzas de la Defensa de la
   República de Panamá
Panamá, República de Panamá

Estimado Inspector Quiel:

Con la presente le envío una lista de las naves de
bandera panameña las cuales fueron abordadas por el
guardacosta de los Estados Unidos desde el 1 de julio
hasta la fecha actual. Ojalá que le pueda ser de
utilidad.

Le agradezco mucho su valiosa ayuda en estos casos
tan difíciles. Espero que nuestros países puedan seguir
trabajando conjuntamente en la lucha, buena y necesaria,
contra el tráfico de drogas y los narcotraficantes.

Atentamente,

James H. Benson
Segundo Secretario

Figure 15.3. Letter dated August 15, 1984, from US Embassy official James H.
Benson to Inspector Luis Quiel, providing a list of Panamanian-flagged vessels boarded
by the US Coast Guard and expressing gratitude for Panama's cooperation in
the joint fight against drug trafficking.

I was receiving many phone calls from Cuba during this time. Some were from within the heart of the nation, Castro's men, his brother, Raul, sometimes himself. The Cubans needed intelligence about CIA dealings in Central America. They were likely then feeding those details to the Russians. I never asked. In return, I would receive information to feed to the DEA and CIA from our end.

"There is rumored to be teams of American pilots who are smuggling weapons and drugs through Latin America and into the US. The CIA knows all about it," I informed my Cuban contacts. It was a strange time. I knew of men who flew for the gringos, transporting weapons all over the Americas on behalf of Uncle Sam. I know some of those men were taking advantage of their covert missions, saving room in their plane for a bundle of cocaine or marijuana to be delivered alongside the weapons. There was an American I knew who did this; we called him Charlie Brown. It became clear that everybody did business with each other, regardless of the boundaries set in place by government bodies and international media. The people needed a narrative to work with. They needed someone to root for and someone to fight against.

Manuel and I did business in Cuba through my company Caza y Pesca. I had to operate under my name alone because of Manuel's relationship with the CIA. If they knew he was openly doing business in Cuba, it would have created leverage for them over Noriega. We didn't need that. I operated a shipping agency in Cuba that facilitated fishing and shipping logistics. It was all part of a broader attempt to bypass international sanctions, particularly the US blockade. I enjoyed making trips to Havana.

The women, the cockfighting, the parties—I loved every minute of it. It truly had become like a second home.

I was a cockfighting champion, a force to be reckoned with. I attended a cockfighting tournament in Havana. The heat was sweltering on this trip. It was one of the hottest days of that year. Castro had a driver come pick me up in an old, yellow Volkswagen Bug. The seats vibrated as the wheels rolled down the cratered Havana suburb streets. He took me to a gallera where I was met with my roosters. They had been transported separately. I didn't want to risk losing out on the prize. Local media were filming the event. I was a superstar. They interviewed me because of my knowledge of the game. The competition attracted powerful men from all over. Many from Panama would attend, like Carlos Duque. We shared many of the same vices at one time.

"Where is Sarmiento?" Duque asked me at the gallera one night.

"I have not seen him in some time," I responded. It was common for business to be done at the gallera. Cockfighting attracted elite businessmen from all over Central and South America. It was a haven from the gringos; they would have never attended matches, and if they did, they stuck out like a sore thumb. We took care of ourselves and our interests, acknowledging that we would all have to feed breadcrumbs of information to the DEA and CIA to keep their fingers off the trigger.

Whenever I was in Cuba, I made it a point to try to see Castro. He was a dear friend whom I admired greatly. We would discuss strategy often. He and Noriega made the decisions, but I was a contributing mind whenever I was needed. After winning the tournament, I met Fidel at a taverna in Havana. His guards gestured to me with a smile as I passed by them and entered the establishment to find Fidel sitting by the bar, pouring himself a drink while the bartender watched.

"Carlitos, welcome, señor. Did you know Ernest Hemingway used to sit on this exact stool?" he said to me.

I had heard many great things about the writer. Cubans looked favorably on the gringo because of his machismo.

"Sit, sit," Castro went on. Fidel always had somewhere to be, but he never seemed to be in a rush. People like me came to him.

"Back in 1959, the CIA helped me overthrow this country. Now, the Soviets give me whatever I need to maintain what we have. Still, all I care about is Cuba," Castro muttered.

"There is always someone looming over us in our part of the world," I responded.

"Over five hundred assassination attempts on my life since 1959! The gringos have tried it all. Poisoning the clams that are retrieved on my ocean floor, bribing my best friends to stab me in the back, turning and training my own soldiers to destabilize the country from the inside out. The CIA creates a radio station to sway Cuban opinion over me, Radio Marti. My people are too smart for such nonsense. If only the world knew how vile they truly are, how they will stop at nothing and have no boundaries with children or family in order to get what they want. The number one cause of death in Cuba is not crime, nor is it famine; it's the United States."

"What they did in Grenada . . . chucha."

"Grenada, Nicaragua, Iraq, El Salvador, everywhere, Carlos. Make no mistake; the CIA will come for you just as they have come for me. Operation Mongoose, the CIA plan to invade my country and slaughter innocent people, it was devastating, so much so that the legacy of the attacks still lingers today. Some Cubans have wanted to flee the issues, and I have let them flee. If they choose to be aliens in a country that detests them, so be it. I do what I must to keep control . . ."

Castro was talking about Plan Bravo. Thousands of Cubans infiltrated the shores of America under the guise of refugees. Most of them were societal opponents, but Fidel saw an opportunity to not only rupture the stability of the Florida economy but also to inject a network of spies on American soil. He turned a negative situation into one that benefited him. He knew so much. The intelligence that circulated on the island of Cuba was palpable, just as it was in Panama. I could feel the gaze and hear the whispers, and I was honored to be able to learn from it all and apply it to my own life at home.

When I returned to Panama, I stepped off the plane in an intense heat. Sweat rolled down my face and dripped to the tarmac. Something was not right. I could feel it in my gut. Men within the National Guard began to murmur behind closed doors. The gringos had been making frequent trips to the city. Men like Oliver North and John Poindexter stepped off jets in suits and walked into our offices with big, swinging dicks. They sat before us in neatly pressed suits, empty-handed, mouths open wide for a taste of knowledge. North was an intelligent brute, a product of traditional American militantism. Poindexter was shorter, fatter. They approached us with smiles.

"Señor Noriega, thank you for your hospitality."

They were polite in the early days. They knew we were aware of their situation. The war in Nicaragua was not going the way they wanted it to. They needed our help to put their man in power, but we didn't agree with the nature of the Contras enough to feel obligated to help in ways other than transporting weapons and cash.

"The Contras are animals," I interjected. I had my diplomat hat on. My word was valuable, but I could still tell North and Poindexter wanted to hear none of it.

"Manuel, we need your help," they begged.

By 1984, we saw the Sandinistas grow stronger. Their leader, Daniel Ortega, looked to soon take the throne of their nation. The gringos may as well have gotten down on their hands and knees for us. If it were the 1970s, we might have helped them, but times had changed. Our position in the world had centered. We were starting to act on our own interests. Ultimately, it was the second Boland Amendment that threatened to break the Contra movement. We were involved in the decisions made behind closed doors that led to President Reagan ordering the National Security Council to continue to help the animals in Nicaragua.

"We need to keep the Contras together in body and soul, no matter what Congress votes for," the Council would relay to Manuel.

Vice-President Bush was outraged with us, and that was obvious. Where once Manuel claimed Bush was a friend, it became clear he was an enemy to us. Noriega would tell me the story often. He would tell many men the anecdote, and it would spread like wildfire through the ranks of G-2 and the National Guard. "I am sitting in a room with Bush and other nameless, faceless robots of the CIA. I am eye to eye with the vice-president. There are wrinkles on his face, veins popping from his forehead. I have never seen a politician show so much emotion. He scolds me for saying no to him. He berates me for my pro-Panama decisions, and he makes no mention of the countless favors I have done for him personally. I give it right back to him. I do not let this man walk all over me; I know too much. Bush can't take it anymore; he stands tall, his lackeys follow suit. He looks me dead in the eyes, and he says, 'You are going to respect me.' It was a threat directed right at us."

As the Cold War shifted over us like clouds during a storm, our work for the DEA remained steady on the ground. DEA administrator Francis M. Mullen signed his name on letter after letter, congratulating our men on yet another seizure of narcotics. We had attended a conference in Brasilia to discuss the ongoing challenges in the narco movement. Manuel was a key voice. He saw the need to create a follow-up conference, but this time on our own Contadora Island. It was clear to the men on the ground, at sea, and in the air that the cartel was expanding in both size and financial strength. Still, our work was being recognized, and we were receiving gratitude constantly.

TRADUCCION

Junio 9, 1984.

Manuel Antonio Noriega
General, Fuerzas de Defensa de Panamà.

Estimado General Noriega:

Reciente inteligencia obtenida por la administración del esfuerzo de droga de los Estados Unidos muestra que desde enero de 1984, Panamá ha sido utilizada por organizaciones de traficantes de cocaína como lugar de trasiego de éter, el cuál ha sido embarcado desde diferentes partes del mundo hacía los laboratorios clandestinos en Colombia y algunos otros lugares de América Latina. Su acción de esfuerzo reciente en el decomiso y destrucción del éter es tan notable el cuál impactará en el mundo ilícito de los suplidores de cocaína HCL.

Así mismo, los Estados Unidos han capturado aproximadamente ?,147 tanques de éter. Conjuntamente con su super esfuerzo, nosotros hemos tenido impactos positivos en el tráfico internacional de cocaína.

Lo felicito por su iniciativa y espero continuar nuestro trabajo conjunto de muto interés.

Sinceramente,

FRANCIS M. MULLEN Jr.
Administrador

Figure 15.4. DEA letter, June 9, 1984, from Administrator Francis
M. Mullen Jr. to General Manuel Noriega, noting Panama's use as a hub for
ether smuggling to cocaine labs, praising Noriega's recent seizures and destruction of
ether as a major disruption to traffickers, and stressing further US and Panama
cooperation after the capture of more than nine thousand ether tanks.

219

Cillian Dunne

Drug Enforcement Administration

Panamá, 27 de Agosto de 1984

General Manuel A. Noriega
Jefatura Fuerza de Defensa
Republica de Panamá
E. S. D.

Estimado General Noriega:

Me complace dirigirme a Usted para continuar el esfuerzo maximo entre los jefes maximos de las Americas en el esfuerzo de combatir el tráfico de drogas. Entre 30 Octubre - 1 Noviembre de 1984 en Brasilia, se va celebrar una conferencia que es como una sequencia de la primera reunión que se efecto en La Isla de Contadora en Panamá.

El Administrador del DEA, Señor Francis Mullen, ha suplicado tener el honor que Usted estuviera presente con los otros funcionarios de los países Americas en el Congreso que fue convocado inicialmente por el General Noriega en 1983.

Tambien, quisiera comunicar a Usted mi profundo agradecimiento por el buen espíritu de colaboración que existe entre los runcionarios de nuestros dos países y manifestarle mi contianza de que esa buena colaboración seguira rindiendo beneficios comunes para nuestros dos pueblos.

Reciba, Señor General, el testimonio de me mas grata consideración y afecto.

Atentamente,

TOMÁS M. TELLES
Agregado DEA

TMT:jl

Figure 15.5. DEA letter, dated August 27, 1984, from Attaché Tomás M. Telles to General Manuel Noriega, inviting him to attend a regional anti-drug conference in Brazil.

220

Protests sparked in the streets. Our people did what they knew best, and they retaliated upon hearing the news of Nicols Ardito Barletta becoming president of our country. "Election fraud in Panama," the headlines lit up. We were being accused of putting our own man in power. It angered me. Nobody understood the devastation a man like Arnulfo Arias would have caused. He was a tyrant, a man whose traditions had turned to ash. He sought to lead a country that had long since existed. The Panama I knew was different from the one that existed in his memory.

Noriega thought more deeply about the bounty on his head. He did not fear death but rather contemplated his position in life. He sat on his throne, pondering through the days. I stood by his side. One afternoon, there was a group of us inside a government building. Manuel and I represented the PDF, along with some armed protection. The president, politicians, and foreign ambassadors stood and conversed over finger food and cool drinks.

Noriega had his back turned to the double doors in the room. They suddenly swung open, and an officer stomped toward Manuel with a pistol held high and out from his chest. His eyes were red, cheeks trembling. His body reverberated so hard I could feel the tremors at my feet. Manuel didn't move an inch. He stayed still, eyes zoned in on the assassin approaching him. The officer's index finger twitched to touch the trigger, but one of our soldiers fired a round into his arm, and he dropped the pistol to the white-tiled floor. Noriega stepped over him, his shadow engulfing the shaking assassin.

"Who sent you?" Manuel inquired calmly.

"N-nobody, please. I'm sorry, Manuel, señor. I'm so sorry—"

"Stop mumbling and give me a fucking answer," Noriega yelled.

"M-my wife . . . she has been whispering in my ear for months . . . 'Kill him. Get the money,' she says. . . . *Chucha*, she is the reason why I am here! I've been taking pills every day to settle my nerves."

"Take him away," Manuel said, turning his back to the officer.

The American interest had burrowed its way into the minds of our people. I knew pawns would come in droves to dethrone Manuel; that was how it always worked, right from the earliest days of our history. Men would overthrow another and rise to the throne, only to be ousted by a younger man with dreams of power. I vowed to always be by Manuel's side. He was my brother, my greatest accomplice. I would do anything for him. He enabled much of my life. Without Noriega, I don't know where I would have been . . . jail, overseas, famished. Manuel and I kept each other in check. I was his guardian; he was mine. Together, we were ready to take on the challenges that swarmed around us, inching closer by the day.

Chapter 16
Women in Uruguay

A unit of us tore through the city like dogs salivating at the mouth. We cleared every taverna in town out of their stock. We bought drinks for every table of beautiful women. We could have had our choice of any of them. They fell at our feet in admiration. We were celebrities. No cost was too grand, no idea too outlandish, and everything felt within reach. We ripped through a dozen bars. I was losing rationality. My eyes adjusted to the light after stepping out from one taverna in San Francisco, and across the street, I saw that an auction was taking place. "Let's go," I yelled to our group. We stumbled in like the slew of drunkards we were, and we did not give a fuck what anybody thought.

An announcer stood on a stage, blinded by a single spotlight. "Our next item is special," the announcer exclaimed.

A pair of red robes on stage pulled open. I watched as the spotlight shone on an adult bull with a ring through its nose. Its legs shook, eyes red and drooping. The fucker was old, too old for good use. Manuel and I broke into fits of laughter. Our beers swooshed and swayed as we grabbed hold of each other. The audience was silent and still.

"Let's start the bidding," the announcer yelled out. Nobody moved a muscle. I shot my hand into the air. "Twenty-five hundred for the *toro*," I screamed out.

Heads turned, and eyes gazed upon me. Lips were pinned shut. Crickets chirped. Even the announcer was shocked. He froze up, delayed in clearing his throat to speak out. "Twenty-five hundred . . . Does anybody have a higher bid for the bull?" the announcer asked.

Liquor fueled my thoughts.

Sold for twenty-five hundred," he bellowed.

My friends fell to the floor in tears as I stepped on stage to drag the bull outside. I didn't know what to do with the fucking thing. It stared at me in the eyes. Noriega slammed his hand on my shoulder as we both gazed at the aged beast.

"You should name it Bush," he suggested with a smile.

The mid-1980s held some of the most exciting times in my life, for good and bad. My heart and soul lay in Panama. I cared little about outside influence. I simply did what I was paid to do. I accepted that the DEA or CIA would soon ask something big of me. The fear was palpable. Colonel Oliver North and National Security Advisor John Poindexter frequented my nation. Their problems were not our own. The people had taken to the streets in protests fueled by men who called themselves revolutionaries. Hugo Spadafora, a name that lights my nostalgia, was one. It was a tragedy what happened to him—mutilation, body found mangled in Costa Rica. He was a lost soul who became involved in drug smuggling for the Contras. I saw the minds and movements of our people change after that. They took to the media. The world labeled us as savages, an authoritarian regime that silenced its opposition with a blade. "MANUEL ANTONIO NORIEGA ACCUSED OF MURDER AND DRUG SMUGGLING," the newspapers said. Cracks formed beneath us all. I would never say a word to anyone as long as I lived. As soon as we chose not to help the United States in Nicaragua, tensions brewed within our government. Barletta had the gringos whispering in his ear while the DEA paid no mind and continued to ask us favors. There was intelligence provided to us about narco shipping through the Colon Free Trade Zone. I was aware of the loopholes people took when it came to shipments. The DEA knew that, too, and they asked for my help. "Large quantities of ethyl ether are reportedly entering Panama. We believe the product is not leaving the country and, instead, is being transported to a lab somewhere on your soil." The war on communism dwindled when the war on drugs raged. While our streets were filled with people who wanted peace, I was on the ground, at sea, and in the air, providing it. There was no other option. We had to perform to maintain peace. Still, my life was good, and I was happy.

I had more trips to Cuba. I was a master trainer and champion. Time spent in the gallera was most important. I had several cocks that propelled me to the top . . . Snoopy, Pipodicio. This was the peak of competition, in my opinion. Cockfighting became corrupted over the years. Once drugs entered the gallera, the sanctity of the event was tarnished. I thrived during the golden era of this sport. My talents took me all over Central and South America. I won tournaments in the Dominican Republic, Mexico, Peru, Ecuador ... the list goes on. Not every fight was about money, however. Some were about pride. When personal matters made their way into the gallera, it raised the stakes.

There was a man named Dario. He was a fucking culebra, a snake. We were introduced by some of the casino people. He was involved in real estate, and he had a proposal for me. I liked the sound of his idea, so I invested time and money into it. Months went by, and not one word from the fucker. I later found out that he cheated me out of eight hundred thousand dollars from the deal. He was a fucking idiot screwing over a guy like me. He knew my inner circle. He was aware of what happened to men who fucked people like me over. From then on, I wanted to terrorize him. I assumed he was smart enough to understand that showing his face was risky, but the fucker did not hide. We found ourselves at the same gallera one night in Cuba. I was there with some friends, Duque and Sarmiento. I held my prized cock, Snoopy. He was a weapon. His claws were sharp like nails, a true champion born from blood. There were no losses on his record; he was a perfect specimen. Dario's rooster was just as impressive. It had a small flesh wound on its wing, but its chest was thicker, and its claws were longer. The wingspan of the bird was almost twice that of Snoopy's. The fucker's beady little eyes had seen terror.

"We fight for the money," I demanded.

"No, we won't," he responded.

I wanted to slam his head through the wall and shove the rooster up his ass. He walked around like he was invincible. No man was untouchable. Dario had made his way to the very top of my shit list with one stupid fucking comment. "You don't have a choice. Put your fucking chicken in the ring," I exclaimed, eyes filled with rage and fury.

I watched as Snoopy launched forward, tearing up feathers. The squawks and squeals of the animals pierced my eardrums. Blood stained the sandy floor. The sounds of slashes and thrashes echoed. Dario sweat bullets. His head rested in his hands. He leaned against the ring barrier, pupils following the movements of his struggling cock. The crowd screamed. Pints of beer and glasses of tequila and seco splashed and sprayed about. I was soaked. I didn't care. Pride bubbled within me. The money was nothing. Eight hundred thousand was enough to buy a luxury home. I didn't need one. Dario gazed at me with wide eyes. I smiled at him, the dance of our roosters coming to a bloody finale between us. Snoopy dug his claws into his opposition's flesh wound. He tore it open, and blood spurted onto the dusty ground. The air stood still. Bodies stayed in place. Dario's rooster crashed into dust, and the crowd erupted. Money fluttered down from the heavens.

I approached Dario.

He took small steps backward until he hit the wall.

I patted the side of his face. "Loyalty is the only thing I asked of you," I stated.

"I'll pay you back, Carlos. I can only give you increments; my money's tied up in a few places," Dario responded, trembling.

I rose through the ranks not because I was a fighter, nor was it because I was intelligent. It wasn't my training with Mossad or the DEA, and it certainly wasn't due to my status as a womanizer. It was all about my loyalty. My word was gold. If a friend needed me to do something, I would get it done. It was simple. No woman, rooster, glass of seco, or stack of cash would deter me from doing my job. I could only sleep at night when I knew I had fulfilled my responsibilities. Men like Dario enraged me. A deal made between men must be honored.

I returned to Panama in chaos. I helped Noriega keep a firm grip on the PDF. It was essential that panic not rumble through the military. We were the heartbeat of the nation, and if we fell, the country would have crumbled into dust. Our chief of staff, Colonel Roberto Diaz Herrera, asked to meet with me in the midst of the outlash. He was important to us, a man who had risen through the ranks just as I had.

"The people are not happy, and things are getting worse," he expressed.

I never said a bad word about Manuel. Herrera wanted me to talk, just like the countless others who had approached me over the years. I would never take another side. Still, his concern was valid. It became clear there were men amongst us, important men like Diaz Herrera, who were dissatisfied. We had to watch our backs. It was in our nature to protest. It was now our responsibility to control what was happening, and to do that, we used the PDF. Our military squashed our problems in the streets while our narco agents extinguished the flames that threatened the United States.

VII.- <u>AÑO 1985</u>

<u>FEBRERO</u>   Las Fuerzas Especiales Antinarcotráfico logran detec-
tar en el Aeropuerto Internacional"OMAR TORRIJOS H.",
un sinnúmero de casos de cocaína, de los cuales, en
5 casos se incautó 11 kilos de cocaína. De igual manera se logra la captura de la chilena MARIA CRISTINA
SALAZAR CACERES, quien intentó introducir en dos gran
des maletas, 5 kilos de cocaína pura en 16 bolsas plás
ticas. El móvil por el cual se procedión a la investi
gación de la señora SALAZAR CACERES, se debió a la des
comunal estructura de confección de las maletas, lo cual
era fuera de lo común.

Figure 16.1. Chronological summary of narco seizures and arrests in February 1985.

229

Pág._____

FEBRERO

Las Fuerzas de Defensa de Panamá entregan in
formación a la Agencia del DEA en Panamá, relacionada
a una de las bandas de la mafia colombiana más grande
que se activaba en ese momento. La información mencio
naba a los colombianos JORGE LUIS OCHOA y GILBERTO RO-
DRIGUEZ OREJUELA como principales cabecillas del narco
tráfico internacional.

Basados en esta información la Agencia del DEA logra
la captura, en coordinación con las autoridades españo
les, de JORGE LUIS OCHOA y de GILBERTO RODRIGUEZ ORE-
JUELA, a quienes les hicieron cargos por narcotráfico
en Estados Unidos, convirtiendose en prófugos de la
justicia norteamericana.

Una investigación realizada por la Fuerza Especial
Antinarcotráfico de Panamá, logró establecer que
OCHOA y RODRIGUEZ OREJUELA, eran dueños del Banco FIRST
INTERAMERICAS BANK,S.A. en Panamá y a través del cual
movían las ganancias del tráfico de drogas.

Las evidencias presentadas por la Fuerza de Defensa de
Panamá ante las autoridades judiciales, conllevaron a
la actuación inmediata contra el Banco que fue interve-
nido, cerrandose sus operaciones en forma definitiva.

MAYO

Se arrestaron a los ciudadanos brasileros REGINA PESCHIE
RO y FRANCISCO BATISTA DA SILVA, quienes procedentes del
Brasil, trataron de introducir al país 5 kilos de cocaína
pura.

Se dá inici a una operación de patrullaje conjunto aero-
naval entre unidades representativas de la Marina Nacional de las Fuerzas de Defensa de Panamá y el Servicio
de Guardacostas de los Estados Unidos de América, con
el objeto de llevar una acción conjunta en interferir
las actividades marítimas del tráfico internacional de
estupefacientes en áreas a lo largo de la costa pacífi
ca de Centro y Sur América, procediendose en base a di
rectrices establecidas por mutuo acuerdo entre la República de Panamá y los Estados Unidos de América, el
abordaje, confiscación del contrabando y arresto de tri
pulación en naves involucradas que enarbolen bandera pa
nameña.

El Inspector LUIS QUIEL, Jefe de la Oficina de Coordina
ción Internacional de las Fuerzas de Defensa de Panamá,
sirvió como testigo de cargo para presentar evidencias
de investigaciones a escala internacional del tráfico
de drogas, en el juicio contra las naves "PACIFIC STAR"
y "SEA DOLPHIN" de bandera norteamericana en la ciudad
de Los Angeles, California.

*Figure 16.2. Chronological summary of narco
seizures and arrests in February and May 1985.*

230

Junio   : El ciudadano panameño FLOYD CARLTON, en aso-
            cio con la organización dirigida por el nar-
            cotraficante colombiano PABLO ESCOBAR GAVIRIA,
            introducen desde Colombia grandes cantidades
            de cocaína a los Estados Unidos de América,
            en compañía del piloto panameño TEOFILO WAT-
            SON. En Panamá, es capturado ALBERTO AUDEMAR
            FARATAY, ciudadano norteamericano de origen
            francés, fugitivo de las autoridades estado-
            unidenses. AUDEMAR FARATAY, representando
            a la organización de ESCOBAR GAVIRIA, inten-
            tó ejecutar actos de violencia en contra del
            grupo de FLOYD CARLTON en Panamá. Ambas or-
            ganizaciones fueron desarticuladas y AUDEMAR
            FARATAY, entregado a la justicia de los Esta-
            dos Unidos.

            En un operativo de la Fuerza Especial Anti-
            narcotráfico llevado a cabo en el Puerto de
            Cristobal en el litoral Atlántico del país,
            se logró la captura de 65 tanques de 55 ga-
            lones cada uno de Eter Etílico, que iban co-
            mo carga de cerveza hacia Buenaventura, Co-
            lombia. En el citado operativo, se detuvo
            a los ciudadanos colombianos CARLOS GUTIERREZ
            y JOSE DIAZ, quienes informaron que éstos tan-
            ques iban destinados a laboratorios clandes-
            tinos del narcotráfico en Colombia.

Agosto   Se logra la captura del avión con matrícula
            boliviana CP-1620 , el cual tenía 8 maletas
            que contenían 12 kilos de cocaína cada una.
            En dicha aprenhensión, fueron arrestados el
            ciudadano panameño PEDRO ROGNONI y los pilo-
            tos bolivianos CARLOS CASTEDO y CARLOS YAMA-
            MOTO.

Septiembre: Las Fuerzas de Defensa de Panamá organizó y
            llevó a efecto un operativo para erradicar
            la presencia de plantaciones de marihuana en
            el Archipiélago de las Perlas. La Agencia

Figure 16.3. Chronological summary of narco seizures and arrests between June, August, and September 1985 (the latter is continued in figure 16.4).

del DEA había comunicado que el Departamento de Estado norteamericano había considerado la realización de un operativo conjunto, FUERZAS DE DEFENSA-DEA, para fumigar y destruir áreas donde hubiesen plantaciones de marihuana en el Archipiélago de las Perlas. El día 12 de septiembre, se inició el operativo conjunto de fumigación, comenzando con 94 hectáreas en la localidad de LA ENSENADA y la Isla PEDRO GONZALEZ. El día 16 de septiembre, se fumigaron un total de 142 hectáreas al norte de la ISLA DEL REY. El operativo de fumigación y destrucción de plantaciones de marihuana, le quitó a la mafia narcotraficante, la ganancia de $144 millones de dólares.

Noviembre : En operativo de la Fuerza Especial Antinarcotráfico de las Fuerzas de Defensa de Panamá, se logra la captura del ciudadano colombiano JAIRO ALBERTO CASTAEÑADA DE LEON, quien en asocio con el panameño ROLANDO ARNETH PEREZ FERNANDEZ, realizaban una transacción de venta de 20 kilos de cocaína refinada y 10.730 kilos de pasta básica de cocaína, droga que fue decomisada al momento del arresto en un centro comercial de la ciudad capital.

Diciembre : En acción coordinada con el Agente Especial a cargo del DEA en Panamá, THOMAS TELLES, se logra la captura de los ciudadanos costarricenses JOHAN LOTZ ARTAVIA y RODOLFO ACUÑA CARCANTE, prófugos de la justicia norteamericana. Los ciudadanos costarricenses en mención, eran requeridos en los Estados Unidos, por su participación directa en el asesinato del Agente del DEA en México, ENRIQUE CAMARENA y por estar vinculados a la organización del narcotraficante mexicano RAFAEL "CARO" QUINTERO.

Figure 16.4. Chronological summary of narco seizures and arrests September (continued from figure 16.3), November, and December (continued in figure 16.5) 1985.

En el año de 1985, las autoridades panameñas decomisaron 39,032.1 gramos de cocaína, 110,820 gramos de marihuana y 4,950 galones de químico de acetona. Se deportaron un total de 33 delincuentes de los cuales fueron entregados 6 fugitivos a los Estados Unidos de América, en coordinación con la Agencia del DEA en Panamá. Asimismo, en coordinación con Agencias Federales y Servicio de Guardacostas norteamericanos, el Gobierno panameño autorizó la captura de 8 naves con bandera panameña e incautado 256, 000 libras de marihuana

VIII-Año 1986

Enero   : Se dió inicio al Segundo Programa de erradicación de marihuana por medio de fumigación aérea en coordinación con la Agencia del DEA en Panamá. Después de llevar a cabo varias faces del operativo, se llegó al exterminio de 199 hectáreas sembradas de marihuana. Las áreas fumigadas fueron detectadas en la ISLA DE PEDRO GONZALEZ y la ISLA DEL REY.

En ese mismo mes, se logra la captura del fugitivo de la justicia estadounidense, OSIRIS SANTIS CORDERO, de nacionalidad cubana, quien formaba parte de una organización de cubanos radicados en Miami, que habían llegado a transportar un total de 600,000 libras de marihuana. SANTIS CORDERO, vivía en el interior del país en compañía de otros cubanos prófugos de las autoridades norteamericanas. Solicitado por las autoridades legales de los Estados Unidos de América, SANTIS CORDERO, fue apresado por las autoridades panameñas y deportado a solicitud de la Oficina del Marshall de Miami. Posteriormente, los socios y compañeros de SANTIS CORDERO, fueron deportados también a los Estados Unidos.

Figure 16.5. Chronological summary of narco seizures and arrests in December 1985 (continued from figure 16.4) and January 1986.

233

After we forced President Vallarino out of office some years prior, our government was under a microscope. We had seen regimes rise and fall all around us, in Central and South America, since the early 1970s. World leaders looked for examples of anti-democratic behavior, and we exhibited it. Men like Jimmy Carter criticized us. We had problems; every nation did. So, as Noriega's trusted advisors, we had to come up with a solution to the problem we faced in the streets and in the media.

"Nicolas Barletta has called for an investigation into the death of Spadafora," Noriega stated. Barletta sat between us and the United States government. He heard it from both sides, but he was Panamanian, and he needed to put Panama first. "Barletta needs to go. He cannot be trusted anymore."

We were being criticized for the act. It needed to happen. Nicolas was cast to the side and lived in obscurity. Noriega thought it was best to put our friend Eric Arturo Delvalle in the position of president. He represented our interests through the Democratic Revolutionary Party, and we felt he was a reliable man in the midst of an international controversy. They were tiring times, and Noriega and I knew we needed to blow off steam. So, when an invite came from Uruguay, Manuel decided to bring me.

Noriega broke out into hysterical laughter when I told him about Dario's downfall on our jet. I spared no details, from the look on Dario's face when I punched him to the sound he made when he crashed into the dirt. Our plane sat on the runway at Tocumen. Uruguay awaited us. We were delayed thirty minutes because of a small rainstorm that was brushing by the central coast of Panama. Manuel and I were beaten down from drinking the night before. The flights for the day would take hours, so it was a good time to sleep. Still, we each had several glasses of whiskey, seco, and beer before the bird could take off. Booze was the only cure for our headaches. Two air hostesses in short skirts, high white socks, and black shoes strutted down the aisles and bent over when they asked us questions. They knew what they were doing. We were powerful men who could take them off that bird at a moment's notice and change their lives. The thrill of lust overcame me often, and I seized every opportunity I had. Most men lost the ability to pull women as they grew older. Not me, not Manuel.

"There are going to be some beautiful women in Uruguay, Carlitos. They have some of the most gorgeous ones in the world."

"Better than Colombia?"

"I don't know about that. But I tell you this because we need to still be smart. Uruguay is in ruins. Its people hate their leaders, the men we are to meet."

"Don't worry, señor. I will make sure you are safe."

"I know you will, my friend. It needed to be said. You and I think with more than one head. At least one of us needs to think with the right head while we are so far from home."

"I understand, señor."

"That doesn't mean we can't have some fun. The last time I came here, I fucked a woman with the biggest tits I have ever seen."

"How big?"

"Inconceivable."

My hands clung to my seat. I could hardly look out the window. I had to shut the blinds and drink ten more whiskeys just so I could fall asleep. Flashes of lightning and torrential winds consumed my dreams. I awoke in a rush of sweat. My chest puffed out with every harsh breath. The lights within the cabin had been shut off. The air hostesses chatted with each other while filing their nails. Manuel rested his chin atop his fist and gazed at the clouds beneath us. He hadn't slept a wink.

We landed in the middle of the afternoon. The pilot personally walked us down to the tarmac, and he shook Manuel's hand. "I will see you tomorrow morning here, yes?" the pilot asked Noriega.

"Let's call it ten a.m.," he responded.

Eighteen hours in Montevideo. I looked forward to it. Every chance to learn was an opportunity to grow. The more I knew, the greater my legacy would become. A private black car took us right to the heart of Uruguay's government. The bricks themselves were older than the United States. I could feel the history, the wars, and the blood all wash over me as the car stopped, and we were led inside to an illustrious room of the minds. Two dozen empty chairs lined the space, and all faced a stage with a golden podium standing tall.

Our Uruguayan contact, Pianta, charged into the room and threw his hands into the air. "Señor Noriega, Señor Wittgreen, it's a pleasure. Welcome to Uruguay," he said.

"Thank you for having us," Noriega responded.

"Señor Wittgreen, would you mind if I stole Manuel from you for one hour? There are some things I wish to speak with him about alone."

"I am not leaving unless Manuel wants me to," I stated.

"It's okay, Carlitos," Noriega said. "Okay, buddy, let's get the business out of the way," and he followed Pianta, leaving the room.

I stood alone with the two Uruguayan guards. They were silent. "What are your names?" I asked.

They looked at each other like frightened puppies, unsure about who should speak first or if they should speak at all.

"Well?"

The larger one stepped forward. His gaze shot over my shoulder; he would not look me in the eyes. "My name is Gabriel," he said before taking a step back and standing upright.

His smaller buddy repeated Gabriel's movement. "I'm Kiko," he muttered.

"Okay. What is there to do here?" I asked.

"Well . . . there isn't much to do right now, señor," Gabriel said. "Señor Pianta is throwing a party here tonight in our ballroom. Until then, I'm afraid there is little to stimulate.

"Chucha madre. So you are saying I have to just fucking stand here until they're finished talking?"

"I-I'm afraid so, señor," Gabriel responded, almost shivering through his words.

Kiko spoke up. "Well, actually—"

"Yes?" I interrupted.

"Actually, there is a television in a room down the hall."

"I didn't come to Uruguay to grab my cock and watch fucking telenovelas all day."

"Roberto Duran is fighting, señor."

"Today?"

"Very soon, señor. Maybe fifteen, maybe thirty minutes from now."

I demanded they take me to the television. Kiko fiddled with the stations as Gabriel fetched me a cool drink. Guards stopped to see what the commotion was. "What is going on?" the guards asked.

Gabriel returned with my beverage. The liquid boasted an amber color, and the cubes of ice crackled against the glass.

"What is this?" I asked.

"*Fernet con coca*. It is an Argentinian drink," Gabriel responded.

The concoction was delicious. I tapped on the glass with my index finger. Gabriel scurried to get me another just as Kiko got the television working, and two gringo broadcasters lit up the screen.

Roberto Duran was just a boy when I met him, an amateur who sold newspapers and fought caballeros in the streets of Panama City. I saw myself when I looked at him, but at that time, Duran had shot to superstardom. He was the pinnacle of boxing, especially in Central America. His name shone in lights on the most impressive stadiums in the world. Duran had just come off major victories at that time. One was against Jose Cuevas of Mexico, one was against Davey Moore at Madison Square Garden, and the other was against Jimmy Batten of the United Kingdom.

There was a relentlessness about him. He always had a goal to achieve, an obstacle to beat. Duran was a dog of brilliant proportions. Rumor has it his trainers would torture him during weight-loss regimes. Roberto would be held down, and a steak would dangle before him, the juices dripping onto his beard and chin, barely getting a taste before the meat was thrown into the trash. Not many people know this, but in 1978, Roberto bought a building in the city with some of his winnings from the world stage. This structure was shit. I assumed it was older than the city itself. Duran wanted to own the place but not have to deal with its problems. Tenants complained, and the police were called. It was a mess, and as a favor to a good friend, I took care of it for him. The property moved into someone else's hands, Roberto got his money back, and I had the satisfaction of helping the very man I watched defeat his opponent on live television. I felt a great pride in my nation.

Manuel's meeting ended, and we were shown to our hotel rooms. They were nothing short of immaculate. A warm hue lit up my bed as I lay atop it and gazed at the beige paint above. My life moved so fast that sometimes, it was hard to recognize the position I was in. There I was, just a boy from Chiriqui, born into a modest family, lying in a silk bed within the walls of Uruguay's most prestigious hotel.

A knock at my door rumbled along the walls, and I jolted up from my bed. Manuel entered in a fine military suit, bearing every badge of honor our nation had to offer. "How do I look?" he asked me.

"Like a general," I responded.

"Good, these fuckers need to know that I'm not all smiles and hugs. A little fear is a good thing, Carlitos."

"Did you hear about Duran's victory?"

"I did. He is the pride of Panama. He represents us well," Noriega stated. "Get ready; we will go to the ballroom soon."

I wore my military uniform, just like Manuel. We were among the first to occupy the ballroom, but after three or four drinks, the entire space had filled up. Several bands played for the crowd and then left. The Uruguayans had invited some of the most important people in South America to this party. That was really why we were there. Noriega must have shaken two hundred hands. From Bolivian businessmen to Peruvian legislators, anybody with a piece of power on the continent was there. Just a few years prior, Uruguay's president, Juan María Bordaberry, closed its parliament and ruled with the assistance of a junta of military generals. They had a coup in 1973, just as we did in 1968.

I found myself in a conversation with the ambassador to Chile in Uruguay. This ambassador was a funny man. After all these years, I cannot remember his name, but I do remember the laughs we shared. He was a dog. When a beautiful woman walked by, he ogled. His hands had a mind of their own. "How did you find the IDEC conference in June?" the ambassador asked.

That conference was important. It was a time for everyone fighting the war on drugs to convene in one location. The DEA had men all over Santiago. We wanted to speak with John Lawn, the DEA administrator, but we were avoided. It was clear our relationship was transactional.

9 de julio de 1985.

General Manuel Antonio Noriega
Comandante Jefe
Fuerzas de Defensa
Republica de Panamá

Estimado General Noriega:

Hago referencia a su carta del 21 de junio de 1985, la cuál me fue entregada en la Conferencia Internacional sobre el Esfuerzo de Drogas en Chile.

Siento mucho que no tuvimos la oportunidad de conocernos en Chile y debo excursarme por no haber podido parar en Panamá en mi regreso hacía los Estados Unidos.

Espero encontrarme con usted tan pronto como nuestra agenda lo permita. Mientras, le extiendo mis mejores deseos en sus continuados éxitos en la lucha contra la amenaza de la droga, la cuál nos afecta a todos.

Sinceramente,

John C. Lawn
Administrador Interino

Figure 16.6. Letter dated July 9, 1985, from Acting DEA Administrator John C. Lawn to General Manuel Noriega, apologizing for not meeting him during the International Drug Effort Conference in Chile, expressing regret for not stopping in Panama on his return, and extending best wishes for Panama's continued success in combating drug trafficking.

I continuously checked on Manuel. I never knew who was a threat, even in a room so pristine. The crowd around Noriega erupted in laughter. A Cuban band took the stage, and their music played. People started to move their bodies along with the rhythm. I had no fucking idea what the song was, but I sang along

241

regardless. Manuel threw his arm over my shoulder and yelled out, "This is the guy who wrote the song!"

Chucha, some fucking people were so gullible that they brought us drinks all night. "You created 'Dos Gardenias'?" they asked in awe.

I lied to every single one of them. "Of course I did," I would say, taking credit from Carrillo.

Everyone got louder as the night progressed. Dancing took the floor, and the tapping of shoes and the laughter of women echoed. Manuel patted the side of my face. "I'm going to show you something, Carlitos. Are you ready?" he asked.

"Yes, señor," I responded.

He closed one eye and pointed into the crowd. Dozens of well-dressed bodies pranced back and forth to the rhythm of the beat. "Look, in the silver dress," he whispered.

My eyes shot wide open. I gulped. The saliva trailed down my throat. I felt it all the way. "Chucha," I mumbled. Standing before me was a woman with the largest tits I have ever seen.

"I wasn't joking, Carlitos," Manuel said.

I practically floated toward her. My head was in the clouds. Manuel stepped off; I didn't see where or with whom. My lady was charming. I made her laugh and smile. We drank together. Every other conversation was blurred. It was static.

"You never asked for my name," she said after some time.

"What is it?" I asked, gaze unbroken.

"It's Penelope," she responded with a perfect smile. Her teeth glistened in the gentle light of the ballroom. A glisten shone in her big, round eyes.

I gripped her gently and led her toward the exit. Her fingers ran up and down my back. Heads turned to watch us exit. Men gawked, and women shifted in jealousy. I stopped at the exit. "Chucha, Manuel," I whispered. "One moment, *bonita.*"

The space was crowded. Waves of suits and dresses fluttered by. I maneuvered through it all. "Manuel? Manuel?" I yelled over and over. He was nowhere to be found. I pulled men to the side. "Have you seen Manuel?" I asked.

"Yes, about thirty minutes ago. He was with a woman," one responded. "Actually, he was with several women," the man added.

Manuel was insatiable when it came to the fairer sex. He always wanted more. He was a dog constantly chasing a bone. "Did he go to the hotel?" I asked.

"He did not. Two of the women he left with live together in an apartment in La Teja. This is not a very nice neighborhood in Montevideo," he said.

I looked at my lady standing by the exit. Her hands were clasped together, gently squeezing her breasts together. She looked at me and only me. I could have had one of the greatest nights of my life, but I knew I had to find my friend.

I was fucking drunk. The cab driver babbled on, but I did not listen. My face was pressed to the glass. The surroundings grew dimmer and dimmer. We passed by a sign that read La Teja. It hung from the iron pole that jutted up from the cracked concrete below. The buildings were made of red brick, and almost half of them appeared to be derelict. Shitty cars were carelessly parked at angles by dirty sidewalks. Vermin of the night stumbled around and screamed obscenities in the street. Thugs gazed at the cab as we pulled to a halt outside an apartment building. I paid the driver and sprinted to the door of the building. It was locked. I rattled it powerfully. A group of men gathered around a taco stand across the street. They watched as I screamed and yelled, trying to rip the door open. "Where is Manuel?" I bellowed to the heavens.

Caballeros across the street set down their food and approached me with malicious intent.

I turned to them with clenched fists. "What the fuck do you want?" I yelled.

"You're making a scene," one of them said. Six big fuckers surrounded me. They wore ragged clothes. My suit sparkled in comparison. The night was loud. Snarling rumbled as if they were a pack of hyenas.

"Nobody is going to touch me," I stated. My fist throbbed as I banged it against the apartment door over and over. Chucha, I was frustrated. The thugs remained. "If one of you fucking assholes touches me, it will not go well," I said.

A step forward caught my attention. The skinniest, slimiest caballero wanted to take me on. His bony arms lifted out from his chest, and his knuckles jutted out from his clenched fists. When the asshole jabbed at me, I swiftly dodged his blow and pummeled him in the nose. He fell backward and slapped the cement with a thud. Two of his amigos picked him up by either arm and knocked him into consciousness.

"Go eat your fucking tacos and leave me alone," I yelled. I wouldn't take any fucking shit. My friend was in that apartment building. It was not safe for him to be in a neighborhood like this alone. All it took was one of our enemies to pay a fucking ladrona with a gun to walk up there and smoke him while his pants were around his ankles. I banged on the door over and over and over.

"Carlos?" Noriega's voice echoed.

"Manuel!" I yelled.

I stepped out into the street and leaned my head back. Three stories from the roof, Manuel's head stuck out from a window with curtains that fluttered in the breeze. His head popped back into the building, and after a moment, he rushed out into the street with his shirt unbuttoned and his belt hanging from his uniform. He embraced me with a hug. We laughed uncontrollably, the thugs surrounding and watching us in confusion. "Thank God you are here, Carlitos. I have no fucking idea where I am," he stated.

The sun soon rose on the horizon as we struggled to stay awake in the back of a rickety cab. When we stumbled into the hotel, we went right to our rooms, grabbed our bags, turned back around, and drove straight to the airport.

"Chucha, what a night," Noriega muttered, closing his eyes and leaning his head against the interior wall of the jet.

I gazed through the Plexiglas at the intersecting runways. Planes full of people landed and took off. The city of Montevideo shimmered along the glowing horizon. Chucha, what a night.

Chapter 17
Crashing the Cocaine Party

A strand of light illuminated particles of dust above my head as a ray struck a whiteboard. Images of shipping containers with the names Yerida Inc., Insumos Químicos Ind., and Depósitos Generales SA written on their sides projected before me. Men coughed at my sides. To my right, Diaz Herrera; to my left, Luis Quiel; and on his left, Lucinio Miranda. The director of DENI, Nivaldo Madrinan, stood at the top of the room; a glow reflected in the lenses of his glasses. Noriega was in the front row.

"A Panamanian-flagged ship by the name of *Sandra* departed Colón on April 19, 1984, with 180 tanks of ethyl ether. Colombian patrol boats intercepted the shipment using electronic trackers. Our intelligence revealed the chemicals were consigned to these companies in Colón: Yerida Inc., Insumos Químicos Ind., and Depósitos Generales SA," Nivaldo read out. "And, then, on June 5, our men uncovered a plot by Méndez, Tribaldos, and Castillo to pay two million dollars for the ether's release. Colombian nationals José Eduardo Zambrano Caicedo and Luis Guillermo Ángel Restrepo were arrested." Images of men in the Medellin

Cartel flashed before me. "Luis is affiliated with Medellín Cartel leaders Fabio and Jorge Ochoa. José Eduardo handles the finances, creating shell companies to launder money."

Colonel Julián Melo, our executive secretary of Defense Command, shot up from behind me. "How do these men keep getting ethyl ether into the country?"

I wondered the same thing. Our operations were airtight. We collaborated with our neighbors. It was rare to have large shipments bypass us.

The images changed on screen, and Nivaldo left us with a photo taken above one of our rainforests. I could tell by the vegetation. "I believe there's a lot more happening in the Darien than we think," Madrinan stated. The gap was an area we all knew of but spent little time near. Noriega had had some experiences out there in his childhood. He knew it better than any of us.

"Our agents have heard rumors, too," Quiel piped up.

"The vegetation is too thick. It would take months to clear up enough space to build a lab. It's not worth it," Melo yelled out.

"Not being seen is worth it," I mentioned.

"Transporting in and out would be near impossible unless there was an airstrip," Lucinio spoke.

"The men in Galeta would have picked something up over transmissions," Diaz Herrera interjected.

"We need to focus on the ports and figure out where all this ethyl ether is coming from. Our resources are not well spent wasting time in the Darien," Melo said.

Noriega and I caught eyes. I shook my head. The bickering got us nowhere. I couldn't stand the back and forth. Some men just wanted to have their voices heard. There weren't many of us who could step outside of our ego and view a problem with objectivity. We all had our own agenda.

"We will send a surveillance team over the Darien to see if we can find anything," Nivaldo concluded. The whirring projector fell silent as we sat still.

Noriega jumped to his feet and turned to us. "I know some of you are concerned with the headlines. The protests against us are natural. It is what our people do. If anybody wishes to speak with me, you know where I am." Manuel was accessible. He wasn't a leader who hid from the light; he basked in it. Yet he made his decisions in the shadows. It was important that nobody knew what we were planning.

The media outside of Panama had been highlighting accusations against Noriega. They were claiming he was using our intelligence and political position to personally benefit from the drug trade. We needed to combat those stories. It was always an iceberg; 70 percent drama, 30 percent truth. I had good standing with our nation's publications. They were not necessarily the problem at first, but rather, it was the foreign journalists. They arrived with prejudice, be it malicious or not. What the public heard was never the full truth, whether it was the gringos who told them or us. We needed to find ways to clean Panama's image in the papers.

"Harvard has invited me to give a speech at the John F. Kennedy School of Government," Manuel said to me with a smile.

"Congratulations, hermano."

"How ironic."

"You deserve the flowers, señor."

"Can I run the speech by you?" Manuel asked.

"Si, of course."

"I have been asked to speak to you today about the role of the military in the Central American peace process," Manuel said. "I will begin by discussing how military leaders can constructively influence the political, social, and economic improvement of the region, focusing on El Salvador, Nicaragua, Guatemala, and Honduras. If you believe that the solution to the current conflicts in Central America is purely military, then I would have nothing further to add. The fact that you are gathered in an intellectual environment like Harvard University suggests you understand that deeper causes must be analyzed and addressed to find more productive and cost-effective solutions. For Panama, the military's responsibility in the increasingly volatile Central American situation is significant, both nationally and globally. Panama, with its interoceanic canal, plays a key role in global security. Actions in Central America directly impact the security and stability of Panama, as well as international norms of security. The role of Central American armed forces is critical in seeking an effective solution. If we desire peace in the region, each country must maintain its dignity and national independence while working to overcome underdevelopment. The armed forces must play a vital role in this broader development.

"Many individuals and sectors simplify the problems of Central America, viewing them in terms of freedom versus oppression or dictatorship versus democracy. However, closer inspection reveals a more complex reality. The real cause of conflict stems from the exclusion of the people from political and economic life. Central Americans have not been given the opportunity to shape their own destinies. To resolve these problems, democracy must be understood as more than just an election. True democracy involves economic and social rights, and the people must have a clear understanding of these principles. Panama, like other countries, should embrace this broader concept of democracy. The root causes of political and military instability in Central America are clear: extreme poverty, social injustice, illiteracy, and ignorance. These societies are largely characterized by subsistence agriculture and single-crop production, low average income and high underemployment, high illiteracy rates and lack of basic sanitation, high infant mortality, malnutrition, and inadequate housing.

"In El Salvador, the military faces a battle against guerrillas who are attracted by poverty and have lost faith in civilian governments. The military is now their only interlocutor. In Guatemala, the military was previously disconnected from the poor and exploited rural populations. However, under President General Mejía Vítores, the armed forces are now working to reconnect with the peasant majority through literacy campaigns and community development. Nicaragua has seen forty-five years of political instability, with a National Guard that failed to serve the people. This failure proved that military defeat is directly linked to the lack of popular support for military doctrine. In Honduras, the military is composed of younger officers with university training. These officers have worked to maintain balance and tolerance despite ideological tensions with neighboring countries.

"The contradiction is clear: Central America needs political, economic, and social reforms to eliminate the causes of subversion and war, but the ongoing conflict prevents meaningful recovery. International economic aid has been insufficient and too conditional, with many programs exacerbating discontent and conflict, as seen in countries like Ecuador and Panama. Amid this situation, I urge agreement on one point: no government can function alone, detached from the military. In Central America and Latin America, the military's role must be clearly defined and aligned with the national mission. When the military's functions are in harmony with this role, its power can be a force for peace. True democracy and human rights must be grounded in the reality of the people, not in demagoguery or empty propaganda. The right to life and the right to not live in hunger are fundamental human rights, and we must ensure that these rights are respected."

Noriega gave an almost exact rendition of that speech at Harvard. I don't believe it worked in changing international opinion, but there was a group of educated young men and women who had the opportunity to see the true colors of a man who was

251

being set alight in the media. In addition to stunts like that, Noriega also went on *60 Minutes* in order to try to show the gringos what kind of a man he was and how the allegations against him were untrue. It was there that he revealed the documents Trujillo would one day own for himself. He flashed them to the camera: Letters of appreciation from John C. Lawn and other DEA administrators. Noriega kept them as proof, collateral in some ways, a bargaining chip he could play if his life or loyalty were at risk. But the interview backfired, and the edit that aired made him look like a Central American devil. There was not much we could do. Castro warned us not to poke the white bear but to feed it; that's what we continued to do.

Men like myself hopped aboard planes to undergo surveillance of the Darien in search of a lab. The transport plane I took was American. The structure was narrow and sleek, but the interior had been stripped of everything but the seats pinned up against the walls. The metal vibrated as we took off. I prayed to God for a safe flight, and I steadied my breathing. My men were silent. I was designated to lead. The boys were young and building experience. We liked to fuck around with them, but we treated our soldiers with respect. We were at the age when the younger guys would look up to us. They would recite our own exploits as if they were folk tales from the days of my *abuelo*. Once the jet rose high enough, we could walk around and look out the windows at the outline of the coast thousands of feet below. I felt vertigo when I set eyes on the land. My heart sank into my stomach as if I was thrown out of the hatch by my enemies.

"Señor Wittgreen?" a young soldier asked.

"Yes?"

"It's a pleasure to meet you, señor," he said, a hopeful shake in his voice.

I was like a celebrity to them. Noriega was the most important man in Panama, and by extension, that made me one of the most important people in the country. My name was known, but I was smart; I rarely let the ink dry. There were no articles focusing on my dealings. I was a successful covert diplomat. A civilian could pass by me on the street and not recognize me, but if people were to look, they would see a man who had been involved in decisions that changed their lives forever.

"You want to hear a story about Noriega?" I said.

Their eyes exploded wide in unison. My words would hold them captive.

"It was some years ago, on November 28 . . . yes, it was November 28. Manuelito and I were in Chorrera. I was challenged to a shootout, and I lost. I wanted to fight the motherfucker who beat me, but Manuel grabbed me and said, 'Chill out, Carlitos. Let's go to a party and talk to some women.' So, we go to this party nearby at our friend Feria de la Cifalunco's house. Manuel starts playing soccer, and I begin talking to women. A man, a cheap little nobody, a buzzing fucking fly in my ear, well, he doesn't like me, and he makes it clear. So, I go to the bathroom, and this motherfucker ambushes me with a woman, and she slaps me. I ask her if she knows who I am. I am mad, ready to break her boyfriend's ugly little jaw. Out of nowhere, Manuel enters and takes everybody's attention. He gets in close to that asshole, and he tells him there was a man he reminded him of, another asshole from his past who crossed his father, and so Noriega strapped C-4 to the underbelly of this asshole's car, and poof. When Manuel speaks the final word of the anecdote, the little fuckers go silent. The woman puts her hands behind her back. They beg to leave with their eyes, afraid of what would happen if they turn. . . . Noriega defused the entire situation with one short speech; that is all it took. Chucha, the moment they left, he broke out laughing and couldn't stop for five fucking minutes."

"What happened after that?" the young soldier asked.

"We went back inside and had our way with the night."

The plane rumbled suddenly. I grabbed hold of my seatbelt straps and inhaled sharply. Men on their feet stumbled forward. "Chucha," I muttered as the aircraft adjusted itself. We had been in that jet for a while. "Let's see where we are," I said as I unstrapped myself. The floor vibrated under the soles of my boots. I walked to the cockpit. The two pilots didn't turn to face me. "How much longer?" I asked.

One pilot turned to me. His mustache hung thinly over his mouth. "We're passing over the Darien now," he said.

The boys unstrapped themselves and turned to get full access to the window. I carefully paced down the aisle toward the back of the plane. The white clouds rushed by the windows every other moment before the never-ending blue opened up. I hunkered down at a window and looked out to where the rainforest met the ocean. I could barely see the white tips. There was no living man or woman within sight. That was an uncharted area. We spent the better part of an hour with our faces to the Plexiglas.

Then a young recruit yelled out, "Señor Wittgreen, I see a helicopter!"

I rushed to his window. The rest of the boys all tried to get a peek, careful not to lean too close to me. My eyes scanned the Darien rainforest. Trees spanned for miles. Hills and ridgetops jutted out from the earth. In the distance, dark clouds hung over the Darien and unleashed thrashings of rain upon all living creatures beneath. Everything I saw was unrelenting, and then I laid eyes upon an AH-64 Apache helicopter sitting in a freshly lumbered block of the forest. Somebody had spent time chopping down those trees and making the earth flat enough to land. The boys swarmed me from all sides, trying to get a look. It was the largest lab I had ever seen. It stood alone in an ocean of green. My eyes fixated on the structure. I could feel my heartbeat slowly rise. "Chucha, look at that," the recruits mumbled. The clouds opened for us long enough to snap some pictures, and in a flash, our jet was covered by white. We turned around and made our way home.

Nivaldo Madrinan immediately received word from us. He communicated our findings to the Colombian military. The lab was closer to their border. Still, we wanted to send men to the site. Inspectors Quiel and Lucinio Miranda put together a team quickly. The next morning, we flew right back to the Darien, and this time, there was no sickness in my stomach. The Colombians were ambushing the site; we wanted a taste. Electricity ran through my veins. I could practically already feel my finger on the pulse of the trigger. My unit was loud. We thunderously hung above the forest, and soldiers climbed down ropes. We spread out through the landing zone, but it very quickly became clear what we were there for. Shrouded by shrubbery, a makeshift laboratory sent smells of gasoline swarming through the air. My foot broke through the door, and my men ambushed the lab from all angles. Cartel men dropped to their knees and held their hands high. I roamed around the facility. It was unlike anything I had ever seen. The money that was needed to build something like that was astronomical. There were paved runways, living quarters nicer than apartments in La Ciudad, warehouses filled with products and weapons, and, of course, thousands of pounds of cocaine.

With the help of the Colombian military, we trashed the lab. There were nine hundred barrels of ethyl ether. We left it up to the Colombians to destroy those. We rounded up the twenty-three cartel men and forced them to watch as we smashed everything they had built. We learned that Otalvaro Cabrera Medina was the mastermind. He was one of our top targets out of Colombia, a name that consistently popped up in intelligence briefings. It was only a matter of time before he was caught. "I spent five hundred thousand dollars on this fucking lab!" he pleaded as we pummeled the structure. I felt pride. We had uncovered one of the largest mass uses of ethyl ether in history until that point. The Americans couldn't have been more pleased. We were heroes in their eyes. Our offices became swamped with gifts and letters of appreciation for our work on the matter.

Office of the Attorney General
Washington, D. C. 20530

August 29, 1984

General Manuel Antonio Noriega
Fuerza de Defensa de Panama
Republic of Panama

Dear General Noriega:

I would like to take this opportunity to congratulate the members
of the National Department of Investigations (DENI) for their
efforts in the investigation resulting in the largest ethyl ether
seizure ever made in the Americas.

Please extend the appreciation of the Department of Justice to
Major Nivaldo Madrinan, Director of DENI, and to Inspectors
Lucinio Miranda and Luis Quiel for their tireless and successful
efforts to remove this chemical from the illicit cocaine market.
Their professionalism, pride, and dedication to the suppression
of drug trafficking are greatly appreciated by our government.

Thank you for your continued support in our mutual efforts to
suppress illicit drug trafficking and to ensure a safer and
healthier environment for all of our citizens.

Sincerely,

William French Smith
Attorney General

Figure 17.1. Letter dated August 29, 1984, from US Attorney General William French
Smith to General Manuel Noriega, congratulating Panama's National Department of
Investigations (DENI) for their role in the largest ethyl ether seizure in the Americas and
praising their cooperation in joint efforts against drug trafficking.

The news outlets rushed to government buildings looking for statements. They came to my office. I told them to fuck off. Some of the soldiers spoke up, and that was okay. The lab smashing was a big deal. The entire world heard about it. From having negative press to the world's spotlight shining on you felt jarring, but it proved Castro's point. As long as we fed the white bear, it would not harm us.

The Colombian military informed us that Otalvaro claimed Colonel Melo had helped them set up the lab. We kept quiet about the news at first. We didn't know its validity and, if it was true, who else was involved. I had known Melo to become increasingly combative in conversation. He contested Noriega more as the years went on. I knew little else of their relationship. Still, Noriega was concerned that one of his supposedly loyal men was acting out of his own interest. We dug deeper and discovered a brewing conspiracy to overthrow the PDF in a coup. Our network of intelligence was too thick for Melo to maneuver through, though he tried and might even have succeeded in another life.

I called Melo's home. He was not there. I broke into his office; nothing was out of the ordinary. I needed intelligence on the colonel's whereabouts. I had ways to track someone through whispers alone. I called several men in my network. Dozens of eyes eventually lay upon the colonel as he stepped into the light. Every move he made and every conversation he had was relayed back to me. I had my own Sayanim [Jewish civilians who help Mossad]. They were men who brushed by him in a corridor, boys who listened. It was a certainty I would find what I needed to hear, and one day, I received a call that Melo's coup attempt had gone underway.

The colonel had attracted a small group of PDFs and turned on us. Our intelligence fed us as we searched for our enemies. I learned that Melo, our own executive secretary of defense, sold information to the cartel.

"He offered them logistical support, you know, immigration favors, free passports, things like that," one of my informants told me. "He's orchestrated this coup with the Medellin Cartel."

It was clear to me how shortsighted Melo was to try such a thing, and it was no surprise the cartel wanted Manuel out. The colonel led a team of PDF soldiers and Medellin Cartel rats. If they wanted to kill him, they would have to kill me.

I tracked down the *sicario* [contract killer] unit in question and kidnapped their leader while my men made sure the other traitors stayed still. I interrogated the fucker. I beat him senseless. "Stop," he would yell before I swiftly smacked him in the jaw. Blood dripped onto his army boots. I gripped my fingers around the base of a handgun and bashed him on the nose. "Tell me everything about the plot to kill Noriega," I demanded. He told me everything I needed. They were going to catch him alone, inside a PDF building, and execute him. Cartel men would disguise themselves alongside PDF officers who followed Melo. I was furious.

The assassination plot was squashed quietly. After I interrogated that sicario bastard, Melo started running his mouth to the news. He wanted the world to be on his side. He claimed

Noriega was involved in drug smuggling and claimed the CIA knew. He spoke with the *New York Times* and *Newsweek*. I guessed that any fucking gringo with a microphone got an interview with the colonel. We loudly put his hands in cuffs, and we threw him into a cell where Manuel, and Manuel alone, would decide what to do with him. Ultimately, he was dishonorably discharged. I did not ask questions, and none of us did, but what I did hear was this. Just before we got to Melo, PDF broke into a warehouse in the Colon Free Trade Zone, and they found seventeen thousand fifty-five-gallon barrels of ethyl ether. I knew these ingredients had to be worth over one million dollars in cocaine. The men in Colon claimed they, too, were approved by Melo to move drugs through the canal. The greedy fuck made money hand over fist, millions of dollars in bribes. That was the nature of this country, and it has always pained me to see no change.

Chapter 18
A Gringo's Last Trip to Panama

Jose and Jack flew into Los Angeles one day in September 2024. They were attending a conference in Anaheim, and on their last day, we met up for lunch to discuss the book.

"The story is great, but if we can get our hands on Trujillo's documents, that would change everything," Jose mentioned.

I knew he was right. Carlos and I had gotten as far as we could with his embellished anecdotes, but Trujillo's documents could prove what I was writing, and maybe even give me the chance to contest Carlos with a spine this time. After all, I found myself listening to the same recording a dozen times to try to find a sense of the truth, but I could never be sure. Carlitos was calculating. His smile made me forget that he was capable of spinning a story in my own mind.

"Come to Panama at the top of the month. We will meet with Trujillo and Carlos to make a deal," Jose said.

I booked my flight when I got home. I was looking forward to returning. It had been a year since my first trip, and my worldview had changed. In many ways, I felt like a different person.

Carlos and Natasha both offered to pick me up from Tocumen. They also mentioned that they had made the bed and prepared for me to stay again.

"Tell Carlos you are staying in my place," Jose told me.

Jack was visiting Panama at that time, too. He had brought an American girl with him for a two-week getaway. They traveled to various parts of the country before I arrived. There was another American man named Dutch, accompanied by Sindo, an older Panamanian man missing half his teeth, who essentially lived in the rainforest and rarely saw civilization with his own eyes. He was in town so he could be taken to a brothel, and it was Dutch's responsibility to make sure he didn't run off or get lost. They both worked for Jose in one way or another. We had a full house. It was an eclectic mix.

Carlos and Natasha came over for breakfast on my second day. He shook my hand and started cracking jokes about my collared shirt. "We need to get you something new," he playfully added before the conversation became serious.

"Carlos, we would like to make a deal with Trujillo to use his documents in this book. We want to show the betrayal of the United States, how they asked you for favors before flipping a switch, and Trujillo's documents do just that," Jose explained.

Carlos was a smart man. He understood what Jose was saying. There were no issues in getting Señor Wittgreen to agree. He and Trujillo were great friends. They spent a lot of time together, especially in their old age. We all agreed that, if Trujillo's demands were reasonable, the addition of proof only strengthened this book. What followed that morning was a pleasant breakfast, where I had the chance to ask Carlos even more questions.

"It must have been quite a blow when you found out Diaz Herrera was conspiring against you," I muttered.

"I had gotten used to it by then," Carlos responded.

"Did Noriega ask Castro for advice when the Americans started to get aggressive?"

"I do not know. In the mid-1980s, Manuel had to inform the CIA station chief in Panama, Don Winters, of his trips to Cuba. If he asked for advice, it was never in a way the CIA could find out. . . . As a younger man, part of my duties was to travel around the world and meet with government representatives and presidents to discuss their relationship with Panama, politically and financially. Panama had become an international hub for money in the 1980s. I was involved in insurance and banking, and many of our clients were based in Asia."

"I heard a rumor that Noriega sent people to China to work out a deal with the Red Army before the invasion," I said.

"Noriega did not know the invasion was coming."

"Did he send men to China?"

"Si, yes, a good friend of mine was one of them. There wasn't enough time to make a deal with the Red Army, but they were ready to jump into the Canal Zone, that is for sure."

"You spent some time working in banking, correct?" I asked.

"Si."

"How did the cartels keep their money here?"

"The same way the Americans did—shell companies, fake names. In the eighties, there was less transparency. Cartels could launder their money through a business with a Panamanian bank account and then transfer the funds to another account anywhere in the world. The cartels had men here who would do this for them. They had people worldwide who would collaborate and send money back and forth to throw off the feds. They called it layering. We knew it was a problem and imposed laws and regulations to fix it. The same issues still happen today. There is always somebody powerful enough to bypass rules. That's how it is everywhere. Plenty of Americans take advantage of our financial system. We are the Switzerland of the Americas. Just look into the Panama Papers scandal."

"Is that what Sarmiento was involved in?" I asked.

"He worked with a group of guys back then in Miami. They would load up these high-powered speedboats in Havana and send them across the channel. One might have gotten seized every so often, but more often than not, the boats would arrive within ninety minutes, completely undetected. He was one of the most successful in the business. He worked with the Costa Ricans, Colombians, Cubans, and eventually, the CIA."

"Escobar really took over the world, didn't he?"

"Escobar was a fool in many ways. The assassination of Colombian politician Rodrigo Lara Bonilla in '84? That was shortsighted. It was a fucking mess, and he had to flee the country. Noriega was the one who helped him, and that is only because Manuel knew Escobar and Torrijos were friends, and he wanted to honor Omar by taking him in. . . . Yes, Escobar was a tyrant to his own people, but he was not what the world thinks he is. Those who actually mattered, like Noriega, Castro . . . these were strong men who took control of a country, not like Escobar, who held it hostage."

"In the eyes of the people, what's the difference between being controlled and being a hostage?" I couldn't believe I said that to a man like Carlos. If it were the eighties, I might not have walked out of that conversation unscathed.

That night, our eclectic group went out in Casco Viejo, where we met with Edgar Noriega and got a table at a rooftop club. I drank tequila all night, and I got home at about four in the morning. Edgar was a fun man. He knew everyone in Casco.

Jose and I were due to meet with Trujillo the following morning for breakfast. He came over at nine. Jose was awake and ready. I jolted out of my bed and immediately jumped into a cold shower before rushing out to the living room where Trujillo sat wearing a neatly pressed shirt, the case containing his documents laid out flat before him. We shook hands. He and Jose conversed in Spanish for some time.

Jose turned to me and explained. "Trujillo's son, Mikhail, has digitized everything," he relayed.

Trujillo was willing to strike a deal, but he did not want to be the one to negotiate. Instead, he referred us to his son, Mikhail. Jose explained to me that it was a tradition in Panamanian culture to let your son do your business when you reach a certain age.

"We can speak about it. Come meet me at my bar," Mikhail told Jose over the phone.

That afternoon, Jose told Jack and me to put on our shoes and to follow him out the door. He was holding a pair of boxing gloves and a framed photo of Roberto Duran.

"Where are we going?" Jack asked.

"Via Argentina. Duran is at a bar, and I want to see if he'll sign this stuff," Jose responded.

We jumped into an Uber and arrived at an empty Galician restaurant that afternoon to find Roberto Duran sitting with his son. They had been drinking, and Roberto was up on his feet, moving around the bar, shaking people's hands, shadowboxing with others. Jose told Roberto that I was a writer.

"You write my book, yes? We will call it Manos de Piedra," he said to me in English before lightly punching me in the chest.

The famous boxer was with his family, so we did not want to bother him any further. Instead, Jose's family came to join us, and we all sat as a group and ate paella.

Edgar joined, as did his father, Ciro, who I could thankfully interview for an hour or so. He was Noriega's brother, and he had lived in Hong Kong as a diplomat for many years. Edgar was partially raised there, too, before being moved to a military school in Florida. Ciro claimed not to have high-level knowledge of Noriega's dealings in Panama. I'm sure he knew more than he let on, especially considering what I learned about Noriega's relationship with the Red Army and how close they came to collaboration. Still, it was clear his life was not the same as

Manuel's and he was detached from much of the controversies surrounding Noriega. "I loved my time in China. It truly was a wonderful country with wonderful people. I feel very lucky to have spent so many years there," Ciro stated.

We met up with about a dozen other men in a cigar club before Jose said we should leave to meet with Mikjail Trujillo and work out a deal for the documents.

Jose, Jack, Jack's date, Dutch, Sindo, and I showed up at Mikhail's bar after the sun fell. It was a real rag-tag group of misfits. I immediately noticed all the patrons were women in tight dresses. Rather than a pub, it was a brothel where men staying in the hotels nearby could come to meet women of the night. I had unknowingly gone there during my first trip to Panama. I had had only one beer before heading home. Paying for sex was never my thing. My first hotel was less than 250 yards from the establishment. This time, with our little crew, the sex workers swarmed us. One rubbed her hands all over my back.

Mikhail stepped out onto the floor and introduced himself to us all with a smile. He wore a tight, black T-shirt and held himself casually. "Come, we will go to the space we conduct business in," he said, leading the way. Mikhail led us into a room with Miami-vice-themed wallpaper and cheap plastic sofas. It reminded me of *Scarface*. I think it was intentional. Jose said that sort of flashiness was common among guys of that age group who were involved in shady dealings. The lights above shone bright, and a little bar was in the corner next to a bathroom. Mikhail got us all a drink of our choice. One of his business partners, who claimed to split his time between Panama and Miami, entered with a tray and handed us each our beverage. We sat back and let Jose start us off.

"These documents that your father has spent his life acquiring are remnants of the only history that can potentially redefine our history. They say something true that has not been said before."

Mikhail and Jose spoke back and forth before us. He sat on a high-top chair in the center of the room. He was upright, whereas Jose was relaxed. It was clear we were watching a negotiation powerhouse in action. Every word that came out of Jose's mouth was intentional. He would press Mikhail one second, and the next, he would pull back and make jokes. I sat in the corner, leaning forward, hands pressed together, just waiting for my turn to speak. It was obvious what was happening. Mikhail was well aware of how valuable his father's documents were, and he wanted to squeeze us for everything he could. Any one of us would have done the same; he didn't owe us anything, and Jose knew that. It was a "would you rather have 20 percent of something or 100 percent of nothing?" question that Jose essentially posed. Trujillo had used the documents before in one of his books, but Mikhail knew, as did Jose and I, that the book hadn't been as successful as it needed to be in order to have an impact. This book would be different. Still, he wanted to play hardball, and I could see the gears shifting in Jose's mind, carefully curating a series of words that not only would reinforce the power dynamic of the conversation but also would fast-forward us to the part where Mikhail would agree to hand over the documents in exchange for a percentage of ownership of this book.

"You know, usually when I do meetings like this, it's at the cigar club downtown. You know the cigar club, don't you?"

"Yes, of course," Mikhail responded.

"We like to do meetings there because if somebody acts out, there's a room in the back where we can shoot them."

I almost spit out my drink. The room went silent. Mikhail choked on his laugh. Nobody else even cracked a smile. The negotiation finished soon after, with Jose, Jack, and Mikhail even discovering new ways to work together in other business areas.

Jose said we should all have a drink at the bar before heading out. "When you negotiate on someone else's home territory, it's important to show you are not intimidated," he explained as we sipped on our beers, the sex workers surrounding the table. "These women are spies. They will listen to what we say and tell Mikhail," Jose warned.

I could see what he meant. I didn't want to be there any longer. We finished our drinks, and Jose sent Dutch and Sindo to a separate brothel where they could do what they came to the city to do.

The day before I left, I made a trip alone to Carlos's apartment to have a bite to eat and a drink. He and Natasha were home relaxing. Carlos had some health troubles then and couldn't join me in a whiskey, but he sat by and cracked jokes while their maid served us a rice and chicken dish. "What I know for certain is that after the Iran-Contra Affair, we became the target. They wanted to make a statement. They knew where Noriega was. They didn't need to drop a fleet onto us. . . . I have listened to the Americans tell the same story over and over. The guilt is riddled in me, a pit in my stomach that hasn't fled since the invasion happened. I should have been there to protect him."

I tried not to ask him too many questions and instead enjoyed his company before I returned to the United States. "What can you tell me about the protests against Noriega?" I asked.

"After '86, it was a slippery slope. Americans like John Maisto used the National Civic Crusade to organize protests for Panamanians to march against Noriega. It couldn't have been more obvious that the gringos were trying to implode our government from within the nation. They pitted top advisors against Manuel, hoping yet another coup would transition leadership of Panama once more," Carlos responded.

I was given a fresh glass of Buchanan's whiskey. I was drunk, and Carlos found that amusing.

When I left his apartment, he wished me good luck and told me he would wake with excitement each day about this book. "When our generation dies, our history will die with it, and all that will be left is the false narrative there is now. I am honored to tell my story."

That feeling seemed genuine. Carlos was highly emotional at certain times, and I could see just how much this project meant to him. Yes, Carlitos did not give me the information behind Noriega's drug smuggling or money laundering operations, but he did tell me a story that came from the heart, one he could recite multiple times without slipping up. It may not have been the full objective truth, but my gut began to tell me that it was the truth Carlos believed.

Mikhail Trujillo and I met one last time in Los Angeles at the beginning of December. We spent nearly two months going back and forth with legal documents. On that winter day, I was flying home to Dublin, Ireland, so we needed to meet and shake hands before he would share the digitized files with me. I told him to meet me at the Fairmont Hotel in Santa Monica. The apartment I was forced to leave was just down the street. It felt like a full-circle moment. A year prior, I was essentially homeless, struggling to maintain confidence in my life and writing ability as I worked on a book that not many twenty-seven-year-olds had the opportunity to write. We shared a nice morning together, and a transfer date was finally agreed upon.

I decided to spend an entire month in Rome, Italy, translating and deciphering the documents. I was sent 481 pages in a PDF, and the majority of it was in Spanish. I chose Rome because it was my favorite place in the world. I didn't want to do the work in Los Angeles, Boston, Panama, or Dublin, the places I had previously been while writing this book. As we all knew, the documents had given us the proof we needed, a fresh angle into a story that had been told thousands of times before.

Chapter 19
The Iran-Contra Affair

anuel and I watched the television as President Ronald Reagan's face flashed on the screen. He wore his signature navy-blue suit and leaned toward the camera with a sharp gaze. I stood by Manuel's cluttered desk. He leaned back in his chair, smoking a cigar, fists resting on the wood.

"I want to tell you a few things tonight about the real nature of the Sandinista regime in Nicaragua," Reagan said. "Shortly after taking power, the Sandinistas, in partnership with Cuba and the Soviet Union, began supporting aggression and terrorism against El Salvador, Honduras, Costa Rica, and Guatemala. And, it's become the stage for a bold attempt by the Soviet Union, Cuba, and Nicaragua to install Communism by force throughout the hemisphere."

Manuel and I turned to each other and shook our heads. The United States framed problems a certain way. It had already been fighting in that war. We were asked to train Contras, and we refused. Every now and again, some money, weapons, or information would pass through the American bases in Panama, and it was our duty to deliver it to Nicaragua. That was business.

The war, that was not our problem. Noriega and I knew that when the American bubble burst, we would catch the debris.

The phone rang for Manuel. He picked it up and smiled, turning to me. "It is your brother, Gaspar. He is calling from his post in France," he said.

My little brother was the ambassador to Panama in France. Chucha, the kid was growing up and doing incredible things. He and Manuel would speak often. They would tell jokes, and then they would discuss business. Many of our affairs seeped into Europe, and there were many times we needed to communicate with representatives of countries like Spain, France, Portugal, and England. Manuel loved to visit Paris.

I saw many planes pass through Panama in the 1980s carrying weapons to Nicaragua, Cuba, El Salvador, and the United States. I found myself aboard these jets often. I was flying weapons, mostly, and sometimes large quantities of cash. Nobody asked questions. In 1985, I flew six million US dollars to Managua in a single trip for the Contras. The CIA paid, and we delivered. I did my job and asked no questions. Never once did I train one of those animals to kill. If they wanted to use gringo weapons, who was I to deny them of that? Because of the civil war in Nicaragua, the American presence in Panama increased dramatically. I felt I was looking into the future. Banks invested in us, businessmen held retreats, tourists stepped off commercial airlines, and the country was changing before my eyes by the day. Economically, we had some ways to go, but I was optimistic. We held leverage over our neighbors in every direction.

In 1985, Manuel and I watched as Daniel Ortega was inaugurated into the Nicaraguan government. Our intelligence told us the Sandinistas were effectively restraining the Contras, who were being driven deeper and deeper into the forests, scattering into the country by the day. The Sandinistas had become knowledgeable in complex military strategy, which they had learned from the Soviets. The Contras were merely ragged drug smugglers who were supplied with the finest artillery in the world. The American-backed militia was losing.

"The Contras are rebels and drug smugglers. The people do not want them in power. The Americans cannot afford to lose another pawn in Central America," Manuel whispered to me behind the scenes of the inauguration.

We maintained our relationship with the Sandinistas, shaking their hands and laughing at their jokes. I have always been fond of Nicaraguans. They were very good people, *buena gente*. The Americans used me to transport this cargo. It was a business from which we all benefitted, nothing more.

My son Ian Carlo and my daughter Romaine had been born to their mother Marta Padilla out of matrimony. Seven children made this time of my life chaos. I was a good father to them. Anything they needed, I provided. At this time, I devoted much of my money to the kids. They had the best education within reach, and I endorsed them wherever they wanted to travel. My children were growing smart, and I was very proud of them. The CIA and DEA kept me busy, so I couldn't see them as much as I would have liked. Intelligence was a 24/7 job.

At that time, we were actively in meetings with the Japanese. There was a major interest when it came to future investment in the canal, when the Americans would be forced to leave. The Japanese were who Noriega wanted to work with most. Their money was good, their manners were clean, and there was an aura of loyalty that hung over our conversations. We liked their proposal to begin buying up land around the canal and ultimately owning certain key areas of the canal. The gringos did not like this. Reagan was very direct with us; even though America would no longer own the canal, they expected to be treated differently from others. We did not care.

The Nicaraguan civil war was loud but not loud enough to take our attention away from our own matters. We continued to help the DEA. We had our own problems in the streets. Manuel's leadership split opinion. The American media slipped its narrative into our society, and no amount of counter-storytelling could effectively squash the lies.

It was November 1986. Quiel tossed a stack of letters on the desk between us. His office was filled with documents. We were both in uniform, actively pursuing fugitives and extraditing the ones we captured. Our unit was a well-oiled machine, even if the surrounding hierarchy of the PDF seemed to be crumbling. I stayed vigilant of my peers. Luis was a devoted worker. His commitment to the job was seen and respected. On that day, he showed no emotion. "The letters they send me," he said.

I reached across and flipped pages over one by one.

U.S. Department of Justice

Drug Enforcement Administration

PCO-85-20

Panamá 17 de Diciembre de 1985

Inspector Luis A. Quiel
Oficina de Coordinación y
 Enlace Internacional
Comandancia de las Fuerzas de Defensa
E. S. D.

Dear Inspector:

 I am writing to extend my appreciation to the DENI for their
professional police work and cooperation which has been shared with
the Drug Enforcement Administration. I am making specific reference
to the December 6, 1985, arrest and expulsion of two U.S. fugitives
wanted for violation of narcotic laws in the United States. The
fugitives were taken into custody by Inspector E. Gomez and other
Panamanian officers at the Holiday Inn in Panama.

 On December 11, 1985, Inspector Alaen Oda and other Panamanian
officers coordinated the arrest of U.S. 'fugitive Alberto AUDEMAR-F.,
a U.S. citizen, and transported him to the United States where he was
taken into custody by U.S. authorities. AUDEMAR, as you are aware,
was wanted for smuggling hundred-kilogram quantities of cocaine into
the United States, using Panamá as a staging area.

 This type of police cooperation is an excellent example of the
international cooperation being practiced to combat the threat of
narcotic trafficking and abuse. Please extend my thanks to the officers
responsible for the above arrests and to Major Nivaldo Aponte-Madrinan,
Director of DENI.

 Cordially yours,

 THOMAS M. TELLES
 DEA COUNTRY ATTACHE

TMT:jl

*Figure 19.1. Letter from Thomas Telles, DEA, to Luis Quiel, December 17, 1985,
expressing that work by this type of DENI (National Department of Investigations)
cooperation is an excellent example of the international cooperation being
practiced in the fight against narcotrafficking..*

TRADUCCION

Agosto 29, 1984.

General Manuel Antonio Noriega
Fuerzas de Defensa de Panamá
República de Panamá

Estimado General Noriega:

Yo quisiera tomar esta oportunidad para congratular a los miembros del Departamento Nacional de Investigaciones (DENI) por sus esfuerzos en la investigación resultante en el gran decomiso de éter etílico jamás hecho en las Américas.

Por favor extienda la apreciación del Departamento de Justicia al Mayor Nivaldo Madriñán, Director del DENI, y a los inspectores Lucinio Miranda y Luis Quiel por sus incansables y exitosos esfuerzos para remover este químico del mercado ilícito de cocaína. Su profesionalismo, orgullo y dedicación para la supresión del tráfico de droga son grandemente apreciados por nuestro gobierno.

Gracias por su continuo apoyo en nuestro mutuo esfuerzo para suprimir el tráfico ilícito de droga y para mantener una seguridad y un ambiente más saludable para todos nuestros ciudadanos.

Sinceramente,

WILLIAM FRENCH SMITH
Procurador General

Figure 19.2. Spanish-language letter from Attorney General William French Smith to General Manuel Noriega on August 29, 1984, congratulating Panama's National Department of Investigations (DENI) for their role in the largest ethyl ether seizure in the Americas and expressing appreciation for their cooperation in efforts to suppress drug trafficking.

EMBASSY OF THE
UNITED STATES OF AMERICA
Panama, July 15, 1986

No. 057

Excellency:

I have the honor to transmit the text of a letter
dated July 14, 1986 from the Assistant Secretary of State
for Inter-American Affairs, Elliott Abrams, addressed to
Your Excellency.

"Dear Mr. Minister:

I was pleased to have had the
chance to meet briefly with you
during your visit to Washington on
June 27. As we are both well —
aware, the United States and Panama
have many shared interests. It is
the intention of my government to
continue to work and consult with
your government, in pursuit of
these many interests and as befits
partners joined in a formal treaty
relationship. We trust that Panama
will also work responsibly and
cooperatively to achieve our many
shared objectives.

His Excellency

Jorge Abadia Arias,

Minister of Foreign Affairs,

Panama, Republic of Panama

38-A-

Figure 19.3. U.S. letter highlighting obligations under the 1977 Canal Treaty, joint anti-drug cooperation, and negotiations for a legal assistance treaty. (The letter continues in figures 19.4, 19.5, and 19.6.)

Our joint efforts cover many fields. Under the terms of the Treaty of 1977, for example, we share in the responsibility to defend and operate the existing canal. My government intends to abide by our various obligations under the Treaty, including the transfer to full Panamanian control of the canal by the year 2000, and expects that your government will act in a similar manner and spirit. In other areas of mutual enterprise, we share aspirations for peace in the region, and we collaborate in the interdiction of illicit drugs. In these and other joint efforts, each needs to be aware of the concerns of the other.

As we discussed during our meeting, a high priority bilateral task at present concerns the negotiation and implementation of a mutually acceptable legal assistance treaty. I am glad that we agree that such a treaty would serve the interests of both our countries, and I am sure you share my disappointment at the lack of results during the recent discussions. I look forward to

Figure 19.4. Continuation of the letter in figure 19.3, addressing press allegations of corruption in Panama while stressing human rights and mutual respect. (It continues in figures 19.5 and 19.6.)

greater progress during the next
round of talks between our
representatives.

    With regard to the concerns
generated by recent allegations
appearing in the press of
corruption in Panama, we both
appreciate the distinction between
such stories and official
statements by authorized
officials. Of course, we continue
to urge respect for human rights
and the full development of
democracy everywhere. Let me say
again what Secretary Shultz told
you last February; namely, that we
wish to maintain a continuing,
constructive and cooperative
relationship based on a spirit of
mutual respect. We expect to
receive similar treatment. My
government would like to be assured
that your government and its
accredited representatives are so
motivated and that the kind of
unfounded statements which are
attributed to at least two of your
diplomatic representatives in the
press of other countries do not
reflect the views of your
government.

Figure 19.5. Continuation of the letter in figures 19.3 and 19.4, reaffirming U.S. and Panama shared interests and urging continued responsible cooperation under a treaty framework. (Final part of the letter is in figure 19.6.)

que la clase de declaraciones infundadas
atribuídas por lo menos a dos de sus
representantes diplomáticos en la prensa
de otros países no refleja los puntos de
vista de su Gobierno.

Sólo cuando los dos países muestren
una actitud responsable y consistente en
sus relaciones bilaterales y en el trata-
miento de los problemas que atañen a
ambos, podremos esperar el florecimiento
de una relación satisfactoria para ambas
partes, tal como nosotros dos lo deseamos.

Sinceramente,

Elliott Abrams
Subsecretario de Estado
para Asuntos Interamericanos"

Acepte, Excelencia, las renovadas seguridades
de mi más alta consideración.

Figure 19.6. Final section of Elliott Abrams's letter (see figures 19.3, 19.4, and 19.5), stressing that only responsible, consistent conduct in bilateral relations can sustain a satisfactory U.S. and Panama partnership.

"Years and years of gratitude," Quiel stated.

"We take care of their problems."

"They're openly accusing us of things they only ever spoke about behind closed doors. They're sending fewer letters of gratitude and more of concern."

I sat in silence opposite Luis for some time while the rest of the building filled with agents and soldiers. We both knew the time would come eventually. The sun rose to its peak. Chatter consumed the hallways. I rushed out to find a half-dozen of our men gathered around a newspaper. I pushed through them and gazed down at the headline of *Ash-Shiraa*; IRAN ARMS SALES REVEALED.

"Chucha madre," I muttered, turning to find Manuel.

The first chance we got to speak about it was shortly after the news broke. Manuel, of course, knew more than anyone. "Bush has egg on his face."

My gut feeling returned. I knew the kind of things the Americans could do if they turned on us.

"They are in trouble because they were selling weapons to Iran during a trade embargo they imposed and then used the profits to secretly fund the Contras. They came to us for help, and we gave them as much as they deserved, which was not enough."

The United States was always in the market for help. We gave them information, we ran weapons for them, and we let their troops on our land. Our arms were open for the gringos, and we wanted something in return. There were men who felt otherwise, men who clearly grew worried as time went on. Roberto Diaz Herrera came to complain to Noriega many times. He would speak about the general behind his back and hope that men like me didn't hear.

"Things need to change, Manuel," Herrera said one day.

"If we change, we are changing for them, not for us. So, why give in?"

I suspected somebody was whispering in Herrera's ear. I knew I was right. There were many of us who felt the change within him, as well as many others who would ultimately rise to try to take Manuel down. Still, the news of the Contra affair rippled throughout our politics. It was an event we did not fully involve ourselves in, yet it felt like we were at its center.

"The Contras are involved in drug smuggling to help fund their militia. They are using the tether attached to the United States as a way to traffic narcotics under the radar. The CIA planes that come to and from the US, they are being loaded with drugs," Noriega informed Diaz.

"I know this, señor."

Herrera was afraid. Noriega and I understood the climate. We all took advantage of our relationships. That was the game. Yet, I was cautious and never took it too far. Castro's warning embedded itself within me. I never wanted to face the wrath of the gringos. Reagan had been publicly embarrassed. The Contra affair proved the US government lied to itself and the people. Manuel and I knew the blame would soon be shifted and imposed elsewhere, and we were a viable target. Several Americans were persecuted, North and Poindexter being the two I was most familiar with. Richard Secord's name was thrown around a lot. He came to Panama, too. I watched from Central America as those men faced the repercussions of covert arms dealing under the nose of Congress. The trials were a joke. I had seen better acting in Hollywood Westerns.

Noriega shook his head and stood up from his seat. He turned the television off. "The United States is taking this very seriously. The CIA will try to lock us in the chains that dangle from this disaster. We must stay strong and not bow down to them," he said before stepping out of his office and jumping into an armed vehicle.

Manuel gave a speech on Avenida Balboa that afternoon. The people came to listen. American soldiers lined the crowd. They sat on camo jeeps, watching over the crowd of thousands. There was no reason to hide.

I was tending to business over the phone during this time. I was busier and wealthier than ever. There was a lot of interest from all over the world in many of my businesses, particularly Caza y Pesca. The business was successful enough to buy Manuel and me two luxury yachts. We named them *Macho 1* and *Macho 2*. I felt I was constantly scheduling flights and appointments. Businessmen wanted to take advantage of our relationships. Smugglers, launderers. We made money from all their illegal activity. I cared little for the transactional nature of people. It showed the worst of humanity. To me, cockfighting was elegant, a bloody sport passed down from generations of important men. I wanted to be at the gallera all the time. It was fulfilling to me. The games gave me time to focus my thoughts on something positive. The world around us had dimmed, and I needed to chase the light however I could. Havana was calling my name. The restaurant I owned with Castro was doing well; people loved coming to it. There was a line out the door in the evenings. Manuel and I had a booth where our friends would sit and watch the dancers.

The flight to Havana moved like molasses. I didn't care what the CIA or DEA would think about me traveling to a Communist nation at such a time. I just wanted to get to Cuba so I could take the fucking stress off my shoulders and relax. I had thousands in my possession and cages of cocks ready to fight. Carlos Sarmiento was to meet me at the gallera. I arrived to see him outside the terminal in sunglasses, white cotton, a short-sleeved shirt, and white pants.

"Carlitos, mi amigo, how are you?" he said with a smile.

I had my roosters transported in another car that would follow us to the gallera.

Sarmiento drove me into the city. He put the windows down, and the warm breeze hit my face. "How long are you in town for?" he asked me.

"Just a few days. I am in no rush," I responded. I hadn't seen him in some time. "Where have you been, chico?" I asked.

Sarmiento was a stoic man who rarely showed an excess of emotion. He smiled, pointing over my shoulder and out the passenger window. "I have been building, Carlos," he confidently exclaimed.

The gallera was packed when we entered. I looked at the dozens of hombres that populated the room. The squeals of roosters ruptured my eardrums. Snoopy was handed to me by the driver of the rooster car. The others, I kept as backup. I saw many impressive creatures that day. Sarmiento and I moved around, taking and placing bets. My stack of cash had grown. Snoopy was a true warrior. His claws were covered in blood; I wiped them off after every battle and prepared him for the next. I must have seen him take down a dozen cocks with ease. He was the talk of the gallera.

"A six-year-old rooster? You're full of shit," people yelled.

I couldn't be touched. I had a dozen men hand me five thousand dollars apiece.

I felt someone tugging on my sleeve. My fist clenched as I spun to the sight of no one.

"Here," a young voice said.

I looked down at a little kid with his fists clenched around loose bills, staring up at me.

"What do you want, kid?" I asked.

"I want to fight your rooster," he responded.

Chucha, I wondered where the kid's parents were. "Are you here by yourself?" I said, kneeling to meet his gaze.

He reached into his pocket and pulled out five hundred dollars. It was all rolled up into a ball. "Five hundred dollars to fight your rooster," he demanded.

I stood to my feet and laughed. "No way, kid," I told him.

Just like that, his father appeared and looked me dead in the eyes. "What are you doing with my son?" he asked.

"The kid asked for a fight; he's a few thousand short," I said.

"He's afraid of losing," the kid blurted out.

"Snoopy doesn't lose."

"You know what . . . I bet you one hundred thousand dollars my rooster can beat yours," the father said.

"Chucha, one hundred thousand dollars for one fight?"

"Si," he said confidently.

"Who the fuck are you?"

"You can call me Juliana."

A golden medallion hung on Juliana's neck; I was entranced by it.

He could see I was immersed in the item's beauty. "You like the medallion?" he asked.

"Where did you get it?" I responded.

He removed it from his neck and handed it to me. The gold weighed heavily in my hands. The engravings were immaculately cut. "This medallion has a story. I live in Miami, you see, and I have a big house in a very nice neighborhood. It was the target of a standard robbery, nothing more. They stole many things, but this medallion? This was the only thing they took that I truly cared about. So I had my men hunt the thieves down and kill them. Now, it stays around my neck," he told me.

"One more fight," I demanded.

I was confident Snoopy could beat anyone. I looked Juliana up and down. The rooster in his cage was fiery and loud. It wouldn't stand a chance against my bird.

"Carlos?" Sarmiento's voice yelled. He rushed over to me and put his hand on my shoulder. "I see you have met Juliana," he said.

Juliana stuck out his hand, and I shook it. His kid looked me in the eyes. Chucha, the little bastard wanted to fight.

I was like that once upon a time. I rustled the little fucker's hair and set Snoopy's cage down. "He just bet me one hundred thousand dollars that his cock can beat mine," I said.

"You do not want to fuck with Snoopy. Trust me, save your money," Sarmiento laughed.

I couldn't take the man's money in good spirit. We fought our roosters, and of course, Snoopy emerged victorious. I never doubted that bird.

"We are going to a party. Come with us, Carlos," Sarmiento offered.

I sent my roosters back to the hotel with a driver. I was taken care of; I knew the cocks would be, too. Snoopy had made me wealthier that day. My pockets were heavy. I loved that fucking bird. Sarmiento roared about him on the drive to the mansion. "Snoopy has won over three hundred fights in his life! What rooster do you know of that has done that?" I drunkenly yelled the entire car ride. It was dark outside. I couldn't tell where we were going, but as the car braked slowly, I could see the immaculate lights of a coastal mansion glowing brighter by the second. It was a colonial Spanish-style home with dozens of trees and flowers around the lawn.

I sat in a hot tub, watching as the women approached me. "Are you Carlos Wittgreen?" they asked. A cigar hung in my mouth. I could see their eyes glancing toward me and cute smiles spreading on their faces. They poured themselves drinks and disrobed, totally naked, to come to join me. I threw my arms over two of them. Their hands caressed my body under the water. "Can I come back with you to Panama?" they whispered sensually in my ear, rubbing the inside of my thigh. It was always like this in Cuba.

"I'll be back; don't go anywhere," I told them as I threw on a robe and grabbed a cigar. I sat on a pool chair, smoking a cigar and looking out at the streak of light created by the moon that rested atop the calm waters of the Gulf of Mexico. Sarmiento came to join me, an unlit cigar resting between his lips. I held my lighter up, and clouds of tobacco smoke washed over me. We faced the ocean.

"What do you think of this whole Contra bullshit?" Sarmiento asked.

"It's a mess," I responded. When I was having fun, I did not want to talk about work. I had enough on my plate as it was. I had come to Cuba for cockfighting, sex, and relaxation, not to talk politics with a businessman.

"How's this going to affect the banks?" he asked. I knew Sarmiento was prying me for intelligence. He was a man who sat in the center of a grand web, tugging on strings when he needed to. My words would help him know which tether to cut and which to mend.

"Why are you asking me this?" I snapped.

Sarmiento took a long drag of his cigar, his body relaxed, still. "I'm doing business with some guys in Miami, and there's concern over the bank transfer," he said.

"What kind of business?"

"Weapons. Cuba to Miami."

"That is a dangerous route." Sarmiento wanted help. I was well-versed in the logistics of shipping under the American radar. It was one of my many businesses, yet I was not stupid. I understood the climate. The intelligence I received brought with it warnings. Things had become different; it was no longer "please and thank you" with the DEA and CIA. There was silence for the first time in our history. Sarmiento was a friend, and I would always help a friend in need.

I left Cuba the next day. I fucked all night and got only two hours' sleep. When I woke up, I arranged for my roosters to be taken to the airport to meet me. I also called a friend of mine who was an artist and asked him to paint me a picture of Snoopy. I felt his days would soon be behind him, and I wanted something to commemorate him. I slept the entire flight home.

A PDF man picked me up, and we drove right to meet Noriega, Lucinio, and some of the other colonels. I entered the office to find my peers standing around an old friend of mine I had not seen since the early 1970s.

"Hello, Carlos," Harari said to me.

I hugged him. It had been many years since we were in the same room.

"Michael will be spending a lot more time in Panama," Manuel exclaimed.

I knew having Harari on our side was a blessing. He was an impressive man, the chief of Mossad's hit squad for many years. I understood his brain revolved around gathering and delegating intelligence to remain powerful. It was a skill I picked up from him during my days in Israel.

"How is retirement?" I asked.

"Business has never been better," he responded.

"I was informing Harari of my dealings with the CIA. They're squeezing me and lying to my face while they are doing it," Manuel said.

"Now that the CIA has been exposed over Iran-Contra, they will be looking for scapegoats," Harari said.

It all happened quickly. One day, we were the greatest accomplices of the Americans. The next, we were their most important target. I looked at a newspaper on Manuel's desk. There was a headline about Hugo Spadafora. The *New York Times* had published some of Hugo's statements about Manuel. It made him look like a devil. Manuel and I knew the truth. Spadafora was helping the Contras. The CIA was using him, and he began to get mixed up in the world of narcotrafficking. Whether his involvement was inadvertent or not, he paid a terrible price. I didn't speak to anyone about Manuel's smuggling allegations because nobody asked me. Yet, for all the chaos surrounding us on the ground, things felt normal. We didn't always clash with the American soldiers. I was very fond of some of them. But we were two opposing forces occupying the same land. Strength and machismo would flare at any moment. Our anger was the flint and stone; the canal was the fuel.

One morning, I awoke in my car, head pounding. I had been out drinking the night before. My face throbbed, and my fist was covered in dry blood. I remembered nothing. My pager beeped. It was in my back pocket. I ripped it out and looked at the screen. "Manuel," I mumbled. I found the nearest payphone and called him with a raspy voice. "Yes, Manuel?" I said into the device.

"Come down to the shooting range right now," he said.

"Yes, señor. I'm on my way." I could hardly see. The cars on the road before me were blurred. The wheel was hot to the touch.

I honked at civilians who ran in the street. When I arrived at the shooting range, I saw Manuel surrounded by a dozen American soldiers. He held a sniper in one hand. The gringos all held semi-automatic weapons.

"Carlitos, come here," Noriega yelled to me.

Twelve white faces turned to face me as I stumbled toward them.

"This is Carlos Wittgreen. He will beat any one of you," Manuel exclaimed with a smile on his face and his hand patting my shoulder.

"Look at him. He looks drunk," an American named Robbie yelled out.

"Who the fuck do you think you're talking to?" I responded.

"Carlos, I brought you here because this man says he could beat anyone with a rifle." Noriega gestured to Robbie.

"I'm a trained marksman with the US military. Of course, I can beat a PDF soldier," Robbie stated confidently.

"He challenged me, but I thought it'd be more fun if you contested," Manuel said with a smile.

I grabbed the gun. The alcohol in my stomach swooshed and swayed against the inner lining of my body. I wanted to puke. My head was pounding. Robbie gripped his rifle tight and approached me with a snarky fucking grin on his face. I knew he thought he was better than me, not just as a shooter, but as a man. He had this elitist aura that a lot of those soldiers had. He took his position, and his bitches followed closely behind.

Manuel paused by me. "You look exhausted." He laughed, patting my cheek.

"Chucha, I woke up in my fucking car this morning!" I responded.

Noriega put his arm around my shoulder. He pointed to Robbie. "That guy is a puta. Look at him. If he wasn't surrounded by those assholes, he'd be on his knees begging to suck your dick," Manuel exclaimed.

I took my place next to the American. Noriega stood amongst the rest of them, arms folded, a smile on his face. "You can go first, *puta*," I told Robbie.

He closed one eye and looked into the lens. I could see six metal cylinder targets a quarter of a mile away. They looked like cans, but they were made of a stronger metal than aluminum. My ears pounded as he fired his first shot. Sparks exploded a quarter-mile away. He turned to me. "Your turn."

I closed my left eye and raised the rifle. The targets blurred through the lens. They danced like a mirage. I fired, and the bullet whizzed through the air and struck the sand behind the targets.

"Chucha madre," I yelled, jumping to my feet.

The soldiers laughed, and I took deep breaths to compose myself. "If you can't do it, you can't do it, Carlos. There's no shame in giving up," Robbie joked.

I closed my fist into a ball. I was ready to strike him, but Manuel intervened. "Why don't you aim for the targets over there instead?" Manuel proposed. He pointed toward a series of metal posts three-quarters of a mile away. I wanted to throw up just looking at them. They were tiny, hardly visible to the naked eye.

"That's not what we agreed on," Robbie complained.

"If you're so great, it shouldn't be a problem for you. Carlos, aim for the far targets," Manuel said.

I lay down and repositioned my aim. I calmed my breathing. Warm air rushed out of my nostrils. The bullet exploded from my rifle. The air was silent for just one moment, and then sparks flew far in the distance.

"Again," Noriega said.

The Americans stood silent, Robbie with wide eyes.

I fired another round, and sparks exploded. I set the gun down on the ground and turned to Robbie. "Your turn," I said.

Robbie fired two shots into the sand. He couldn't see the fucking targets for shit. His face was red with rage and embarrassment. He jumped to his feet and threw his arms in the air. "You're a cheat, you Panamanian bastard," he yelled. The gringo was a sore loser.

Manuel and I laughed at the asshole. We sent them all back to Howard with their pussies between their legs.

"These new gringo soldiers ... chucha, they're cocky bastards," I said to Noriega.

"Their government tells them we are untrained animals. They come here, and they think they are better than us."

"Let them assume."

The streets were beginning to move more slowly. I sat behind the wheel, listening to the radio. The announcer spoke English and Spanish. It was for the Americans. I changed the station. "Dos Gardenias para ti" blasted from my car's speakers. I sang along to it, reminiscing about my days in Uruguay with Manuel. I drove into the city to check on my restaurant before the dinner rush. My hostess stood by the door in a tight dress. I kissed her on the cheek and rubbed against her waist as I entered.

"Good afternoon, Señor Wittgreen," she said softly. "There is an American man sitting at the bar waiting for you."

I walked into the space and saw the back of an American man in a black suit. He turned to me, hearing my footsteps. "Carlos Wittgreen?" he asked.

"Who are you?" I responded.

He revealed to me a set of papers. "Termination Notice" was written on the first page.

"What is this?"

"We're shutting down the restaurant. Everything is explained in these papers."

"For what reason?"

"It's all explained in the papers, Mr. Wittgreen."

"Fuck you; tell me why you think you can just come here and do this."

"Fidel Castro is an enemy of democracy, Mr. Wittgreen. The US military needs all hands on deck. Read the papers."

I jumped at him with rage. My fist cracked against his jaw, and he stumbled and fell onto a table. I grabbed him by the collar and punched him again. My knuckles ached. Blood sprayed across my skin. The man kicked me in the knee, and I stumbled. Before I could get up, the man had vanished. I stood alone in the empty restaurant, blood on my hands and on the floor.

The papers were filled with fucking legal jargon, but I understood the only reason for the closure was that Fidel owned a stake in the place. The fucking cabrons couldn't stand the fact that he remained in power, even after all the time and resources the US had invested in destroying him. I went to Noriega, eyes red with fury. I wanted to fight every fucking American man I saw. They carried their bodies like kings. The arrogance was incredible. I burst into Manuel's office. He stood alongside Harari.

"The gringos told me I have to close La Bodeguita del Medio," I yelled.

"This is how it starts. They no longer see you as an asset," Noriega stated.

"In 1999, when ownership of the canal returns to Panama, the United States will have to leave for good. It does not take a smart man to realize that doing so is not in their best interests," Harari said.

"The soldiers that walk these streets will soon start to patrol them if we do not protect ourselves," Manuel exclaimed.

Manuel strengthened relationships with the Libyans, the Japanese, and the Chinese. Gaddafi was an ally. Plenty of information, weapons, and money had been transferred between our two nations. Our knowledge kept us centered. We had allies to draw from if we needed them. We had given up for decades, and it was finally time to take.

"The Americans are using your relationship with Castro and Gaddafi against you," Harari said. "They're wondering what information you are selling to the enemies. They not only want to make sure their money is being well-spent; they also want to find a way to take back the canal and to make it your fault."

"They train me, they pay me, then they want to kill me. Chucha, where is the honor?"

"Intelligence is a business, Manuel," Harari stated.

"Reagan knows not to pull the trigger too fast. He knows this. Bush, on the other hand, will put me in the guillotine if he wins the 1988 election," Manuel said.

I was in rooms where important decisions were made. I heard ideas that blossomed into action, and I witnessed the consequences, all with my own eyes. That's why, when I first saw the picture of Eugene Hasenfus in Sandinista chains after being shot down over South Nicaragua while transporting American weapons to the Contras, I knew everything would change. That photo proved the CIA was not telling the truth, not even to their own government. If they would lie to their people, they would certainly lie to Manuel, and they would lie to the rest of us, too. We had to keep the canal. It needed to stay in Panamanian hands. The gringos loomed over the fifty-mile stretch like a shadow. I never questioned the direction Manuel brought us in. I would die for the Panamanian flag.

Stepping into my home, I felt tense. I couldn't help but think about all the gringos in our streets that could snap at a whim and turn their weapons on us. I sat in my armchair with a glass of whiskey, watching the world news. Every report coming out of the United States revolved around drug trafficking. It was the new issue; Communism was a thing of the past. I couldn't take my eyes away from the device. Not even a knock at the door attracted my attention. A fist thumped against the wood over and over.

My wife stormed out of the bedroom wearing a nightgown and ripped the banging door open. "Carlitos, there is somebody here with a painting," she yelled before strutting back into the bedroom.

I arose from the chair and approached the door. My eyes jolted wide open when I saw the painting. I almost dropped my glass. "Is this Snoopy?" I asked, excited like a child on Christmas morning. The delivery man handed the canvas over to me. I could have cried. It was so beautiful. Rich colors of red, orange, and blue with shades of black and brown boasted brightly on the piece of art. The brush strokes and attention to detail were phenomenal. Snoopy, my favorite rooster, was immortalized.

Chapter 20
The Trap

I arrived at the airport too late. The plane took off without me. I could see it in the air until it broke through the clouds. My gun sat in my holster, and I had eleven thousand dollars burning a hole in my pocket. The casino was close by. I could see the slight hue emitting from its neon exterior. It was bright out when I entered. The clock's hands spun like a fucking propeller. By the time I lifted my head, the sun had already begun to fall. I walked through the doors of the casino with my bag in my hand and five hundred dollars in my pocket. I lost $10,500 in one day. I don't even remember how it all went. I needed that money for Mexico. I was waiting for the next flight out of Tocumen. Noriega was already in the air. He also had his accommodation taken care of. By the time I made it, I had to find my own room and rush to meet the others. The hotel I stayed in was disgusting, so I found a woman to spend the first night with.

Noriega had a meeting with the president and his people. I had helped him arrange it. On the second night, Noriega and I drank with the president and his men in an old *taverna* with a mariachi band playing. It was a relaxing night at first. We were away from the tensions of home. A break was needed.

The drunker we got, the busier the taverna became. A flood of hombres in cowboy hats and sombreros entered, stirring up noise by the bar. One man started to scream and yell. It irritated me. Everyone at our table visibly detested this man's outcry for attention. He sang out of tune with the band.

"Shut the fuck up," I yelled to him. The music was beautiful, but the singing along ruined it.

The man did not stop. He continued to drink and yell and sing. When he started to move around the room, I became nervous. He was sloppy and stumbled into people. It could have been an act. I needed to be on guard.

"Carlitos, President de Gortari says they have been experiencing more DEA involvement in Mexico," Noriega said.

"Many drugs are coming through my country and into the United States. They think they can solve it, but they cannot. We will always be outnumbered," the president said.

Since Operation Tigre, we have worked closely with the Mexican government. Drug routes often started in Panama, and if they did not go through Cuba, then they typically went through Mexico. The border was an issue for the DEA. Gangs in Mexico had begun working with the cartels in Colombia. It was an issue that both of our governments were tackling.

U.S. Depart, ıt of Justice

Drug Enforcement Administration

PCO-85-08

Panamá 9 de Julio de 1985

Inspector Luis A. Quiel
Oficina de Coordinación y
  Enlace Internacional
Comandancia de las Fuerzas de Defensa
E. S. D.

Estimado Inspector:

El día 20 de Marzo del presente año, La Corte Federal de Laredo, Texas, expidió la orden Federal de Arresto número L 850078M 01 contra el ciudadano norteamericano Alberto AUDEMAR-Fareatai por violación de las leyes Federales de narcóticos de los Estados Unidos.

Con fecha Marzo 5 de 1985, las autoridades Federales arrestarón a AUDEMAR-Fareatai en la cuidad de Nashville, Estado de Tennessee en relación con la incautación de 300 kilogramos de cocaína decomisados por la policia en Laredo, Texas. Investigaciones anteriormente realizados identificaron a AUDEMAR como la fuente de suministro de 385 kilogramos de cocaína (90% de pureza) que se incautaron el día 31 de Octubre de 1984 en Nuevo Laredo, Tamaulipas, Mexico.

La Corte Federal ha formulado cargos contra AUDEMAR-Fareatai por violación de los siguientes artículos del Codigo Penal Criminal de los Estados Unidos de Norteamerica:

(1) Artículo 21 U.S.C. 841 - Posesión de cocaína con intención de distribuirla

(2) Artículo 21 U.S.C. 846 - Conspiración para poseer y distribuir cocaína

(3) Artículo 21 U.S.C. 952(a) - Importación ilegal de substancias controladas

El ciudadano AUDEMAR-Fareatai es actualmente fugitivo de la Justicia penal norteamericana. En la eventualidad que la presencia de este fugitivo se logre detectar en la República de Panamá, le solicitamos la cooperación de las autoridades competentes Panameñas para arrestar a este narcotraficante y ponerlo a disposición de los tribunales para que responda a los cargos que se le emputan por tráfico internacional de estupefacientes.

Figure 20.1. DEA memo, July 9, 1985, requesting Panama's cooperation in the capture and expulsion of a fugitive wanted in the United States on drug charges. (Memo is continued in figure 20.2.)

301

```
PCO-85-08
Inspector Luis A. Quiel
Panamá 9 de Julio de 1985

Le adjunto copia de el pasaporte norteamericano Número Z-4507600
expedido a favor de ALBERTO FAREATAI AUDEMAR el día 20 de Junio de
1984.

Agradeciendo la atención que se digne prestar a la presente me
suscribo de Ud. como su atento servidor y amigo


                                    Tomás N. Telles
                                    Agregado del DEA
                                    Embajada de EE.UU.AA.

TMT:LEG:jl
```

Figure 20.2. Continuation of the memo in figure 20.2, providing identification details and expressing gratitude to Panamanian authorities for their assistance.

The drunk man sang louder. He shifted through the crowd and stumbled into Noriega's back. "*Lo siento, amigo,*" the drunk man mumbled, trying to pat Manuel on the shoulder but swaying and missing.

I was fed up. My chair screeched against the wooden floor as I jumped to my feet. I grabbed him by the back of the neck with one hand, and with the other, I shoved my pistol right into the back of his rib cage. His eyes shot wide open.

"Are you going to kill me?" he asked hysterically.

"You and I are going to leave. Stay calm," I whispered, pushing him toward the door. I kicked him outside, and he stumbled into the dust. A single floodlight lit us in the dirt parking lot. Two hombres were smoking cigarettes by the entrance. They didn't bat an eye. "If I see you in there again tonight, I'll use this," I stated, showing him the glisten of my gun.

It was my job to protect Noriega. It wasn't intelligence or military servitude; it was protection. Motherfuckers like that drunk asshole were dangerous. He didn't know who Manuel was. Otherwise, he wouldn't have stumbled into him. If a fight broke out, he would not think twice about drunkenly using his pistol. I couldn't let anything happen to my friend. We returned to Panama safely.

Noriega asked me to come to headquarters one afternoon. He looked distraught.

"Everything okay, señor?" I asked.

Noriega pulled out a copy of *La Prensa*. "They're publicly scolding me," he said.

"It is time to do something about it," I responded. I was ready for Manuel. *La Prensa* was our largest opposition voice in the media. It reported everything Noriega did; the opposite should have been done. Even in 1984, when our friend Barletta won the election, *La Prensa* was calling for fucking Arnulfo Arias to take the seat!

"Eisenmann has already fled the country," Manuel muttered.

"Roberto Eisenmann? Chucha, he created *La Prensa* only seven years ago and put us through hell to suddenly decide to flee from us," I complained.

"Eisenmann is a traitor to the nation," Noriega said.

"I will talk to Governor Velazquez about a raid."

"In due time. Right now, we need to worry about Diaz Herrera. He is out of order."

I wasn't shocked that Diaz Herrera spoke out against Manuel. He was retired because we foresaw that he would do something shortsighted, but I was shocked that the culebra had the balls to amplify his voice as loud as he did. He wanted Manuel's head on a stick; he had a real hard-on for him. I think he always did. Domestically, we made statements like Herrera's as quietly as we could in the media. I was seeing our people slowly turn against their government because a respected man inside the PDF, once close to Manuel, accused Noriega of drug smuggling and murder.

"The CIA is plotting something," Noriega said. "They're using men I have confided in against me, men I spent years with building this country. . . . I know they are," he muttered.

There was only so much we could stop. Herrera's words had been captured by the American media and the BBC. He had become a spokesperson. He finally got the spotlight that he wanted.

One night, my wife passed out and fell asleep in bed. I sat in the kitchen, by the open window, smoking a cigar with a single reading light illuminating the room. My finger moved along the page of the Diaz Herrera report we acquired from a source in Washington. Everything he said about Manuel was there—drug trafficking, election manipulation, wire fraud, murder. Reading it disappointed me. He was our chief of staff, Manuel's second-in-command. His words cut deep. I collected everything I could about him. Intelligence files were kept secret. I had access to the knowledge that others didn't. He served us all over the world; he even negotiated part of Torrijos's treaty deal. Everything I read contradicted the character of the man I thought I knew. I was deeply immersed in his words when the phone rang.

"Carlos?"

"Who is this?" I asked.

"This is Carlos Sarmiento."

"Sarmiento, mi amigo. How are you?"

"Listen, I do not have long to talk. Remember those friends I told you about in Miami? There is a deal I want to cut you in on, a big one."

"What kind of deal?"

"It is one shipment. They need help with the transport. Fly to Cuba, meet them, have dinner, drink, go to the club… If you don't like them, just come home. You do not even need to see the boat."

I trusted Sarmiento enough to tentatively accept. I was a weapons trafficker for much of my life, and I never got caught because I was smart. I operated through legal means, and I rarely left behind a signature. Sarmiento's line cut, and a static dial tone rang in my ear. I knew I would have to vet his men, but with the revenue from the restaurant cut, I was open to making some extra cash.

Our problem with Herrera had reached its peak. We couldn't sit back and watch the headlines roll. We secretly developed a plan to solve our issue. Everything was in place, and not a soul outside the one hundred soldiers and our leaders knew.

I watched the sunrise. My uniform slipped onto my body seamlessly. The streets were empty; I could drive as fast as I wanted. A smell lingered in my nostrils as the sky grew brighter. I joined Noriega. We listened to our military radios as one hundred of our men stormed Diaz Herrera's house.

"They have thirty men guarding him," our soldiers yelled through the radio.

Gunfire echoed through the speaker. I listened as our men on the ground and in the air overpowered our opposition and took Diaz Herrera forcibly from his home to be put on trial.

Diaz never stood a chance in court. "Please, have mercy, Manuel," he pleaded. Noriega didn't even want to see the motherfucker's face. I knew his trial would be swift, but there would be mercy. We had known him for years, and we were not monsters. His accusations upset Noriega, and Manuel simply did what he had to do. President Delvalle met with Noriega after this raid and tried to negotiate with him. It was no use. Diaz Herrera was put under house arrest. We felt this was more than fair. He continued to garner some support, and we felt that was a threat, so Herrera was moved into a prison before being exiled to Venezuela. My contacts at the CIA and DEA weren't returning my calls; my only interaction with either organization was opening the envelope they licked shut with my paycheck inside.

I scheduled a flight to Havana to meet with Sarmiento's contacts, but I wanted to speak with Noriega before I flew out. Something didn't sit right in my stomach. I didn't know if it was smart of me to assume I could still work under the radar. Reagan's War on Drugs had escalated. The American people were fully on board. The aggression they held for Communism, they now had for drugs, and to catch a trusted advisor of Noriega doing something illegal could have been detrimental to our cause. For all I knew, I was the most recent addition to a list in the Oval Office.

Noriega sat behind the wheel of his car when I arrived in the rural village where he was to give a speech that evening. "Get in, Carlos. Let's go for a drive," he said. Manuel liked to be among the people as often as he could. We drove slowly, and locals turned as we passed them by.

"I need some advice."

"About what?" Noriega responded.

"My money is drying up. There is an opportunity in Cuba through Sarmiento, but I have a bad feeling about it."

"Smuggling?"

"Si, señor, weapons, Havana to Miami."

"And they want help with the logistics, yes?"

"Yes."

Noriega understood I had to go to Havana to see what the opportunity was. If Sarmiento's men were trafficking weapons, I could make enough to fix my problems. I left Panama for Havana. I didn't want to reach out to anyone while I was there. It was to be a quick trip. Sarmiento's men would contact me at my hotel. I spent two days sitting at the beach, drinking and talking to beautiful women. They liked the way I spoke. It was an aphrodisiac for them. I spent my time in good company. On the third day, I sat in a breakfast cafe alongside my beauty from the night before. A thin cigarillo sat between my lips, a crisp beer in a green bottle before me.

"I'll be right back, baby," the chick said to me.

I lit up my cigarillo with a match. The television in the corner of the room caught my attention.

"The Reagan administration is moving closer to open confrontation with Panama's de facto leader, Manuel Antonio Noriega, after five thousand supporters of the general came marching on the US embassy in Panama City. It is believed that Noriega incited this riot himself. The United States closed the consular section and library of the US Embassy yesterday to protest the Panamanian government's involvement in demonstrations at the embassy."

I watched as images of protestors swarmed the US embassy in my home city. I jumped from my seat and rushed for the payphone by the bathroom. The dial tone sounded in my ear. Nothing. "*Chucha*," I muttered. I needed to get back to Panama.

My chick stepped out of the bathroom; her eyes lit up when she saw me.

"I'm leaving. I'll call you a cab," I said. The driver dropped me off at the hotel, and I ran inside. When I opened my room, the blinds fluttered in the hot breeze that entered through the open window. The phone was ringing. I picked it up.

"Carlos Wittgreen?" a Cuban voice said.

"Who is this?" I responded.

"This is Sarmiento's friend. Are you free to come meet us at our marina this afternoon?" he asked.

I worried for Manuel. Every TV I watched and each radio station I listened to spoke of the demonstration. The gringos were outraged. They saw it as a sign of aggression. My people were loyal and had become fed up with the American presence. It was a tale as old as time. I always believed Panama was founded in protest. There was a change coming.

The sun blasted me in the eyes when I stepped out of the cab at the marina. My bag was over my shoulder. I set it down by my feet. There were boats docked everywhere. I didn't know what I was looking for. Three men in the distance whistled at me. They were standing by a tourism boat with hourly prices painted onto the vessel's exterior.

"Carlos?" one of them bellowed.

"You must be Sarmiento's friend," I said, taking off my sunglasses.

They jumped down to the dock to meet me. All three caballeros were beaten by the sun; I could see the early blemishes of skin disease riddled along their bodies.

"Sarmiento speaks highly of you," one yelled out.

"Where is he?" I asked.

The men had no answers for me. Carlos hadn't been seen in Cuba for weeks.

"I want to see what you're transporting," I demanded.

They all turned to each other, confused. "Why?" they asked.

I felt a rush of warm air circumnavigating my ankles. Something hadn't felt right about those guys from the first second. They looked drawn out, beaten, like druggies. "The weapons, are they already in the boat?" I asked.

"Not yet," one responded.

A sinking feeling fell in my stomach. I scanned around. I couldn't stay there any longer.

"Hey, where are you going, man?" they yelled out to me as I turned and walked off the dock.

I had to get home. History was happening in Panama, and I needed to be there.

I was distraught when I arrived home; my mind was churning at the rate of my heart. I kept rationalizing the thought that the CIA and DEA were going cold on me because they were trying to pin me with something to take me out of the picture. I was a trusted aide, a loyal confidant for Manuel and my government. I had secrets they wanted. It made sense. I made some calls. Manuel had told me something a long time ago, something that made sense at that moment—my training in Israel, in Washington, and in Cuba gave me connections all over the world that I could call at a moment's notice. My ear was red. I called and I called until I finally found the answer that I was looking for. Sarmiento had been caught by the CIA. They had been on his trail for years, and they finally seized him for his financial involvement in narcotrafficking. They knew of his connection to me, so they did what any good intelligence agency would do, and they asked him to trap me. My name was officially on some list in the Oval Office. I was a target, just like Manuel.

"Fuck," I whispered to myself.

Each morning, I woke up worried about what would happen that day. Everywhere I drove, there were protestors, either in favor of us or in opposition. The PDF was controlling the situation as best it could. I met often with men for Noriega and gathered intelligence. The sentiment toward our nation and its leaders was split in different directions. I could see it all with my own eyes, and with my ears, I heard things such as the fact that US assistant secretary of state, some fucking culebra named Elliott Abrams, was calling for Delvalle to overthrow Manuel. I heard this standing right by Noriega.

"Military leaders must remove their institution from politics, end any appearance of corruption, and modernize their forces to carry out their large and important military tasks in defense of the canal," Abrams stated publicly.

We lost our military funding from America. It was a toxic, brutal period in my history. The Americans knew the power they had over us, and they abused it. We would have to fend for ourselves with fucking sticks and rocks while our enemy camped by the canal ten fucking miles away.

"Do not worry, Carlitos. Our people are strong. We will persevere," Noriega reminded me.

I drove through the city one morning in the summer of 1987. It was June 26, to be exact. I could feel the earth shake under my tires. The radio was muffled. Through the windscreen, I saw dozens of young men and women holding signs and wearing riot clothing. They were heading somewhere as a unit. I followed them. The streets had become empty. No vehicles joined mine. The humming purr of my car entranced me as I scanned my surroundings for activity, and then I heard the yells. "Out with Noriega!" The chants consumed the air around me. I parked as close as I could to the noise. Ahead of me, hundreds, thousands of protestors stepped out onto the street with bullhorns and signs, and they were red with rage. My eyes jolted wide open; I wanted to fight every fucking one of them. They were calling for the destruction of my friend, the man who cared most about Panama. I wanted to stop them myself. I could hear the sirens of the PDF vehicles approaching from a distance. I knew they would arrive with rubber bullets and smoke bombs, all manufactured by the United States government. I needed to find Manuel.

After several hours of hunting, I learned that Manuel was at the house of a man named Jorge. He was an arms dealer wanted by the United States. I interrupted their conversation. Manuel shook Jorge's hand, and Noriega and I stepped outside to his armed car with a driver.

"Let us talk in the car," he said.

I felt sick. The chants, yells, and gunshots could be heard for miles. It sounded like a war out there.

"This is fucking Diaz Herrera's fault," Manuel said. "His words sparked this. And now the United States refuses to back us because of this? Chucha, after all I have given, I received nothing."

We drove along the outskirts of the city to avoid the growing protests. Manuel's gaze lingered through the glass. "Our intelligence tells us there are over one hundred thousand people protesting around the city today. That is almost a quarter of the population." It saddened him to see his people revolt. We were supposed to have the greatest and longest dynasty of leadership in Central America.

The gringos did what we knew deep down they would; they reevaluated relationships and made new friends, tossing the old ones away forever. Manuel couldn't show his face in public without someone screaming. Even when I went to a taverna, a boxing match, or a gallera, somebody would approach me. One man, several weeks after the first riot of one hundred thousand, pushed me at a cockfight. I almost broke my hand, jabbing him in the nose. His airwaves clogged, and he gasped for air at my feet. I wanted to spit on the culebra. I could feel the tension everywhere I went. Noriega knew he needed to make a decision that would have long-term effects. The people needed to realize that what they were doing was treason, one hundred thousand counts of treason, spurred on by the American media machine.

I watched on the news as our PDF soldiers contained the riots with force. Noriega pivoted, and his speech included anti-American sentiment. It was all for a reason. They were fucking us in front of the world and calling us human rights violators, drug traffickers, tyrants. . . . Chucha madre, the world had no idea what we did for the gringos. Nothing would have materialized without men like me or Noriega. We were their golden eggs in Central America. We built the foundations of the relationships that they leaned on. I met with Gaspar to gather intelligence from his sources in Europe. He had connections all over the world through the embassies.

"Bush has made Noriega his primary target," Gaspar told me. He was smarter than I was, and he understood world politics better than anyone, with the exception of Manuel. My brother sat before me in his clean suit and a cigar in his hand, the waters of the Colon's Caribbean coast rippling before us. He said to me, "Carlitos, you need to be careful. You're not just some pawn in the PDF. You're an aide, a right-hand man for one of America's greatest threats in recent history. . . . Think of the secrets Manuel knows. Think of the secrets you know. . . . It does not matter how much you helped them in the past. You need to be protected, hermano."

Gaspar was clear and direct. The world was talking about us. My name even started to appear in *Los Angeles Times* articles. I needed to figure out where I stood in that spotlight. The CIA was avoiding me, and the DEA was out of sight. I had trusted sources of intelligence that I could call. So I picked up the phone and called a friend from my days in Israel.

"I need to ask you for a favor."

"Anything for Carlos Wittgreen."

"Tell me if my name is showing up anywhere."

"I can do that, señor. I can do that. . . . Is everything okay?" he asked sincerely.

"I just want to know which shoulder to look over."

I trusted my sources to report their findings in a timely fashion. My friends were often the spiders that spun the web world agencies perched themselves on. I needed to stay alert in the meantime. Enemies were everywhere. Eyes were on us. I kept to my own dealings. Politics was always adjacent to my life. I sensed the PRD [Partido Revolucionario Democrático, or Democratic Revolutionary Party] growing greedier, constantly asking of the

PDF. The government and military were growing apart. My suspicions of politicians' cooperation with the United States in order to take Noriega out were heightened. Some party members never looked us in the eyes. We trusted many of them over the years. I stood by Noriega's side as these people shook his hand and reaffirmed their loyalties, only to swing to the other side like a pendulum when Uncle Sam came stomping. Everything I had seen Manuel build was coming crashing down on him.

Every day, I saw Panamanian citizens screaming for change. I couldn't take it. I charged out into a crowd of young men yelling out for "something different," and I laid out three of them with my fists. One of the fuckers pulled a knife, he waved it in front of my face. I grabbed his wrist and snapped the bone in two, and the weapon fell between my boots. "*Malditas traidoras,*" I said with disrespect. They deserved to be on Coiba with all of the other ladronas. Every fucking one of them.

The women in my life continued to grow worried for me, but I didn't fucking care what they thought. Some of my children left the country and went off to foreign nations with no political tensions. I received calls from them often. I had a son in Switzerland studying engineering and a daughter in the United States who was building a life for herself. By the beginning of 1988, I had seen everything I loved about my nation vanish, and what took its place was a hellscape created by the strong arm of the United States.

I gathered intelligence while Manuel was meeting with his allies in the Legislative Assembly to understand the state of internal affairs within our government. Traitors and two-faced spies were slipping through Panama and dripping onto US soil; I knew we would be stained by their disloyalty to everything we had built. Manuel often told me how this is what the United States has been doing in Latin America for years. We had seen it with the invasion of Grenada. I understood that continually displacing governments in our region would help the gringos keep control over our affairs. The Monroe Doctrine was fully at play. No one family or man could stay in the same seat. No amount of phone calls or secret meetings with the American elite could change the trajectory of our future, even when Reagan told Manuel to walk into exile.

"Ronald Reagan has asked me to flee my own country. He says I will not be harmed if I do this. Chucha, he does not understand. I will never leave my post willingly. If they want to negotiate, I am here."

Bush was looking like he would become the next leader of the United States. We could see it all the way in Panama. We all knew that was not good for us. Reagan was giving Noriega an out, and as I knew he would, Manuel tossed it back in his face.

"There is a solution," Manuel said. "We negotiate with China so it will put troops on our land, the Red Army."

"That would put us in a war zone."

"We are already in a war zone."

My mind barely had time to process what was happening around me. It felt as if we were in a never-ending storm. The seas around us were tumultuous, their waves thunderous and unrelenting. The core of the PDF shielded Manuel from external threats. I knew I would die for the man. Still, there was hope. Our intelligence arm was so strong that it would have ruptured the CIA if it fell. Our connection to the Middle East was vital. The Americans needed us and Mossad to supply them with intelligence. When it came to the Colombians, it was our boats and planes that seized more smugglers than any other Central American nation. All we wanted was self-governance. We did what was necessary to attain respect, yet we never received it.

In the midst of the turmoil, I pulled up to the gates of Manuel's residence. The guards shone a flashlight in my face.

"Let me in, fucker," I demanded. The gates opened for me, and I drove through.

Manuel sat at his desk on the phone when I entered his office. He raised his index finger to me. I stopped, the floorboard creaking below my feet. "Indict me? I am not even a fucking American citizen. How can they indict me?" Noriega declared loudly for me to hear. "Chucha," he followed with a whisper. He gestured to the unopened bottle of seco atop a file cabinet against the room's wall.

I uncorked it and poured two glasses as Manuel intently listened to the voice on the other side of the call.

"Do you know how much information I have on these fuckers? I know the people they worked with. I have evidence of their involvement in issues they should never be involved in. Don't they know this?" Manuel asked.

I wanted to know who he was talking to. It could have been anyone, but I knew the person was important.

"Harari, Harari, listen, listen. Just tell me whom I have to speak with to resolve this," he said, ending the call.

His Nicaraguan housemaid sprinted to the door. "Is everything okay, señor?" she asked.

"Yes, go downstairs," he responded.

We drank our seco in silence for only a moment.

Then he arose from his seat and paced back and forth. "How are your parents, Carlitos?" he asked me.

"Good, señor," I responded.

"Good, and your children?"

"They are well, señor. . . . And you?"

"I'm fighting, Carlos."

A storm surrounded us, but Noriega and I felt at ease at its center. Women and drinking were good distractions, but they weren't enough. I understood that I didn't know everything about Manuel. I didn't want to know everything. A man lives for his own purpose, and I am no judge. I devoted myself to Noriega because I knew that I would follow him into the darkness. He was my best friend, my brother. I couldn't fuck without wondering if he was safe. The CIA was plotting something, I fucking knew it.

"Our own people are trying to cut us at our feet, Carlos. Either we show strength, or we die," he told me.

"The DEA Indicts Manuel Noriega on Charges of Drug Smuggling, Racketeering, and Money Laundering." The newspapers sang these words as loud as they could. I tore up every copy I saw. Some of our friends in the PDF fucked up the head office of the newspaper *La Prensa*. It was finally happening. They were coming for Manuel and would not stop until a public display of justice was presented before the American audience. The Americans also put an economic sanction on us. They had gripped our throats. I helped Noriega put out whatever fires I could, but the flames were raging too hot and bright. Those who were once our allies began to refuse collaboration, and caballeros we once considered friends failed to return our calls. Harari had one foot in the room and one out the door. Ever since Munich, he had been a notable figure in Mossad, and his association with our allies made him a target in US publications. I knew he was trying to be smart, yet he continued to provide us with intelligence whenever he could. We heard nothing about plans of an invasion. We knew it was a possibility after Grenada. I didn't know where I stood in my own life until I received a call one winter's night.

"Tell me you have information for me," I responded.

"I do. . . . Carlos, you are, in fact, a target, but it is not the CIA who set the task."

"The DEA? Chucha, puta bandejos."

"It is not the DEA, either, Carlos. It is Interpol who is after you."

"Interpol?"

"Si, Carlos."

"Under what charges?"

"Robbery, sixty-three thousand dollars. They think you acquired it during a vacation you had to Spain several years ago."

"Chucha madre. If I wanted sixty-three thousand, I would have robbed a fucking chino! This is bullshit."

My heart sank into my stomach. I wanted to throw up. The bottle of seco in my cupboard called my name. I finished it, thinking about what to do. There was no out for me. I had safety only at home, which I knew would be fleeting even then. I could feel the charge in the air, the stench streaming from the military bases along the banks of the canal. Tensions brewed over there; I knew it. I had intelligence at the ground level. My days in Mossad taught me that the best intelligence came from everyday conversation. US soldiers talked bullshit over drinks. The bartenders would overhear statements of war and terror, but the drunk word of a gringo was more likely a show of ego rather than the truth. There was more talk than action. I listened closely until a yell sounded, and the truth came.

"Eric Andre Delvalle is a fucking traitor. Who does the fucker think he is?" Noriega said, containing his fury.

We learned that Delvalle had cooperated with the United States government. He tried to gather support within the PRD to democratically remove Manuel from his position as general. He declared this to the world. Our fucking president stood on a stage and demanded that Panama hand Manuel over to the DEA to stand on trial for the crimes he was accused of. I wanted to kill the man. Manuel fired orders to PDF soldiers to track him down, but he had vanished. I showed up at his residence, and there was not a soul to be seen. I sauntered through the home alongside a half-dozen PDF soldiers. It looked like they had left in a hurry. Items were carelessly strewn about, the sink full of dishes. The bastard had fled to the United States. Just like that, we had no president, half of the PRD resented us, and the people who protested in the streets sang louder and louder.

Noriega called for an immediate gathering of his supporters. I helped spread the word, contacting news stations and radio stations to attend. The room was filled with hundreds of men and women. They smiled and cheered for their leader, who stood with me behind the stage. His machete hung from his belt. I spiffed up his white shirt. Several of my peers, Manuel's advisors who remained, whispered things into his ear. I knew he didn't want to hear anything. I could see the reflection of the cameras in his glistening eyes. This speech would be for the world. I shook his hand and patted him on the shoulder, and he stepped out onto the stage and stood in the spotlights that shone down on him from above. I scanned the crowd as they erupted in cheer. For all I knew, the CIA could have planted a bomb under the stage or could have hired an assassin to sneak through the crowd. I didn't know; none of us did. This was Noriega's last chance to speak his voice. I looked at my greatest friend stand before the world, and I watched as he ripped the machete free from its holster and raised it high above his head.

"This machete represents the dignity and courage of the Panamanian people," Noriega said as he held the gleaming weapon. "It says, 'Not one step back.'"

The crowd erupted; I could feel the reverberation of their cheer at my feet.

"Delvalle's words are those of a fleeing coward. I will not be relinquished in my position," he said.

I could see the reporters steadying their cameras. My gut told me the words spoken that day would shake the earth. The energy in that room incited a reinvigoration of love for our leader, my friend. Yet I knew what the media did with words, with statements of power . . . they turned them into symbols of aggression. After that day, there was no going back for us. America wanted Manuel's head on a stick; Interpol wanted to put me in chains.

Chapter 21
The Storm

I had to listen to the claims that Noriega was part of an international conspiracy to import cocaine and materials used in producing cocaine into the United States.

"If only William Casey were still alive, he would be able to back me up. He knows all about Bush's drug pilots," Noriega said on occasion.

I looked out my window often, and I saw nothing but growth. I gazed upon the banks that Noriega welcomed with open arms, I saw the US soldiers that Manuel allowed to train on our land, and I fucking personally spoke with the CIA, who Noriega worked tirelessly for over twenty years. The theories about racketeering and money laundering made me laugh. I knew firsthand that the Americans were giving us their capital to keep safe in our haven. Those fuckers were the ones who were laundering money, not us. I thought it was a joke. I was hysterical. It didn't help that Interpol had a bounty on my head, too. The accusations against me were mostly true. I did traffic weapons. I did things the Americans did not like, but I didn't care because what I did for them was far more illegal. It was a slap in the fucking face that I was now being hunted for crimes I was paid to do. The 1980s were coming to a close, and every ounce of hope and prosperity I held at the beginning had washed away by the end.

Muammar Gaddafi phoned Noriega once a week during that time. He knew what it was like to be a target of the United States, and so he offered Manuel support and advice. I found it to be a caring act. It yet again opened my eyes to the true size of the world. We were thousands of miles apart, yet in 1989, we were neighbors.

By '89, Panama was a beehive for all of us. It was chaotic. I couldn't walk in the street without seeing poverty. I couldn't enjoy a moment of silence in my own home because people protested and screamed in the city. Manuel had to send the PDF out frequently to contain riots. I wanted to be there; I wanted to help my friend. I spent much time providing intelligence and aid to him. There was an election coming up, and Noriega feared the CIA was plotting to overturn the government. Arnulfo Arias's party was still loyal to his name, and its vocal anti-Noriega message was louder than ever, but luckily, he died in 1988 and left the Arnulfista party without its leader. The Alianza Democrática de Oposición Cívica was our opposition coalition, and the members nominated Guillermo Endara for the 1989 presidency. In the past, Manuel exiled him due to his relationship with Arias. I knew the United States was whispering in Endara's ear. So we put our man, Carlos Duque, in the running for the PRD. He was someone we could trust.

Noriega was frantic the day before the election. His phone wouldn't stop ringing. I picked up calls for him. Everyone wanted to know what was happening with the presidency. I remember seeing the statue of the Virgin Mary in his office. Its marble eyes stared into my soul. I could feel the tremors, but nobody was speaking.

"Has my contact in the Pentagon called?" Noriega asked.

"Not yet, señor," I responded. We had allies everywhere, but as the decade came to a close, they stopped picking up our calls. It was as if they had been warned not to.

"Jimmy Carter will be in Panama for the election," Manuel said.

"Why?"

"He started an organization called The Carter Center. He promotes democracy, and so we will show him that our candidate is who the people want."

Carter being in Panama brought with it unwanted attention. I knew Harari and Manuel met often to discuss intelligence. Harari had become Noriega's highly trusted advisor.

"You find yourself in a position of importance, Manuel," Harari said. "The US wants to make an example out of you. They did not do this for Jorge Rafael Videla in Argentina or Banzer in Bolivia, and they didn't even do this for Pinochet in Chile; he was removed from his throne, but he still sits in government. They are after you because they fear you the most. The canal sits on the land that you control. You have decades of intelligence that could topple entire countries, including America. Think of it. You acquired knowledge from figures like George Bush, Oliver North, and countless American spies whom you won over in one way or another. You, sir, are feared, and the only way to stay in power is to balance your fear and love in the eyes and hearts of the Panamanian people. Look at what Castro does. He has been in power for nearly thirty years, and he sits ninety miles from American land."

I was Manuel's right-hand man, and Noriega looked out for me. But there were discussions where I didn't need to be present; there were things I didn't need to know because if I did, then I would be squeezed just as was being done to my friend. There was nothing I wouldn't have done to be there for him. I would have gladly stood in front of a rifle held by George Bush himself. Our intelligence told us to stay calm, but my gut told me to prepare for war.

I decided to visit the casino the night before the election. My chick at home waited for me, but I couldn't just sit. I needed action. As I pulled into the parking lot, I noticed the neon lights that had once glistened in the sky were dimmed to darkness. The door was locked. I shook it violently. "Ballerna, let me in," I yelled. I was confused. Why wouldn't I have been informed? I needed an answer. My car rattled as I drove over uneven pavement. A slew of cars was stopped before me. "What the fuck is going on?" I asked myself as I peered over the wheel to see. Drums beat a hundred feet ahead. The red brake lights on the stationary cars cast a red hue on my face as I charged along the line of vehicles toward the beating drums. A half-dozen caballeros in dirty clothing protested before me. The first car in line honked loudly and consistently. "Let us fucking through," I yelled, approaching the largest man in the group.

"Fuck you," he responded to me.

I could feel the gun in my pocket growing heavy. I wanted to bash the fucking culebra's face in, but instead, I jabbed him in the fucking nose. He fell to the street, and I kicked him in the stomach twice. Two of his amigos lunged at me. I elbowed one in the jaw, grabbed the other by his hair, and dragged him face-first into the concrete. Three men squirmed at my feet. I breathed heavily, one hand slowly reaching for my gun.

"Okay, okay, we'll move," they cried.

I stomped back to my vehicle.

The people in the line of cars honked and cheered for me.

"What the fuck do you mean you're permanently closed?" I yelled into my house telephone the moment I returned home.

"I'm sorry, Carlos. I don't know what to say. Business is not good; I have no choice," Ballerna responded nervously.

Everything was chaos. I didn't blame any business owner for having to shut down during those times. Protests put our nation at a standstill. Corporations were bleeding capital. It was happening with casinos all over Panama and the rest of Central America, too. I went to bed that night and did not close my eyes. My wife lay next to me as I gazed at the ceiling, thinking about what was going to transpire after the next day. All the accusations against me were putting me on edge. I waited for Interpol agents to kick down my door and drag me to court. What a fucking joke.

"And the new president of Panama is . . . Carlos Duque of the Coalición para la Liberación Nacional!"

I listened as the news of the election results swept the nation. People were outraged; they took to the streets again. Chucha madre. I was fucking sick of it all. Noriega and I watched them grow in numbers by the thousands. "Guillermo Endara has been robbed," they chanted. I saw Jimmy Carter himself shake his head and publicly announce that "the government is taking the election by fraud." Claims of marriage and voter fraud were sung in the media; I didn't want to listen to it. Carlos Duque was a friend and a former business partner of Noriega's and mine, and we trusted him. Manuel and I learned that Endara's people were monitoring voting booths, and they claimed that as of the night before the election results, he was winning. I called bullshit. I never saw any fucking numbers that proved that. Even the Catholic Bishop Conference had jumped on the anti-Noriega train and doubled down on claims of tampering with an election.

I was by Manuel's side when the country turned on him, and I will never forget the look of loss that struck him when it became obvious it would take an even stronger arm to put the people in check. Manuel didn't want to demolish any part of his nation. I knew in my heart that he cared deeply for the people. Still, he was a leader and a vitally important man, and I helped him send the PDF onto the streets like hunting dogs. A thick layer of riot smoke hung in the air; I looked at the devastation from the Palacio. The radio played, and the words of Marcos G. McGrath, the archbishop of Panama, echoed in my ears. "This election has been stolen," he said over and over. I didn't want to leave Manuel even for a second.

Noriega had initially planned to declare Duque the winner, regardless of the result. Duque rumbled into Noriega's quarters, filled with hysteria. "I know I have been beaten; I refuse to go along," he began saying.

I stepped out of the conversation; it was not one for me.

The next day, Endara, Arias Calderón, and Guillermo Ford really pissed us off. It seemed as if every day, some fucking guy we used to drink with was holding a microphone and screaming obscenities into it. I was expecting further chaos in the streets, but when it came to diplomacy and politics, I had assumed discussion and conversation would run the engine of democracy. These fuckers rolled through Casco Viejo atop a fucking motorcade screaming, "We won the election. Noriega is a fraud," loud for all to hear. Journalists, cameramen, authors, and politicians all ran to the scene.

Chucha, Noriega was infuriated, and yet again, he had to send the PDF out to reprimand them publicly. Manuel needed to send a message that was stronger than those who had fallen before him. The Dignity Battalions [paramilitary militia units that supported PDF] were used, and I stood amongst inferior officers and watched as Endara and his amigos were beaten to a bloody pulp in the middle of the busy street. I could see the flashes from cameras shining, and I knew it would add to the weight I felt on my shoulders for Noriega.

It was no surprise that another coup was attempted that October. The protests had bubbled to a pop. The motorcade beatings did not help our case. Our own Lieutenant Colonel Moisés Giroldi Vera staged the insurrection with the help of several of our junior officers. I instructed those still loyal to us to squash and capture these traitors, and within days, we did. The PDF mainly remained true to their word. Manuel often stood on stages with cameras pointed at him while these riots ensued below him. He yelled in the streets and screamed for change in media halls. Everything was documented. I turned a blind eye as Giroldi Vera and his men were taken far from the city and executed for their crimes against the government. After months of countless arrests, killings, protests, and attempted insurrections, Noriega looked like a deflated balloon barely holding onto a string during a vicious windstorm. I would like to think that I held that string.

At the beginning of December 1989, Noriega entered my home and kissed my woman on the cheek. I grabbed a bottle of seco, and we sat in my study. My home had thick walls, and the sounds of the outside world were muffled. "You and I are going to Coiba tomorrow," he said.

"Okay, señor," I responded. The alcohol barely numbed a muscle. My brain was pumping; I could see Manuel's was, too.

So much had happened in what felt like a short amount of time. No leader wanted to act the way Noriega was acting, but he didn't have a choice. If he rolled over, the CIA and DEA would rip him from his nation and shoot him on live television for the world to see.

"I need to get away from all of this shit," he said. "Besides, it has been some time since I have checked on things on Coiba."

"Chucha, a break sounds nice, señor. If only there were women on Coiba," I joked.

Noriega laughed.

It wouldn't have been difficult whatsoever to bring a dozen beauties to the prison, but neither of us was in the mood. For once, the thoughts of fucking and debauchery vanished from our minds. All we could focus on was the downfall of what we had built.

"It all happened so suddenly," I said to Noriega.

Manuel was a man of many words, but when he chose not to speak, that was when I knew he struggled to see the moves ahead.

A chopper escorted Noriega and me to Coiba. I believe it was the morning of December 14. I gazed at the red sky the entire ride.

Domingo met us at the landing point. "Just in time," he bellowed and pointed to the clouds on the horizon. "A red sky in the morning, a sailor's warning."

Noriega and I stomped through the prison. Inmates stayed put. I looked into every pair of eyes I passed, and none blinked.

"As you can see, General, everything is fine," Domingo exclaimed.

Noriega was never convinced by words, but the prison did look to be functioning normally. The cells were filled with men who had committed crimes on the mainland; we didn't care about their conditions as long as they were sufficient for survival. As I walked by the last cell on the block, a hand reached out to me. The man had overgrown, yellow fingernails with various slices and cuts visible on his forearm. I slapped it away before he could open his mouth.

"Don't touch me," I muttered to him before catching up with Domingo and Manuel.

"Everything is fine, see?" Domingo pleaded.

"Yes. ... Now, leave us. We have to speak," Noriega responded.

"Yes, señor," Domingo said, turning to leave us.

"Actually . . . get us a bottle of seco. No. Two bottles of seco. Bring them to us by the shore," Noriega said.

Of all the drinks I have had in my life, that seco was the one that hit the spot just right. My ass sank into the white sand of the Coiba shore. Manuel sat next to me. We both held crystal-clear bottles of seco and sank back shots in silence. I was entranced by the swirling red hue in the sky and the gray clouds that were slowly approaching.

Manuel gazed at the horizon; I could see the reflection of the swooshing waves in his glistening eyes. He wiped his mouth and dug the base of the glass a few inches into the sand. "My days in Chiriqui were incredible. Everything afterward seemed to move fast. But not my days in Chiriqui," he stated. I could tell Manuel was filled with nostalgia.

"Do you remember the time we were drinking in that taverna in Guatemala with some of our officers, Herrera and Paredes, and the lights went out?" I mentioned.

"Chucha, how could I forget? The electricity failed, and you thought it was an assassination attempt, so you jumped on me and fired your pistol into the darkness," Noriega added.

"When the fucking lights came on, the bartender was so fucking pissed with me that he wanted to kick us out."

"It's a good thing we were there visiting the president."

I did a lot in my time, things that even some of my closest friends and family have no idea about. Noriega knew everything. He was my confidant, who understood me to my core and kept my darkest secrets safe. We could be anywhere together—a whore house, a church, a fucking library—and we would always manage to laugh and enjoy the moment. That evening, as we watched the red hue fade into the night, we sat in total serenity, staring as the gray clouds approached us.

"Señor Wittgreen!" Domingo's voice echoed.

My neck creaked as I turned, and I saw the warden sprinting toward me in the sand.

He skidded to a halt and panted with heavy breaths.

"What is it?" I asked.

"I just received a message from one of your officers, señor. Your son has been in an accident in Switzerland," Domingo stated.

My heart sank into my stomach. My eyes shot wide open.

Manuel placed his hand on my shoulder. "We will get you back to the city in an instant," he said.

As my brain thumped to the rate of my heart, a thunderous boom echoed from a distance. All three of us looked to the horizon, where sparks of lightning had begun to strike the waters.

Noriega charged into Domingo's office and made dozens of calls to our men in the military. "I need a bird to take me back to the city right now," he yelled, screaming orders into the phone.

Nobody could do it; nobody wanted to. "The storm is too powerful, General Noriega. No helicopter can fly," they told him. No matter how powerful my dear friend was and how hard he tried to get me off that island, there was no way it was happening until the storm lessened.

Noriega took me under his wing, just as he always did. There were quarters for us to sleep in and plenty of alcohol for us to drink. I worried deeply for my son. I thought about how he was alone thousands of miles from home.

"Keep your mind straight, Carlitos. We will get through this storm," he told me.

I was distraught. We lit candles in the room when the electricity ran out. The howling winds shook the walls, and dust fell atop our heads. I gazed through the glassless window as shards of rain sliced into the sand of the island. The worst of it all was that I didn't even want to leave my friend. My gut told me I needed to be here with him, but Manuel said otherwise. He eased my worries.

However, on that Saturday night in Panama City, hundreds of kilometers away from us, a killing occurred that would change everything. Members of our military brigade shot down a US Marine at a roadblock. To add fuel to the fire, the wife of an American soldier would also be harassed by members of the PDF.

At that moment, all I cared for was the well-being of my son.

"You know, Carlitos . . . I am lucky to have you by my side through all this," Noriega began.

"Thank you, señor," I responded.

"The information I have is more valuable than the canal itself right now. Bush has done things he hopes the American public will never know. He worries I will make them known."

Noriega went to the grave with many of his secrets. I wouldn't have dared ask him what sat in his memory. A true friend would never. I don't think anybody ever could get him to speak. There are countless conspiracies surrounding him. People have brought them up to me my entire life, such as the theory that Noriega had secret recordings of Bush acting against the American interest. I never heard these tapes, if they did exist. But, in our Latin circles, we knew Bush to be a bull, a man who said one thing to your face, then stabbed you in the back when you turned. Then George Sr. became president, and he had the power to do anything he wanted without recourse. Under Reagan, we were Bush's most wanted target, but he didn't have the full power to do what he wanted. So, during the first year of his term, we expected something big to happen.

"If they want to come and get me, they know where I am," Manuel said.

"I won't let them kill you, señor."

"Do not worry about me, Carlitos. Worry about your son, and you let me know how I can help."

"I'm your right hand, señor," I responded.

"This storm will end eventually, and life will continue. Remember that, mi amigo."

Noriega was right. The storm did end, and we made it back to the city. I flew to Switzerland to be with my son, Carlos Jr., and thankfully, he turned out just fine in the end. His mother and I were there for him, and I will always have Manuel to thank for that. Every time I have seen a storm since that day, I have thought about Manuel and how he helped me weather the torrential winds and swirling emotions that came with them. A drop of rain could not fall on my head without thinking of the general, the man who, in many ways, saved my life. That was the last time I saw my friend as a free man because, several days later, the United States invaded Panama with the intention of extracting Manuel Noriega to be put on trial for his crimes in Florida. Part of me thought Manuel knew what was coming for him, so he told me to leave. But that is only part of me. . . . When news of the invasion broke, I scrambled to find a way home.

Chapter 22
The Red Notice

My son was healthy. I thanked God. He would need to lie in a hospital bed for only a few more days. I was by his side when I heard word about the invasion. A call had come to the facility for me.

It was Gaspar. "The Americans invaded the city," he told me.

I turned on the TV to catch whatever footage I could. The Swiss news stations showed images of my people lying dead in the street. My finger ached as I clicked through stations. BBC, CNN, and TF1 all told the story of an evil dictator finally facing the repercussions of his actions. The United States was the hero, of course. I grew frantic immediately.

"You need to go. I will be fine," my son said.

The streets of Geneva were ignorant of the terror that was happening in my home. I hysterically sprinted through crowds to reach the nearest cab.

"Where to?" the cabbie asked.

"The airport." I hadn't heard a word from Manuel. They were coming for him; I needed to know that he was safe. "Turn on the news," I told the driver.

He fiddled with the dial until the BBC sparked on the radio. I understood English enough, and they were talking about Manuel as clear as day.

"Turn this up, cabbie," I demanded.

The fucker put his arm around the headrest of the passenger seat and turned his head to me. We were still propelling forward, the airport in the near distance. He was acting like I had insulted his fucking grandmother.

I wanted to fucking nail him, but I didn't. "Please, fucking, please . . . chucha," I muttered.

The cabbie turned the volume dial, and the voice of a British man echoed in my ears. "The United States has invaded Panama with the intention of extracting its de facto leader, General Manuel Antonia Noriega. US President George Bush has called this Operation Just Cause. In our most recent updates, it has been revealed that after the war declaration, four US military personnel, including Marine Captain Richard E. Haddad, Navy Lieutenant Michael J. Wilson, Army Captain Barry L. Rainwater, and Marine First Lieutenant Robert Paz, faced a roadblock near the PDF headquarters in El Chorrillo, a blue-collar neighborhood of Panama City in proximity to the canal. The PDF alleged that the Americans were armed and conducting reconnaissance. Tragically, Paz was fatally shot, and Haddad sustained injuries. Following this event, US Navy SEAL Lieutenant Adam Curtis and his wife, Bonnie, were taken into custody by PDF troops. Bonnie was allegedly sexually threatened, and Curtis reportedly endured physical abuse during detention. President Bush then commanded the implementation of the Panama invasion plan, scheduling H-hour for 0100 on December 20. Stay tuned for regular updates from our correspondents in Panama."

When I arrived at the airport, a feeling in my gut told me not to go inside. Interpol had a target on my back. I did not know if I would be arrested at any moment. I scanned the airport, looking for anyone who seemed suspicious. My top targets were every man or woman with a pair of sunglasses, a hat, a scarf, or anything that concealed a feature. It could have been anyone. I had to be smart. There were no direct flights from Geneva to Panama. I would have to pass through Madrid, Spain. I looked at the board of scheduled flights. There was a flight to Paris that was taking off soon. I had contacts in France, some through Gaspar, some through my own friendships. I could get there and have a friend do some reconnaissance for me. However, I knew that if I had enemies in Switzerland, I wouldn't be allowed to step onto the plane for France. The flight was at half-capacity; I sat far down the back, scrutinizing everyone as they passed by my shoulder to use the bathroom.

It was a rainy day in Paris when I arrived. A thin layer of fog covered the runway; I couldn't see the ground until the last second when the plane stopped. I clung to the armrests. Part of me thought an agent would be waiting for me at the gate. I stepped out to find normality. My eyes scanned the bustling terminal. I had no bags, nothing to weigh me down. There were faces everywhere, people I would never recognize. Sweat perspired on my palms. I needed to get a hotel and find out what the fuck was going on.

I loved Paris. It was a beautiful city. At this time, I barely knew where I was. My mind was in Panama, fighting with the men I had vowed to die for, standing by Manuel's side. I burst into my hotel room and jumped for the phone. "Come on," I whispered to myself as the dial tone echoed. No answer. Chucha, I had to speak to someone at home. Gaspar was my next call. "Mi hermano, how can I get home?" I asked.

"You cannot get in or out of Panama right now, Carlos," he told me over and over.

There had to be a way. I could not just sit in my hotel room night after night with my eyes peeled to the television as footage of my home in flames consumed my sight. I needed an answer directly from the source. I called countless contacts, but nobody could find me a way in. My eyes were forced to watch the news unfold within the confines of a small room, and my ears had to listen to the beratement of my friend as he feared for his life behind the walls of the Vatican Embassy. The Americans were laughing; the news highlighted footage of US soldiers playing rock music—Van Halen's "Panama" and Kenny Loggins's "Danger Zone"—at full volume outside the gates where the essence of our religion was held. It would take several days to get an answer, but when my phone finally rang, I fucking jumped for it.

"It's over, mi amigo. There are over thirty thousand American troops. . . . They brought with them heavy artillery, and my intelligence tells me they are even testing weapons on our people."

"What kind of weapons?"

"Chucha . . . lasers, for one. I heard one story about a PDF soldier who was shot by a US laser, and his gun melted to his body."

"Why isn't anybody talking about this?"

"It's the United States."

"I don't care what you say. I'm finding a way home, one way or the other."

"Listen to me very carefully. You have a red notice. Do you understand? Interpol has informed international law enforcement of your crimes. The French authorities likely know you are in their country, and if you go to Charles de Gaulle, they will be notified, and you will be arrested."

"So what? It is my home. I cannot return to it?"

"Not until your case is overturned. I have a man for you to meet. His name is Pablo, and he lives in Madrid. Go see him. . . . I'm sorry, Carlitos."

I had to smuggle myself across the border of France and into Spain. For such a beautiful journey, I didn't pay attention to any of it. My mind beat at the rate of my heart. I could think of nothing but Manuel hiding from US soldiers as they fired rounds at our people in the streets and bombed housing complexes with families inside. The terrifying thoughts consumed my mind. I have done many things in my life that my Lord and Savior would likely not approve of, but I have repented for them. This invasion sickened me to my core. My people were frustrated. They had problems with Manuel, but that was mob mentality, and I knew the tides would change, just as they always did. The invasion was personal, a statement made to the rest of the world that the United States was in charge.

Christmas Day came and went, and I had spent it alone. The glistening winter lights of Madrid instilled in me a feeling of disgust. I was surrounded by serenity when everyone I knew was either fighting or hiding for their lives. The United States would not back down.

President Bush took to the media every day, and I watched with clenched fists and alcohol rushing to my brain. "Our efforts to extract Noriega from the Vatican Embassy are proving worthwhile, with all fighting surrounding the area to have seemingly faltered."

The PDF was outnumbered, out-weaponed; I knew that as much as any man who took to the battlefield. America gave us our money to fund the military. Barely any of what we armed ourselves with was manufactured in Panama. We relied on our "allies" for such things.

I had gotten Pablo Munoz's number and address. It was a short ride from my hotel on the Metro. On December 26, I thought about paying him a visit, but I knew I had to at least try to make it home to my country, my people, my friend. No matter what, I would eventually have to stand trial and be persecuted by Interpol. It sounded like hell. I knew I couldn't bring myself to give up while my friend needed me. I had to try to save him. So I decided not to pay Munoz a visit on December 26. Instead, I called in favors from every spy, diplomat, and politician who ever owed me. Mike

Harari didn't pick up at first, but I received a call from him in Israel some days later. He had made it out of Panama the night before the invasion, and he was facing scrutiny from all angles. I do not think Mossad was involved in the invasion. Harari could not help me, nor could the rest of my contacts in Cuba, Nicaragua, Argentina, Uruguay, Brazil, Peru, or the United States. Nobody could fucking help me, and I grew tired of hiding in hotel rooms every night and covering my face when I walked outside.

New Year's Eve had approached, and my desperation grew uncontainable. The only way I would get home would be by boat. An airline would have my information on file, and Interpol would intervene. A boat was more covert. I could jump on and hide in the stowaway. I needed to find one that was heading for the canal. From there, I could sneak off and find a way to get to Noriega. I didn't know how I would protect him. That plan would have to be formulated on the trip. I gazed out my hotel window. The streets of Madrid were bustling for the festivities. A new decade was beginning, the 1990s, and the change felt palpable. Transition lingered in the air that I breathed. The elevator doors opened for me, and I stepped inside. Christmas music played softly. I gazed at my own warped reflection in the chrome walls. The lobby appeared before me; it was empty. I carefully walked through it and out onto the street. People rushed by, cars honked, busking musicians sang. . . . I whistled for a cab, sticking my hand out. In the corner of my eye, I could see three men in suits walking on the sidewalk. They were staring at me, hands in their pockets. One of them had a cigarette in his mouth; I could smell the tobacco stench from where I stood. I lowered my arm and began walking. I turned the first corner and picked up my pace. My neck creaked when I looked back. They were still trailing me, walking faster than they had been. Chucha, I knew they were after me. I had to be smart; there were only three of them. The block was tight, with four busy streets surrounding it. I sprinted around all four corners and rushed back to the hotel. The three agents squeezed through the spinning doors as I ran through the lobby. The elevator doors opened for me; I stood there, waiting, as the agents dusted themselves off and stepped in alongside me. All four of us panted with heavy breaths, silent with words. I pressed the button to take us to the penthouse. The clock was ticking, and the chrome doors slowly started to close, but right before they did, I slipped out at the last second and turned to watch as the elevator shut completely and rose to the top floor. Fucking idiots.

The New Year rang in with the news that I couldn't leave the country. No ships were heading to Panama due to the conflict, so I would have to wait. The world's supply chain was at a standstill for weeks. It was evident how powerful the canal was when nothing passed through it.

On January 1, I felt more isolated than I had ever felt in my life. I sat in a quiet taverna, watching the news. The owner sat by me and changed the television when I asked. The news did not cover the conflict in my country. They were too focused on the festivities. They cared only for their own speculations as to what the nineties would bring for us all.

"You are from Panama, yes?" the owner inquired.

"Si," I responded under my breath.

The owner nodded his head and stepped into the backroom for a moment. He popped out with a bottle of seco in his hands. He blew the dust off the glass and handed it over to me. It was old; the date was registered seven years prior.

"Chucha, where did you get this?" I asked.

"I have a good friend from Panama; he gifted it to me," he responded.

The taste reminded me of home, and it relaxed my muscles for a short while. The TV that played irreverent news suddenly switched, and footage of my home appeared on the screen. "Turn it up," I yelled.

Media teams swarmed as US soldiers had Noriega in handcuffs. My friend had been caught. My heart almost stopped beating. I could not taste the liquor on my tongue. They yelled and screamed out to Manuel, looking for a statement, before the footage vanished and a news reporter flashed on the screen.

"The United States has officially captured Panamanian General Manuel Antonio Noriega. He is being extracted from the city and taken to Miami, where he will stand on trial before a grand jury. After eleven days of terror, things are finally back to normal in Panama."

I will never forget how I felt hearing that news. I was not there for my friend. There was no point being covert anymore. I had to contact Pablo Munoz and work through my trial. Munoz took my case in the end. All of that fucking trouble over sixty-three thousand dollars. It was a joke, but I was a man, and I stood tall when they berated me with words of theft. I would, of course, return to Panama within my lifetime, but in the early 1990s, it was not necessarily safe for me. My crimes had caught up to me. I had prison time to undergo, I had people to pay back. . . . I had come so far, only to be dragged to the dirt and pinned down, forced to watch my country turn inside out and start all over again.

Chapter 23
France

For six months, I sat in a Peruvian jail cell. I was accused and convicted of murder. Interpol put me there. Those bastards had had it out for me since the incident in Spain. Panama wanted to extradite me. It was the worst fucking prison in the world. Inmates shit on open floors, they pissed anywhere they wanted, and the clothes we wore were torn and ragged. I hated every moment of it. While I sat in my own filth, Manuel was in the early stages of serving his forty-year sentence on American soil. The DEA got him, and to nobody's surprise, he was found guilty of the majority of his crimes, even if there was no evidence to support the drug trafficking charges against him. Not one piece of viable evidence. I knew they wouldn't treat him fairly, but I didn't expect them to withhold evidence that further proved his cooperation with the DEA and CIA.

The fuckers in Washington were lying about the invasion, too. I wasn't there, but I trusted the men who recounted their experiences to me. They were people who had never had reason to lie. They spoke about executions in the streets, the abuse of Panamanian women, some teenagers, and chucha, the most fucked up of all, they broke into my house, stole all my money, and killed my dog. I was infuriated, but I could do nothing but move on. I worked hard for that money, I loved that dog. . . . What the fuck did it matter? Everything had turned upside down, and I found myself in hell, looking forward to my single phone call per week. Noriega and I had worked to schedule a conversation through our prisons. I had finally gotten approval, as did Manuel. I walked along the shit-staunched corridor of my unit. Dirty Peruvian inmates yelled to me, showing their incomplete sets of teeth and shredded lips and skin.

"This is a collect call from the Federal Correctional Institution of Miami. Do you accept?" a woman's voice said.

"Chucha, yes!" I responded.

"Carlitos?" Manuel's upbeat voice suddenly echoed.

"Manuel, can you hear me? Manuel?"

"I can hear you, mi amigo."

"How are you, señor?" I asked.

"How do you think? They finally see that I am a prisoner of war, you know, because of the Geneva Convention. . . . But they treat me worse than any of the ladronas in here!"

"I'm sorry to hear."

"Ah, it is okay, Carlitos. I have made good friends here. I am like a king to them. How are you doing?"

"Chucha, this place is a fucking nightmare. I cannot believe I am going to be here for six fucking months. . . . I want to kill the fucking guards, but that's how they get you to stay longer."

"Six months? Stop being a bitch! I'm here for forty years, cabron!"

Noriega and I laughed hysterically. The inmates waiting around me fidgeted with themselves, anticipating their time with the phone. I paid no attention to them. "This is funny, isn't it, Carlitos? You in jail, me in jail. Think of our lives only three years ago. . . . We could fuck the most beautiful women in the world at the whim of a wink, and now, our cellmates want to fuck us in the ass!" Manuel could make me fall over in fits of laughter, no matter what was happening in my life. The man was funny; he used jokes to disarm tough conversations. He was a born politician and raised a soldier. I missed him dearly. He managed to make me forget where I was.

"Listen, Carlos . . . we will see each other again. This will not be my life. It will not be the way I die."

In a way, he was right. As time progressed, I moved back to Panama, and I worked in a number of different fields. Most of my contacts remained, and they liked me. I had a personality that people trusted, and whenever I wanted work, there was work. Yet, unlike many others, my loyalty to my friend, the general, never faded. By the end of 1999, the canal had officially returned to Panamanian hands, and I watched as US soldiers vanished from their military bases. It was a change that I wish Manuel had been there to see in person. Panama was inching closer to standing on its own two legs, and whether people knew it or not, it was because of the work that people like me and Omar, and Manuel did. I was proud, but I wasn't convinced the days of puppeteering were over.

Our presidents had representatives from all over the world whispering in their ears. They were weak, slimy men who acted more like a fucking culebra than a leader.

Noriega called me one day in 1999 to tell me the French government was requesting his extradition. "Can you believe it? They're saying I laundered three million dollars in drug proceeds by buying real estate in Paris," he exclaimed.

I learned the French had convicted him in absentia. What kind of a backward country can prove you guilty without first hearing what you have to say? I was shocked.

But Gaspar proved to be the voice of reason. Gaspar, mi hermano, had left his post as the Panamanian ambassador to France to become the Panamanian ambassador to Germany at this time. Still, he, like many others, would make sure Noriega was taken care of as much as possible. "He will be a prisoner, but there will be people with their eyes on him," Gaspar told me.

I didn't have the legal brain that he did, but the way I saw it was that Noriega had cut a forty-year sentence in America down to seventeen in favor of a seven-year sentence in France, a country which he loved to visit as much as I did. In fact, I had a woman in France, a beautiful yet timid woman with a strict father. The news excited me, and on April 26, 2010, Manuel was transported to Paris to be incarcerated on their soil. They froze his accounts and would not let any of his relatives or friends like me touch a cent. I did not expect to, but that money deserved to go somewhere and not into the hands of the French government.

"Things aren't much better here, Carlos. I feel like a fucking sardine. My lawyers are looking to get me moved," he first told me. "Chucha, how ironic it is that the French made me a commandeur in the Légion d'honneur only twenty years ago. And now, I sit in one of their cells with this prestigious badge pinned to my chest."

I sat in my apartment overlooking the San Francisco district of Panama City, thinking to myself that there was nothing for me at home at that moment. My children had all grown up, and they could take care of themselves. I was even a grandfather, and I had security in knowing my family dynasty would continue. I gazed out that window, looking at the ocean gently rippling toward the small harbors in the city's bay, and I knew I had to go to France. After so many years of being unable to visit my friend in America, I now had a window of opportunity to reunite with the man who helped make me who I was. My bags were packed in an instant.

A cool, crisp glass of whiskey rested in my hands as I leaned back on my flight. Families and business people surrounded me. I rested my eyes and breathed through my nose, thinking of the moment I would see my friend. It didn't matter that a set of iron bars would separate us. I was his right-hand man, his *mano derecha*, and I would be by his side.

Gaspar had arranged for a car to pick me up at Charles de Gaulle. The back door opened for me, and when I entered the luxury vehicle, Gaspar sat in the back with one leg over the other.

"Mi hermano, look at you!" I yelled. He looked very dignified, like the true politician he was.

"Everything is good, Carlitos. I checked in with our whole family, and there are no concerns. I hope you got the chance to see everyone before you left," he said as we drove through the outskirts of the city toward the center.

I could see the Eiffel Tower standing tall, its shadow stretching through the streets. Manuel was one of millions there.

When we arrived at La Santé Prison, Gaspar had his driver open my door while he stayed in the car. "I cannot go today, mi hermano. Tell Manuel I will see him soon," he said before shutting the door. I watched as the car sped off.

The prison was not a nice place, not quite as bad as Peru, but the conditions were not good enough for a man who should have been considered a prisoner of war. The French somehow bypassed that, and I do not know how; it was unfair, but Manuel was a man nonetheless. There was a room designated for meetings; that's where I was escorted to. I sat at a metallic table, feet tapping, watching the door. When it did open, Manuel came stomping toward me with his wrists in chains but a smile on his face.

"Carlitos! Mi amigo. It is good to see you," he said.

"It's good to see you too, señor. In person, and not on the news," I responded.

"Chucha, I know. . . . You do not look as old as I thought you would," he joked.

The man hadn't seen the light of day in almost two decades and could still make a joke. We caught up on all affairs. I informed him about the state of the government at that time and how I did not like where it was heading. There were positives, of course, but

Manuel liked to know their weaknesses. I understood that knowing a person's weaknesses gave you strength over him.

"Is the Torrijos boy still president?" Manuel asked.

"No, we have a new one. He was inducted recently, and the people seem to like him," I responded. I had seen some incredible politicians walk through our government, but I had also seen some terrible, corrupt ones. It took time for me to trust the person in power. Before Manuel and I knew it, our time was up. Manuel had to return to his quarters. I returned to a hotel in the city and pondered what to make of everything. I was in Paris, and I knew I needed to stay there.

The next morning, I walked the streets, jumping in and out of restaurants, looking for work. I finally fell upon a restaurant named Petite Fleur. It was a beautiful establishment, a single room with two dozen tables and a kitchen in the back. The manager gave me a position as a busboy and a waiter. I did what I had to do; I only cared about getting paid. In the morning, I would come in early to set up, and then I would work until late afternoon. I was paid once per week. The evenings were spent at La Santé with Manuel. We would talk about anything we wanted to. If I saw a chick on the street, he wanted to know if I could see her through her shirt. We joked and we laughed; it was a way for both of us to decompress. Working in that restaurant was a fucking experience. It had been some time since I had worked like that. Sitting with Noriega put me at ease.

"The French are speaking with our government right now, Carlitos," Manuel told me one day.

"An extradition?" I asked.

"They wish that I serve time on home soil."

"For how long?"

"Sixty years. All of it at El Renacer."

"Chucha . . ."

"It will be better at home. This is how it is."

Noriega was extradited back to Panama on December 11, 2011. I tied everything up with the restaurant in Paris. They were good to me. It was a humbling experience, but an experience nonetheless. Where Noriega went, I went, and it was time for me to return to my home. The Panamanian media had eyes focused on Manuel from the moment he arrived at El Renacer, and about a year later, when he suffered his first brain tumor, they zoomed their lenses on his character.

"Manuel Noriega has been diagnosed with a brain tumor. Further details are not known. Could this be an end for the once-leader of Panama?"

I had been to that hospital many times to visit loved ones and colleagues. I had known it to be a fine institution of medicine my entire life, and that didn't change when Manuel lay in one of its beds. Our friend, Roderick Purcell, blood of Alberto, was Noriega's private chef. He was a fine boy who deeply cared for his leader. He was the man who served Manuel his last meal on earth.

I was by his bedside constantly. I was there when the doctor told him his tumor was benign and he would continue to live. The following five years were filled with nostalgic visits. We both knew Manuel would die incarcerated, and we tried to make the best of a bad situation. Noriega had women slip through the bars of his cell whenever he wanted. He could live like a king behind bars, but he could not leave. His health had deteriorated by 2017. We knew a life-or-death surgery was imminent. Manuel was allowed to spend his sentence under house arrest. Chucha, even in his condition, the man was a hound. We drank like we were young men. Young women caressed our aging bodies like we were still kings. "Life is good, Carlitos," he would continue to say.

On March 7, 2017, I got the call that Manuel had suffered a brain hemorrhage. I rushed to the hospital. They were keeping him at Hospital Santo Tomas. I waited by his side day after day. Onlookers came to take a glance at the once-great leader of Panama. They fucking snarled and laughed at him.

I couldn't take it. I would rush out to the hallway where they stood and physically push people away. "Get the fuck out of here!" I found myself screaming every other day. Fucking news reporters and journalists slithered into the hospital like snakes. I stood guard, standing at the end of Manuel's bed with clenched fists, ready to fight. "Put those fucking cameras away," I demanded. Armed guards were supposed to keep him safe, but they didn't; it was only me.

Noriega's family came to visit him often. I was close with them all. When Manuel had the strength to wake up, he would crack dirty jokes to his nephews. He wanted his last image in their heads to be a positive one and not that of a dying old man.

Manuel's life was fading before me. He turned and opened his mouth. Every other noise around me suddenly became muffled.

Purcell dragged me out of the room one day and told me he had overheard the doctors talking about the surgery. "Señor, señor . . . I must tell you something," he said, panting.

"What is it?" I asked.

"This surgery . . . it is not necessary." Roderick was hyperventilating. The orders were in place, Manuel was a prisoner, and whether we liked it or not, he was having surgery in the morning.

"Do not worry for Manuel, kid. He's stronger than any bull I have ever seen."

Purcell's chest deflated. He breathed through his nose. "If Señor Noriega needs anything, please call me."

I patted him on the shoulder and told him to go home. He had done enough for our sick friend. After the boy left, I turned to the door of Manuel's room and realized he and I were all alone. The hinges creaked as I entered and sat by his bedside.

He turned to me with dead eyes and shaky hands. "This surgery, Carlitos . . . it will be the end of me," Noriega muttered.

"You have a tumor, señor," I responded.

"It is benign. I feel deep within me that it is benign, just as it was before. . . . There is no need for surgery. . . . But, you know just as I do that nothing will change. . . . I am a prisoner in my own country. . . . Chucha, who would have thought?"

"Something can be done, señor. I'll bolt these doors and guard you with a rifle. Just say the word."

"You are a good friend, Carlitos."

It was May 29 of that year when Manuel passed away. It was a hemorrhage that killed him in the end. The surgery tipped him over the edge. It wasn't the CIA, the DEA, the Colombians, the Contras . . . he died right here in Panama. My life paused at that moment. Seeing his lifeless body on a hospital bed enraged me. My heart beat against my chest. The news had been spread, and three members of the PPF [Panamanian Public Forces] strolled up in their uniforms alongside journalists with their cameras held high.

"What took so long?" one from the PPF joked as journalists' cameras began flashing.

"What the fuck did you say?" I yelled, picking up a metal tray. The item soared across the room like a frisbee. It cracked against the fucker's forehead, and blood dribbled down to his nose. I rushed at the other two, salivating with rage and tears in my eyes. "I'll fucking kill you!" I screamed.

Hospital staff restrained me as if I were a pit bull attached to a metal leash. They dragged me down. "Señor Wittgreen, relax, please," they begged.

The fucking soldiers stood tall, smiles on their ignorant fucking faces. My best friend lay dead fifteen feet from where I lay. I was a beehive of emotion. After almost fifty years of friendship, he had finally passed. That day will be forever etched in my memory.

Chapter 24
The End of a Memory

I watched Carlos from afar as he stood ankle-deep in the rising and falling waters at Jose's beach house. It was the day the storm rolled in, all the way back during my first trip to Panama. I hardly knew anything about him then, but I could sense that he was deep in his nostalgia. That happens often during this process. Carlitos gazed out at the shuddering streaks of lightning sparking through the sky over the horizon. The gray clouds were barreling in. Señor Wittgreen stood in place as the rain fell over the Pacific. He was entranced by the sight.

I found it difficult not to feel for the man. Telling me this story took the life out of him. He wore his heart on his sleeve, at times, and he opened himself to me. It was difficult not to have been swayed by his beautiful words. The man was a poet in another life, I am sure of it. Yet, in this reality, Carlitos was a soldier, a smuggler, a loyal follower who, in many ways, wished he had been taken alongside his friend during the American invasion in 1989. He would have laid down his life for Noriega. I am more than certain of that. Carlos's own daughter made claim to Jose shortly after I wrote the book that she found it unlikely Carlos told me the full truth about what he and Noriega did behind closed doors. I think what she meant was that her father had committed some atrocities on behalf of his beliefs, and Carlos knew better than to include those in something—this book—that would allow his legacy to live on. Still, I was given the confidential documents, I was allowed to interview anyone I wanted. An Irish journalist, Graham, reached out to me and told me about an Irishman named John O'Toole, who was jailed for importing cocaine nearly three decades before the release of this book. Graham said that John was married to the daughter or niece of one of Noriega's inner circle. Graham claimed he wasn't sure if Wittgreen knew John or not. I was told that John and his wife, Gabrielle, were representatives of Noriega's government during the 1980s in Europe, but in reality, they were a front for cocaine smuggling. Graham said he knew this because John was previously married to an aunt of his and remained friends with his parents in Bray, Ireland, before any of this came to light.

I firmly believe that if the narrative of one side is taken into consideration, then so must the other—this story, Carlos's story. Do I believe every hand was clean? Of course not. But the American government didn't have as much evidence as it led the public to believe. That is evident from the way Noriega's drug trial was unjustly conducted.

Carlos had this ultra-machismo, just like most older Panamanian men I met, especially the soldiers. Yet, beneath the surface, there was an emotional man who cared for the arts and prioritized the preservation of his culture.

Noriega once told Carlos that the stories about him were 70 percent drama and 30 percent truth. "This is always the case. Every story is embellished to some degree," Carlitos relayed to me.

I felt the irony of that statement rush over me many times. The old man had delusions embedded deep within his mind. They had been pressed in there for decades, too deep to be removed. Señor Wittgreen's words were those of an old man filled with nostalgia. A great story told by an objectively great man. Still, much of what he said was corroborated by others, and in many cases, Trujillo's documents directly backed up a story Carlos delivered to me. There were times I was surprised by the parallels. Yet it was Carlos's personal narrative that appealed to me most. It's what made my heart beat for this book over the course of two years while writing it. I rarely felt struggle during this process. I felt as though I knew the man completely, even though I likely did not.

"Gaspar . . . my little brother, how I miss him. I would give anything to once more sit by his side in our family home, watching our parents' friends get drunk and stumble, dancing to Tamborera. I was surrounded by so many in those days. . . . I'm lucky not to be alone in my old age."

After such an eventful life, sitting in rooms with the men who ruled the world and making decisions that had an effect on people across the globe, all he seemed to care about in the end were his family and friends. That's where every story went, every little conversation over a glass of whiskey. He knew when I caught on to a lie, and he didn't really care. He told me what he wanted to tell me, and in some cases, he actively held information from me. There was one moment, in his apartment, during my second trip to Panama, where he began to speak about the Mexican government, which was run by Andrés Manuel López Obrador at the time, when he suddenly stopped speaking, turned off my voice recorder, and told me to delete the file. "This will get you killed," he said in English. In moments like that, the curiosity in me typically wins over, and I want to know the truth regardless of what it may do to me. Yet I look back and I recognize that Carlos was looking out for my safety. Whenever I did contest him, he would simply double down on what he said in the first place. I could see how impressive his mind was, controlling rooms and people like it was nothing, but I also felt he would have given his life to someone if he considered the person a friend, and I still wholeheartedly believe that.

Carlos Wittgreen passed on March 23, 2025. He died of a heart attack while at home in Panama City. I was in Boston, Massachusetts, finishing this book when Jose informed Jack and me of the devastating news. I couldn't help but think of my time with Señor Wittgreen. I wish he could have been alive to read this book. I think he would have been surprised by what I ended up writing. He saw this project as his legacy. I wanted the book to tell a truth greater than one man's personal narrative, and I am confident I did that. I am proud. Not only do I feel grateful to have been the one to tell this explosive story, but I am glad I had the chance to know such a truly great man. His experiences may help pave the way for a new narrative, one that contests the lies of the

American government and the CIA and shows the world what happens when the United States backs a strongman to lead a nation, before extracting everything from that person, the government, and the country, before ousting the leader by backing a coup and repeating the same process again.

Something that always interested me about this whole thing was that, after Noriega's removal in December 1989, drug trafficking in the region surged. Recorded cocaine seizures in Panama rose from 1,728 kilograms in 1989 to 3,959 kilograms in 1990. The 1990 total included a record 2,118-kilogram seizure in Colón directed by the DEA. Seizures continued upward into early 1991, with more than 1,300 kilograms seized from January to March, compared with 418 kilograms in the prior three months. However, Noriega could never have continued to sit on his throne. He held too many secrets, had too many personal vendettas with powerful Americans, and made too many mistakes because of an inflated ego, ignoring the advice given to him by Fidel Castro, the only example of a Latin leader who took on America and won.

Saddam Hussein, Osama bin Laden, and Augusto Pinochet. These are all once American-backed names we know. There are many, many more. Nothing is coincidental. Every strongman is put into place for one reason—to do what the American government says. At its core, this book is a tale of what happens when a power-hungry dictator and a vulnerable nation become expendable to an empire, and how and why that pattern still echoes through global politics to this very day.

Carlitos will be missed by many, and his name will forever be associated with what makes Panama, Panama.

Acknowledgments

Special thanks to:
Jose Goldner
Jack Moran
Jose Hilario Trujillo
Diego Goldner
Mikhail Trujillo
Michael Frick
Mark Gildea
Miriam McDonell
Dr. Neel Anand
Rod Robertson

Sources

Archibold, Randal C. "Manuel Noriega, Dictator Ousted by U.S. in Panama, Dies at 83." *New York Times*. May 30, 2017.

Archibold, Randal C. "Noriega Back in Panama for More Prison Time." *New York Times*. December 11, 2011.

Castaneda, Jorge G. "What Did We Want from Noriega?" *New York Times*, June 16, 1991.

Cullather, Nicholas. *Secret History: The CIA's Classified Account of Its Operations in Guatemala, 1952–1954*. Stanford: Stanford University Press, 1999.

Dinges, John. *The Condor Years: How Pinochet and His Allies Brought Terrorism to Three Continents*. New York: The New Press, 2004.

Fiedler, Tom. "2D Ex-aide Says Bush Was Warned about Noriega." *Philadelphia Inquirer*. September 23, 1988. Accessed via Central Intelligence Agency, CIA-RDP99-01448R000401580035-3. Declassified May 25, 2012. https://www.cia.gov/readingroom/docs/CIA-RDP99-01448R000401580035-3.pdf.

Gleijeses, Piero. *Shattered Hope: The Guatemalan Revolution and the United States, 1944–1954*. Princeton: Princeton University Press, 1991.

Hersh, Seymour M. "Panama Strongman Said to Trade in Drugs, Arms and Illicit Money." *The New York Times*. June 12, 1986.

Isikoff, Michael. "Drug Activity in Panama Has Increased, GAO Says." *Washington Post*, July 23, 1991.Koster, Richard, and Guillermo Sánchez Borbón. *In the Time of the Tyrants: Panama, 1968–1990*. New York: W. W. Norton, 1990.

Koster, Richard. Author archive. *La Prensa*, Panama City.

Langley, Lester D. *The Banana Wars: United States Intervention in the Caribbean, 1898–1934*. Lexington: University Press of Kentucky, 1983.

Lindsay-Poland, John. *Emperors in the Jungle: The Hidden History of the U.S. in Panama*. Durham: Duke University Press, 2003.Perkins, John. *Confessions of an Economic Hit Man*. San Francisco: Berrett-Koehler Publishers, 2004.

Long, William R. "He Sees Plot Aimed at Canal Control: Accusations Put Spotlight on Panama's Strongman." *Los Angeles* Time., July 18, 1986.

Marshall, Jonathan. "Operation Just Cause's Unjust Aftermath: Drug Trafficking and Money Laundering in Post-Noriega Panama." Lobster, no. 87 (2023).

Marshall, Jonathan. "Unjust Aftermath: Post-Noriega Panama." The Real News Network. December 29, 2019.

Monroe, James. "Seventh Annual Message to Congress." December 2, 1823.Muse, Kurt, and John Gilstrap. *Six Minutes to Freedom: How a Band of Heros Defied a dictator and Helped Free a Nation*. New York: Citadel Press, 2006.

Nintendo87 (blog). "Manuel Noriega 60 Minutes Presentation (1988)." *The World History Archive and Compendium*. July 13, 2023. https://worldhistoryarchive.wordpress.com/2023/07/13/man uel-noriega-60-minutes-presentation-1988/.

Noriega, Manuel Antonio. *Sin temor a la verdad*. Bogotá: Planeta, 1997.

Noriega, Manuel Antonio. "Speech at Harvard University: The Military's Role in Securing Democracy." Medium. February 28, 1985. https://manuelnoriega.medium.com/the-militarys-role-in-securing-democracy-by-general-manuel-noriega-b62c2a5e7b41.

Noriega, Manuel, and Peter Eisner. *America's Prisoner: The Memoirs of Manuel Noriega*. New York: Random House, 1997.

"Peru Releases Carlos Wittgreen in Spite of Panama's Extradition Request." *International Enforcement Law Reporter* 8, no. 11 (November 1, 1992): 448.

Rohter, Larry. "Noriega Sentenced to 40 Years in Jail on Drug Charges." *New York Times*. July 11, 1992.

Roosevelt, Theodore. "Annual Message to Congress." December 6, 1904.Secord, Richard V. *Honored and Betrayed: Irangate, Covert Affairs, and the Secret War in Laos*. New York: John Wiley & Sons, 1992.

Simon, Scott. "The Return of Manuel Noriega." Weekend Editon Saturday. NPR. August 18, 2007. https://www.npr.org/2007/08/18/12899531/the-return-of-manuel-noriega.

Staff Report of the Select Committee to Study Governmental Operations with Respect to Intelligence Activities United States Senate. Covert Action in Chile, 1963–1973. Washington, DC: US Government Printing Office, 1975. https://www.intelligence.senate.gov/wp-content/uploads/2024/08/sites-default-files-94chile.pdf.

Treaster, Joseph B. "After Noriega: Noriega; Military Command Belittles General." *New York Times*. December 27, 1989.

Trent, Barbara, dir. *The Panama Deception*. Written by David Kasper. Narrated by Elizabeth Montgomery. United States: Empowerment Project, 1992.

Trujillo, Jose. *George H. W. Bush vs. Manuel Antonio Noriega: Centro financiero internacional; narcotráfico invasión Panamá papers*. Editora Sibauste, 2021.

US Department of State. "Remarks on U.S. Policy in the Western Hemisphere." John Kerry, Secretary of State, Organization of American States, Washington, DC, November 18, 2013. https://2009-2017.state.gov/secretary/remarks/2013/11/217680.htm.

US Department of the Treasury, Office of Foreign Assets Control. "Issuance of 2001-Era Cuba Licensing Guidelines (no longer current)." April 11, 2001. https://ofac.treasury.gov/recent-actions/20010411.

US Department of the Treasury, Office of Foreign Assets Control. "Venezuela Sanctions General Licenses and FAQs, 2023–2025."

US General Accounting Office. *Drug Control: U.S.-Supported Efforts in Panama Have Achieved Some Success but Challenges Remain*. Washington, DC: US Government Printing Office, July 1991.

Zito, Tom. "Delegates Get a Taste of Panama Canal Lox." *Washington Post*. August 13, 1980.

www.ingramcontent.com/pod-product-compliance
Lightning Source LLC
Chambersburg PA
CBHW060403130626
46555CB00005B/1983